DirectX Demystified: A Comprehensive Guide to Game Development Essentials

Kameron Hussain and Frahaan Hussain

Published by Sonar Publishing, 2024.

DIRECTX DEMYSTIFIED: A COMPREHENSIVE GUIDE TO GAME DEVELOPMENT ESSENTIALS

First edition. April 9, 2024.

ISBN: 979-8224562589

Written by Kameron Hussain and Frahaan Hussain.

Table of Contents

Chapter 1: Introduction to DirectX

1.1 The Evolution of DirectX: A Historical Overview

The Early Days (DirectX 1-3)

DirectX 5-7: Maturing and Expanding

DirectX 8-9: Graphics Revolution

DirectX 10-11: Vista and Beyond

DirectX 12: Low-Level Access

The Ongoing Evolution

1.2 Understanding DirectX and Its Role in Game Development

The Importance of DirectX

Multimedia Functionality

Cross-Platform Considerations

DirectX Versions

DirectX and Game Engines

DirectX in Modern Game Development

1.3 DirectX Versions: From Past to Present

DirectX 1-3: The Foundation

DirectX 5-7: Building Blocks

DirectX 8-9: The Graphics Revolution

DirectX 10-11: Modern Graphics

DirectX 12: Low-Level Access

DirectX Today

Choosing the Right DirectX Version

DirectX and Windows Compatibility

Future of DirectX

DirectX Alternatives

1.4 Setting Up the Development Environment for DirectX

Windows Operating System

Visual Studio IDE

DirectX SDK

Graphics Drivers

DirectX End-User Runtimes

Debugging Tools

DirectX Samples and Tutorials

DirectX Community and Forums

Project Configuration

Development Assets

Version Control

1.5 Key Concepts in DirectX: An Overview

1.5.1 Graphics Rendering

1.5.2 Shaders

1.5.3 Textures

1.5.4 Input Handling

1.5.5 Audio Management

1.5.6 Networking

1.5.7 Game Physics

1.5.8 Shader Language (HLSL)

1.5.9 Cross-Platform Considerations

1.5.10 DirectX and Game Engines

Chapter 2: The DirectX Graphics Infrastructure

2.1 Diving into Direct3D: Rendering 3D Graphics

Direct3D Basics

The Rendering Pipeline

Vertex Processing

Geometry Shading

Rasterization

Pixel Shading

Output Merger

Shaders in Direct3D

Direct3D Versions

Creating a Direct3D Application

2.2 Understanding Shaders and the Graphics Pipeline

What Are Shaders?

Vertex Shaders

Geometry Shaders

Pixel Shaders (Fragment Shaders)

Shader Compilation

Shader Constants and Variables

Shader Stages in the Pipeline

Shader Effects and Visual Realism

Shader Optimization

2.3 Textures and Materials in DirectX

Textures in DirectX

Texture Coordinates

Common Types of Textures

Texture Filtering and Mipmaps

Materials and Shading

Diffuse, Specular, and Normal Mapping

Texture Compression

Texture Loading and Management

Dynamic Texturing

Shader Integration

2.4 Lighting and Shadows: Techniques and Implementation

Lighting in 3D Graphics

Types of Lighting

Light Sources

The Phong Lighting Model

Shadow Techniques

Shadow Mapping in DirectX

Normal Mapping for Realistic Lighting

Shader Programming for Lighting

Optimization Considerations

2.5 Advanced 3D Modeling and Rendering

Model Complexity

Level of Detail (LOD)

Terrain Rendering

Particle Systems

Procedural Generation

Instancing

Virtual Reality (VR) and Augmented Reality (AR)

Deferred Rendering

Post-Processing Effects

Global Illumination

Chapter 3: DirectX and 2D Graphics

3.1 2D Graphics with Direct2D

Introduction to Direct2D

Key Features of Direct2D

Initializing Direct2D

Drawing Shapes and Paths

Working with Brushes

Text Rendering with DirectWrite

Layered Composition

3.2 Integrating 2D and 3D Graphics

The Need for 2D and 3D Integration

Using Direct3D for 3D Graphics

Direct2D for 2D Graphics

Overlaying 2D Elements on 3D Scenes

Billboarding

Depth Testing and Blending

User Interface (UI) Integration

DirectComposition

Cross-Device Integration

Conclusion

3.3 Text Rendering and Font Management

The Importance of Text Rendering

DirectWrite for High-Quality Text

Initializing DirectWrite

Rendering Text with DirectWrite

Font Management

Text Effects and Animation

Conclusion

3.4 Image Processing and Manipulation

The Role of Images in DirectX

Texture Mapping

Sprites and 2D Images

Image Filters and Effects

Image Loading and Compression

Dynamic Image Creation

Image Memory Management

Conclusion

3.5 Implementing User Interfaces with DirectX

The Importance of User Interfaces

DirectX for UI Implementation

Integration with Direct2D and DirectWrite

UI Frameworks and Libraries

Input Handling

Layout and Rendering

UI Responsiveness and Performance

Transition Effects and Animations

Cross-Platform Considerations

Testing and User Feedback

Conclusion

Chapter 4: Sound and Music with DirectX

4.1 Introduction to DirectSound

The Role of Audio in Applications

DirectSound Overview

Key Features of DirectSound

Initializing DirectSound

Loading and Playing Audio Files

Advanced Audio Effects

Performance Optimization

Conclusion

4.2 Loading and Playing Audio Files

Supported Audio Formats

Loading Audio Files

Streaming Audio

Managing Audio Resources

Sound Cues and Triggers

Advanced Audio Features

Error Handling

Conclusion

4.3 3D Audio Effects and Spatialization

Understanding 3D Audio

Spatialization and Positional Audio

Positioning Sounds in 3D Space

Doppler Effect

Environmental Effects

HRTF (Head-Related Transfer Function)

Sound Occlusion and Obstruction

Performance Considerations

Conclusion

4.4 Integrating Sound with Game Physics

Audio Feedback for Actions

Collision Sounds

Footstep and Movement Sounds

Object Interactions

Environmental Effects

Synchronization with Physics Engine

Performance Considerations

Conclusion

4.5 Advanced Audio Techniques and Optimization

Streaming Audio

Real-time Effects Processing

Dynamic Sound Mixing

Multithreading and Asynchronous Playback

Latency Reduction

Profiling and Optimization Tools

Conclusion

Chapter 5: DirectX for Input Management

5.1 Handling Keyboard and Mouse Input with DirectInput

Overview of DirectInput

Initializing DirectInput

Acquiring and Releasing Devices

Polling for Input

Handling Keyboard Input

Handling Mouse Input

Custom Input Handling

Error Handling

Conclusion

5.2 Implementing Game Controllers and Haptic Feedback

Recognizing Game Controllers

Initializing Game Controllers

Polling for Game Controller Input

Game Controller Input Data

Haptic Feedback

Custom Input Handling

Error Handling

Conclusion

5.3 Touch and Gesture Recognition

Touch Input Basics

Handling Touch Messages

Processing Touch Input

Gesture Recognition

Handling Gestures

Custom Gesture Recognition

Multitouch Support

Error Handling

Conclusion

5.4 Custom Input Devices and DirectX

Custom Input Devices Overview

Using DirectInput for Custom Devices

Example: Motion Controller Integration

Custom Input Challenges

Conclusion

5.5 Input Processing and Game Loops

The Role of Input Processing

Input Handling in Game Loops

Input Polling vs. Event Handling

Managing Input States

Input Buffering and Debouncing

Handling Multiple Input Devices

Error Handling and Robustness

Conclusion

Chapter 6: DirectX Networking

6.1 Basics of Network Programming in DirectX

Understanding Networking in Games

Key Concepts in Network Programming

DirectX Networking APIs

Setting Up a Basic Networked Game

Conclusion

6.2 DirectPlay for Multiplayer Games

Key Features of DirectPlay

Setting Up a DirectPlay Multiplayer Game

DirectPlay vs. Modern Networking Libraries

Conclusion

6.3 Synchronizing Game States Over a Network

The Challenge of Synchronization

Techniques for Synchronization

Code Example: Interpolation

Conclusion

6.4 Handling Latency and Network Issues

Understanding Latency

Challenges of High Latency

Strategies for Latency Compensation

Handling Packet Loss

Code Example: Lag Compensation

Conclusion

6.5 Building a Simple Multiplayer Game

Designing the Game

Setting Up the Development Environment

Networking Implementation

Code Example: Player Movement Synchronization

Testing and Debugging

Deployment and Scaling

Conclusion

7.1 Introduction to High-Level Shader Language (HLSL)

Understanding Shaders

Purpose of HLSL

HLSL Syntax

Code Example: Simple Vertex Shader

Conclusion

7.2 Creating Basic Vertex and Pixel Shaders

Vertex Shaders

Pixel Shaders

Shader Compilation and Integration

Shader Debugging

Conclusion

7.3 Advanced Shader Techniques

Tessellation Shaders

Geometry Shaders

Compute Shaders

Shader Libraries and Code Organization

Shader Debugging and Optimization

Conclusion

7.4 Optimization Strategies for Shaders

1. Minimize Memory Accesses

2. Reduce Branching

3. Optimize Register Usage

4. Loop Unrolling

5. Precompute Constants

6. LOD Management

7. Profile and Measure

8. SIMD Optimization

9. Avoid Costly Functions

10. Use Compiler Directives

Conclusion

7.5 Using Compute Shaders for Non-Graphics Tasks

1. What Are Compute Shaders?

2. Parallelism in Compute Shaders

3. How to Use Compute Shaders

4. Applications of Compute Shaders

5. Memory Access and Synchronization

6. GPU Compute Programming Languages

Conclusion

Chapter 8: DirectX and Game Engines

8.1 Overview of Popular Game Engines with DirectX Support

1. Unity

2. Unreal Engine

3. CryEngine

4. Godot Engine

5. Lumberyard

8.2 Integrating DirectX with Game Engines

Benefits of Integrating DirectX

Steps to Integrate DirectX with Game Engines

Example Integration Code

8.3 Customizing Engine Features Using DirectX

Advantages of Customization

Steps for Customizing Engine Features

Example Customization Code

8.4 Case Studies: Successful Games Built with DirectX and Game Engines

1. Halo: The Master Chief Collection

2. Forza Horizon 5

3. Gears 5

4. Ori and the Will of the Wisps

5. Flight Simulator (2020)

8.5 Future of Cross-Platform Gaming with DirectX

1. DirectX 12 Ultimate

2. Cloud Gaming

3. Mobile and Streaming

4. Cross-Play and Cross-Save

5. Emulation and Retro Gaming

6. Advanced AI Integration

7. Open Standards and Collaboration

9.1 The Role of DirectX in Modern Windows Applications

1. Graphic-Intensive Applications

2. Multimedia and Entertainment

3. Business and Productivity Software

4. CAD and Engineering Applications

5. Mapping and Geographic Information Systems (GIS)

6. Virtual Reality (VR) and Augmented Reality (AR)

7. Cross-Platform Development

8. Future Windows Programming

9.2 DirectX for Desktop Application Development

1. Graphical User Interfaces (GUI)

2. Data Visualization

3. Simulation and Modeling

4. Multimedia Integration

5. CAD and 3D Modeling

6. Cross-Platform Development

7. Performance Optimization

9.3 Integrating 3D Graphics in Business Applications

1. Data Visualization and Analysis

2. Product Design and Prototyping

3. Training and Simulations

4. Geographic Information Systems (GIS)

5. Virtual Conferencing and Collaboration

6. Cross-Platform Compatibility

9.4 Performance Considerations and Best Practices

1. Hardware Compatibility and Requirements

2. Efficient Resource Management

3. Render Batching

4. Multithreading

5. GPU Performance Profiling

6. Dynamic Level of Detail (LOD)

7. Memory Management

8. Error Handling and Recovery

9. User Settings and Optimization Profiles

10. Continuous Testing and Profiling

9.5 DirectX and the Future of Windows Programming

1. DirectX as a Catalyst for Graphics Innovation

2. Integration with Emerging Technologies

3. Ray Tracing and Realism

4. Cross-Platform and Cloud Gaming

5. Developer Community and Ecosystem

10. DirectX for Virtual Reality

10.1. Understanding the Basics of Virtual Reality

1. What Is Virtual Reality?

2. Key Components of VR

3. DirectX and VR

4. Optimizing Performance

5. VR Development Platforms

10.2. Implementing VR Support in DirectX

1. VR Hardware Integration

2. Stereoscopic Rendering

3. Head Tracking

4. Input Handling

5. Audio Integration

6. Performance Optimization

7. VR Development Platforms

10.3. Optimizing Performance for VR

1. Maintain a Consistent Frame Rate

2. Reduce Latency

3. GPU and CPU Optimization

4. Adaptive Quality

5. VR-Specific Rendering Techniques

6. Regular Testing

7. User Feedback

10.4. User Experience Design in VR Applications

1. Comfort and Motion Sickness

2. Interaction and Input

3. User Interface (UI) Design

4. Performance and Optimization

5. Comfort and Accessibility

6. Testing and Feedback

10.5. Future Trends and DirectX in VR

1. Improved Graphics and Realism

2. Eye Tracking and Foveated Rendering

3. Enhanced Haptic Feedback

4. Wireless VR and 5G Integration

5. AI-Driven Interactions

6. Social VR and Collaboration

7. Health and Wellness Applications

8. Cross-Platform VR

9. Ethical and Privacy Considerations

Chapter 11: Debugging and Profiling DirectX Applications

Section 11.1: Tools and Techniques for Debugging DirectX Code

1. Debugging Tools

2. Debugging Techniques

3. Profiling Techniques

4. Debugging DirectX Errors

5. Best Practices

Section 11.2: Profiling and Optimizing DirectX Applications

1. Profiling Tools

2. GPU Timings

3. Frame Analysis

4. GPU Shader Profiling

5. Optimizing Techniques

6. Continuous Profiling

Section 11.3: Handling Common Errors and Issues

1. HRESULT Error Codes

2. Debugging Tools

3. Resource Leaks

4. Invalid Shader Code

5. Driver Compatibility

6. Memory Management

7. Threading Issues

8. DirectX Version Compatibility

9. Third-Party Libraries

10. User-Friendly Error Messages

Section 11.4: Advanced Debugging Scenarios

1. Debugging Graphics Pipelines

2. GPU-Related Issues

3. Memory Corruption

4. Multi-Threading Debugging

5. Performance Profiling

6. Remote Debugging

7. Memory Debugging

8. Custom Debugging Techniques

9. Collaboration and Documentation

10. Continuous Learning

Section 11.5: Case Studies: Debugging Complex DirectX Applications

Case Study 1: Flickering Shadows

Case Study 2: Random Crashes on Certain GPUs

Case Study 3: Multiplayer Synchronization Issues

Case Study 4: Memory Leaks in a Complex Scene

Chapter 12: DirectX in Mobile Development

Section 12.1: DirectX on Windows Mobile Platforms

DirectX on Windows Mobile:

Development Environment:

Challenges in Windows Mobile Development:

Code Sample (Setting up a Direct3D Mobile Device):

Section 12.2: Design Considerations for Mobile Graphics

1. Optimized Graphics Assets:

2. Responsive User Interface:

3. Adaptive Rendering:

4. Battery Efficiency:

5. Device Compatibility:

6. Performance Profiling:

7. Screen Orientation:

8. Input Handling:

9. Offline Play:

10. Cross-Platform Considerations:

Code Sample (Adaptive Rendering):

Section 12.3: Optimizing DirectX for Mobile Devices

1. Texture Compression:

2. Mesh Simplification:

3. Shader Optimization:

4. Batching and Instancing:

5. Dynamic Resolution Scaling:

6. Texture Atlases:

7. Resource Streaming:

8. Reduced Overdraw:

9. Memory Management:

10. UI Performance:

11. Testing on Real Devices:

12. Profiling and Monitoring:

Section 12.4: Touch and Sensor Integration

1. Touch Input Handling:

2. Multi-Touch Gestures:

3. Accelerometer and Gyroscope:

4. Orientation Sensors:

5. Proximity Sensors:

6. Light Sensors:

7. GPS and Location Data:

8. Vibration Feedback:

9. Testing and Calibration:

10. User Experience Design:

11. Energy Efficiency:

12. Documentation and User Guidance:

Section 12.5: Case Studies: Successful DirectX Mobile Games

1. Asphalt 9: Legends

2. PUBG Mobile

3. Alto's Odyssey

4. Genshin Impact

Chapter 13: DirectX and the Cloud

Section 13.1: Cloud Computing and DirectX

Section 13.2: Leveraging the Cloud for Enhanced Graphics Processing

1. Distributed Rendering

2. AI-Enhanced Graphics

3. Scalability and Performance

4. Cloud-Based Assets

5. Dynamic Environments

6. Cost-Efficiency

Section 13.3: DirectX in Cloud-Based Game Streaming Services

1. Cloud Gaming Infrastructure

2. Low Latency Rendering

3. Device Agnosticism

4. Multiplayer and Social Features

5. Scalability

6. Security and Data Privacy

Section 13.4: Security Considerations in Cloud-Based DirectX Applications

1. Data Encryption

2. Authentication and Authorization

3. Code Obfuscation

4. Regular Security Audits

5. Secure Communication

6. Regular Updates

Section 13.5: Future of Cloud Gaming with DirectX

1. Improved Latency Reduction

2. Enhanced Graphics Quality

3. Cross-Platform Gameplay

4. Augmented Reality (AR) and Virtual Reality (VR)

5. Enhanced AI Integration

6. Evolving Cloud Services

Chapter 14: DirectX and Artificial Intelligence

Section 14.1: AI in Game Development: An Introduction

1. The Role of AI in Games

2. AI for Realistic Game Worlds

3. Integrating AI Engines with DirectX

4. Procedural Content Generation

5. Future Directions for AI and DirectX

Section 14.2: Using DirectX for AI Visualization

1. Debugging AI Behavior

2. Visualizing Decision Trees

3. Displaying Sensory Information

4. AI Animation and Expression

5. Creating AI Debug Tools

6. Enhancing Player Experience

Section 14.3: Integrating AI Engines with DirectX

1. Choosing an AI Engine

2. AI Model Training

3. Exporting AI Models

4. DirectX Integration

5. Inference and AI Behavior

6. Handling AI State Changes

7. Debugging and Testing

Section 14.4: Procedural Content Generation with DirectX

1. Understanding Procedural Content Generation

2. Terrain Generation

3. Texture Synthesis

4. Dynamic Level Design

5. Particle Systems and Effects

6. Debugging and Visualization

Section 14.5: Future Trends and DirectX in VR

1. Evolving VR Technologies

2. DirectX and VR Rendering

3. VR Audio with DirectX

4. Mixed Reality and AR Integration

5. DirectX Ray Tracing in VR

6. Social and Multiplayer VR with DirectX

Chapter 15: Advanced Texturing Techniques

Section 15.1: Detailed Look at Texture Mapping

1. The Basics of Texture Mapping

2. Types of Textures

3. UV Mapping

4. Tiling and Texture Coordinates

5. Texture Filtering

6. Anisotropic Filtering

7. Texture Compression

8. Shader Effects and Texture Blending

Section 15.2: Bump Mapping and Normal Mapping

1. Bump Mapping

2. Normal Mapping

Section 15.3: Environment and Reflection Mapping

1. Environment Mapping

2. Reflection Mapping

Section 15.4: Dynamic Texturing Strategies

1. Procedural Texturing

2. Video Textures

3. Render-to-Texture (RTT)

4. Texture Streaming

Section 15.5: Texture Compression and Management

1. Importance of Texture Compression

2. Texture Compression Formats

3. Texture Streaming and Level of Detail (LOD)

4. Mipmapping

5. Texture Atlases

Chapter 16: Real-Time Rendering Techniques

Section 16.1: Understanding Real-Time Rendering

Section 16.2: Implementing Real-Time Shadows and Lighting

Shadows in Real-Time Rendering

Lighting Effects

Performance Considerations

Section 16.3: Particle Systems and Effects

Understanding Particle Systems

Particle Effects

Optimization and Realism

Section 16.4: Real-Time Environmental Effects

Reflections

Refractions

Depth of Field

Ambient Occlusion

Global Illumination

Dynamic Weather and Time of Day

Section 16.5: Optimizing Real-Time Rendering Performance

1. Level of Detail (LOD)

2. Occlusion Culling

3. Batch Rendering

4. GPU Instancing

5. Deferred Rendering

6. Texture Compression

7. Multithreading

8. GPU Profiling

9. Dynamic Resolution Scaling

10. Resource Management

Chapter 17: Physics in DirectX

Section 17.1: Basics of Game Physics

1. Newtonian Physics

2. Rigid Body Dynamics

3. Collision Detection

4. Collision Response

5. Constraints and Joints

6. Fluid Dynamics and Soft Bodies

7. Performance Considerations

8. Integration with DirectX

Section 17.2: Implementing Physics with DirectX

1. Physics Libraries and Engines

2. Integration with DirectX

3. Collision Detection

4. Physics Materials and Properties

5. Ragdoll Physics

6. Joint and Constraint Systems

7. Performance Optimization

8. Debugging and Visualization

9. Integrating Physics with Gameplay

Section 17.3: Collision Detection and Response

1. Collision Detection Algorithms

2. Handling Collisions

3. Continuous Collision Detection

4. Optimization Techniques

5. Collision Response in Game Mechanics

Section 17.4: Simulating Realistic Environments

1. Physics Simulation

2. Particle Systems

3. Realistic Lighting

4. Weather Effects

5. Terrain Generation

6. Sound and Environment

7. Optimization and Performance

Section 17.5: Integrating Physics Engines with DirectX

1. Choosing a Physics Engine

2. Setting Up the Integration

3. Synchronization

4. Callbacks and Events

5. Debugging and Visualizing

6. Performance Considerations

7. Advanced Features

8. Examples

Chapter 18: DirectX and Cross-Platform Development

Section 18.1: Challenges of Cross-Platform DirectX Development

1. Platform Dependencies

2. Graphics API Variations

3. Hardware Differences

4. Input and User Interface

5. Testing and Debugging

6. Codebase Maintenance

7. Performance Optimization

8. Deployment and Distribution

9. Third-Party Library Compatibility

10. Version and Update Management

Strategies for Cross-Platform DirectX Development

Section 18.2: Strategies for Writing Portable DirectX Code

1. Abstraction Layers and Frameworks:

2. Conditional Compilation:

3. Feature Flags:

4. Cross-Platform Libraries:

5. Separate Platform Modules:

6. Testing and Continuous Integration:

7. Cross-Platform Development Tools:

8. Documentation and Community Resources:

9. Version Control and Collaboration:

Section 18.3: Leveraging DirectX in Cross-Platform Game Engines

Integration of DirectX:

Benefits of DirectX Integration:

Cross-Platform Abstraction:

Engine-Specific DirectX Support:

Testing and Quality Assurance:

Conclusion:

Section 18.4: Case Studies: Successful Cross-Platform DirectX Projects

1. Hollow Knight:

2. Ori and the Blind Forest:

3. Stardew Valley:

4. Risk of Rain 2:

5. Dead Cells:

Section 18.5: Future of Cross-Platform Gaming with DirectX

1. DirectX 12 Ultimate:

2. Cloud Gaming:

3. Cross-Platform Play:

4. VR and AR Integration:

5. Machine Learning and AI:

6. Evolving Hardware Standards:

Chapter 19: The Community and Ecosystem around DirectX

Section 19.1: The DirectX Developer Community

1. Community Forums and Websites:

2. Open-Source Projects:

3. Tutorials and Educational Content:

4. Meetups and Conferences:

5. Development Communities:

6. Online Courses and Certifications:

7. Developer Tools and Utilities:

8. Beta Testing and Feedback:

Section 19.2: Resources and Learning Materials for DirectX

1. Official Documentation:

2. Books and eBooks:

3. Video Tutorials:

4. Online Forums and Communities:

5. GitHub Repositories:

6. Online Courses and MOOCs:

7. API and SDK Samples:

8. Blogs and Articles:

9. Online Courses and Certifications:

10. Documentation in Game Engines:

Section 19.3: Contributing to the DirectX Ecosystem

1. Open-Source Projects:

2. Code Contributions:

3. Answering Questions:

4. Tutorials and Documentation:

5. Sample Projects:

6. Contribute to Frameworks:

7. Technical Blogs and Presentations:

8. Mentoring and Collaboration:

9. Feedback to Microsoft:

10. Participate in DirectX Communities:

Section 19.4: DirectX in Academia and Research

1. Teaching Graphics Programming:

2. Research Projects:

3. Academic Projects:

4. Thesis and Dissertations:

5. Collaboration with Industry:

6. DirectX Research Publications:

7. Hackathons and Competitions:

8. Guest Lectures and Workshops:

9. Collaborative Projects:

10. Industry-Academia Partnerships:

Section 19.5: The Business Aspect of DirectX Development

1. Cost Considerations:

2. Revenue Generation:

3. Intellectual Property (IP) Protection:

4. Market Competitiveness:

5. Marketing and Promotion:

6. User Engagement:

7. Monetization Models:

8. Distribution Platforms:

9. Community Building:

10. Legal and Regulatory Compliance:

11. Long-Term Support:

12. Revenue Sharing:

13. Indie Development:

14. Global Reach:

15. Evolving Business Models:

Chapter 20: The Future of DirectX

Section 20.1: Emerging Trends in Graphics Technology

1. Ray Tracing Advancements:

2. Real-Time AI Integration:

3. VR and AR Evolution:

4. Cross-Platform Development:

5. Cloud Gaming Integration:

6. Advanced Multi-GPU Support:

7. Real-Time Collaboration Tools:

8. Advanced Rendering Techniques:

9. Enhanced Developer Tools:

10. API Efficiency:

11. Machine Learning Integration:

12. Dynamic World Generation:

13. Global Illumination:

14. Haptic Feedback Integration:

15. Environmental Sustainability:

Section 20.2: DirectX and Next-Generation Hardware

1. Ray Tracing Acceleration:

2. Advanced Tensor Cores:

3. High Refresh Rates and Resolution:

4. Variable Rate Shading (VRS):

5. Hardware-Accelerated Machine Learning:

6. Advanced Memory Management:

7. Hardware Ray Tracing in Consoles:

8. Realistic Physics Simulations:

9. Mesh Shaders:

10. Advanced Audio Processing:

Section 20.3: Evolving Standards in Game Development

1. Cross-Platform Development:

2. API Abstraction Layers:

3. Open Standards and Open Source:

4. Web Integration:

5. VR and AR Standards:

6. Accessibility and Inclusivity:

7. Real-Time Ray Tracing Standards:

8. Globalization and Localization:

9. Security and Privacy Standards:

10. Ethical Game Development:

Section 20.4: The Role of DirectX in Future Gaming Experiences

1. Realistic Graphics and Ray Tracing:

2. Virtual Reality (VR) and Augmented Reality (AR):

3. Cloud Gaming:

4. Artificial Intelligence (AI):

5. Cross-Platform Play:

6. Accessibility Features:

7. Blockchain and NFT Integration:

8. Sustainability and Energy Efficiency:

9. Ethical Game Development Practices:

10. User-Generated Content and Modding:

Section 20.5: Preparing for the Next Wave of DirectX Innovations

1. Continuous Learning and Skill Development:

2. Hardware Upgrades:

3. Adaptability and Flexibility:

4. Collaboration and Networking:

5. Ethical Considerations:

6. Environmental Responsibility:

7. Market Research and Player Feedback:

8. Security and Data Privacy:

9. Accessibility and Inclusivity:

10. Innovation and Risk-Taking:

Chapter 1: Introduction to DirectX

1.1 The Evolution of DirectX: A Historical Overview

DIRECTX HAS A RICH history that spans over two decades, playing a pivotal role in shaping the world of PC gaming. It all began in the early 1990s when Microsoft recognized the need for a standardized API (Application Programming Interface) that would provide game developers with direct access to hardware acceleration on Windows-based systems. This move aimed to simplify game development and improve performance.

The Early Days (DirectX 1-3)

IN 1995, MICROSOFT released the first version of DirectX, DirectX 1. It included libraries for basic graphics and sound support. DirectX 2 and DirectX 3 followed shortly, introducing incremental improvements. These early versions laid the foundation for what would become a critical component of the gaming industry.

DirectX 5-7: Maturing and Expanding

WITH DIRECTX 5, MICROSOFT introduced Direct3D, a dedicated graphics API that enabled developers to create 3D games. DirectX 6 and 7 continued to evolve Direct3D, enhancing features and capabilities, while also adding support for audio and input devices.

DirectX 8-9: Graphics Revolution

DIRECTX 8 BROUGHT SIGNIFICANT changes to the graphics landscape with the introduction of programmable shaders.

This allowed developers to create more realistic and visually stunning games. DirectX 9 continued to build on this foundation, delivering even more advanced shader capabilities and improved graphics quality.

DirectX 10-11: Vista and Beyond

DIRECTX 10 DEBUTED with Windows Vista, introducing a new graphics architecture known as the Windows Display Driver Model (WDDM). DirectX 11 extended support for tessellation, multi-threading, and other modern rendering techniques, pushing the boundaries of graphics realism.

DirectX 12: Low-Level Access

WITH DIRECTX 12, MICROSOFT shifted its focus towards low-level hardware access and reducing CPU overhead. This version aimed to harness the full potential of modern GPUs by providing developers with more direct control over hardware resources.

The Ongoing Evolution

DIRECTX CONTINUES TO evolve with updates and new features. Its importance extends beyond gaming into areas like virtual reality, augmented reality, and professional applications. As technology advances, DirectX remains a fundamental tool for developers seeking to harness the power of modern hardware.

In this chapter, we'll delve deeper into the world of DirectX, exploring its role in game development and how to set up the development environment. We'll also introduce key concepts that serve as the foundation for the rest of the book. Let's embark on this journey through the world of DirectX and its exciting possibilities.

1.2 Understanding DirectX and Its Role in Game Development

DIRECTX, DEVELOPED by Microsoft, is a collection of APIs (Application Programming Interfaces) that facilitate multimedia and gaming development on Windows-based systems. Its primary role is to provide developers with a unified platform for accessing various hardware components, including graphics cards, audio devices, input devices, and networking capabilities. Understanding DirectX is crucial for anyone involved in game development, as it forms the backbone of multimedia applications on the Windows platform.

The Importance of DirectX

DIRECTX SERVES AS A bridge between the hardware and the game or multimedia application. It abstracts the complexity of hardware interactions, allowing developers to write code that works across a wide range of hardware configurations. This abstraction layer is vital for ensuring compatibility and ease of development in the ever-evolving world of PC gaming.

Multimedia Functionality

DIRECTX ENCOMPASSES a wide range of multimedia capabilities, such as 2D and 3D graphics rendering, audio playback and recording, input device management, and network communication. These features make it an all-in-one solution for game developers, eliminating the need to rely on multiple disparate libraries or APIs.

Cross-Platform Considerations

WHILE DIRECTX IS PRIMARILY associated with Windows, its influence extends beyond the Microsoft ecosystem. Many game development engines, like Unity and Unreal Engine, offer DirectX support on multiple platforms, including Windows, Xbox, and even some mobile devices. This cross-platform compatibility allows developers to leverage their DirectX skills on various platforms.

DirectX Versions

DIRECTX HAS GONE THROUGH several iterations, each introducing new features and capabilities. As of the book's publication, DirectX 12 is the latest version, offering low-level access to hardware and improved performance. However, it's essential to consider the target audience and platform when choosing a DirectX version for your game.

DirectX and Game Engines

MANY POPULAR GAME ENGINES, such as Unity and Unreal Engine, provide integration with DirectX, making it easier for developers to leverage its capabilities. Understanding how DirectX fits into your chosen game engine's workflow is crucial for optimizing performance and achieving the desired visual and audio effects.

DirectX in Modern Game Development

IN CONTEMPORARY GAME development, DirectX plays a pivotal role in creating immersive experiences. It enables realistic 3D graphics, advanced shader effects, high-quality audio, and responsive input handling. Whether you're an indie developer or part of a large studio, a solid understanding of DirectX is essential for pushing the boundaries of game design and delivering captivating experiences to players.

In the following chapters, we will explore various aspects of DirectX in more detail, from graphics rendering and sound management to input handling and network communication. By the end of this book, you'll have a comprehensive understanding of DirectX and the tools to create impressive games and multimedia applications for Windows-based systems.

1.3 DirectX Versions: From Past to Present

DIRECTX HAS EVOLVED significantly since its inception, with each new version bringing improvements, features, and optimizations to the world of game development. Understanding the history and progression of DirectX versions is crucial for game developers as it directly impacts the capabilities and performance of their applications.

DirectX 1-3: The Foundation

THE INITIAL VERSIONS of DirectX, including DirectX 1, 2, and 3, laid the groundwork for multimedia and gaming on Windows. They provided basic support for graphics and audio, marking the beginning of DirectX's journey.

DirectX 5-7: Building Blocks

DIRECTX 5 INTRODUCED Direct3D, a significant milestone in DirectX's history. This version set the stage for 3D graphics in games. DirectX 6 and 7 continued to enhance Direct3D, improving its capabilities and making it more accessible to developers.

DirectX 8-9: The Graphics Revolution

DIRECTX 8 WAS A GAME-changer with its introduction of programmable shaders. This innovation allowed developers to create visually stunning and realistic graphics effects, significantly enhancing the gaming experience. DirectX 9 expanded upon this by introducing more advanced shader capabilities, pushing the boundaries of what was possible in terms of graphics quality.

DirectX 10-11: Modern Graphics

DIRECTX 10 ARRIVED with Windows Vista, bringing the Windows Display Driver Model (WDDM) and improved graphics performance. DirectX 11 built on this foundation, introducing support for tessellation, multi-threading, and other advanced rendering techniques.

DirectX 12: Low-Level Access

DIRECTX 12 SHIFTED the focus towards providing developers with low-level access to hardware resources. This version aimed to reduce CPU overhead and maximize the potential of modern GPUs, leading to significant performance improvements.

DirectX Today

AS OF THE BOOK'S PUBLICATION, DirectX 12 remains the latest version, widely used in Windows-based gaming and multimedia applications. It continues to receive updates, bug fixes, and new features, ensuring that it remains a relevant and powerful tool for game developers.

Choosing the Right DirectX Version

SELECTING THE APPROPRIATE DirectX version for your project is essential. Factors to consider include your target audience, hardware requirements, and desired features. DirectX 12 offers the latest advancements but may not be suitable for all scenarios, especially if you need to support older hardware or different platforms.

DirectX and Windows Compatibility

DIRECTX IS TIGHTLY integrated with the Windows operating system. This means that DirectX versions may be tied to specific Windows releases. It's essential to check compatibility and ensure that your target audience can run your application without issues.

Future of DirectX

WHILE DIRECTX REMAINS a vital component of Windows gaming, the landscape is continually evolving. New technologies like ray tracing, machine learning, and real-time ray tracing are shaping the future of graphics. DirectX will likely adapt to incorporate these innovations, ensuring its relevance in the ever-changing world of game development.

DirectX Alternatives

IT'S WORTH NOTING THAT other graphics and multimedia APIs exist, such as Vulkan and OpenGL, which offer cross-platform capabilities. Game developers should also consider these alternatives, depending on their project's requirements and target platforms.

In the upcoming chapters, we will explore the practical aspects of using DirectX, regardless of the version you choose. We will delve into graphics rendering, audio management, input handling, and other critical topics to empower you as a game developer in creating compelling and immersive experiences.

1.4 Setting Up the Development Environment for DirectX

BEFORE DIVING INTO DirectX game development, it's essential to set up the proper development environment. This environment includes the necessary tools, libraries, and configurations to ensure a smooth and productive development process. In this section, we'll guide you through the steps to set up your development environment for DirectX.

Windows Operating System

DIRECTX IS TIGHTLY integrated with the Windows operating system. Therefore, you'll need a Windows-based machine to develop DirectX applications. The exact version of Windows you require may depend on the DirectX version you plan to use, as some versions are tied to specific Windows releases.

Visual Studio IDE

MICROSOFT VISUAL STUDIO is the preferred Integrated Development Environment (IDE) for DirectX development. It provides a comprehensive set of tools and features for creating, debugging, and optimizing DirectX applications. You can download the latest version of Visual Studio from the official Microsoft website.

DirectX SDK

THE DIRECTX SOFTWARE Development Kit (SDK) is a collection of libraries, headers, and tools that you'll need for DirectX development. However, it's important to note that starting with Windows 8, the DirectX SDK is no longer a separate download. Instead, the necessary headers and libraries are included with the Windows SDK. Make sure to install the Windows SDK that corresponds to your target Windows version.

Graphics Drivers

TO LEVERAGE DIRECTX'S graphics capabilities fully, ensure that you have up-to-date graphics drivers installed for your graphics card. Check the website of your graphics card manufacturer (e.g., NVIDIA, AMD, Intel) for the latest driver updates.

DirectX End-User Runtimes

IF YOU PLAN TO DISTRIBUTE your DirectX application to end-users, they will need the DirectX End-User Runtimes installed on their systems. These runtimes provide the necessary DirectX components for running DirectX applications. You can include the DirectX End-User Runtimes installer with your application's installer for convenience.

Debugging Tools

DEBUGGING IS A CRUCIAL part of game development. Visual Studio includes powerful debugging tools that allow you to diagnose and fix issues in your DirectX applications. Familiarize yourself with these tools, such as the Visual Studio Debugger, to streamline the debugging process.

DirectX Samples and Tutorials

MICROSOFT PROVIDES a wealth of DirectX samples and tutorials to help you get started. These resources offer code examples, documentation, and best practices for various aspects of DirectX development. Exploring these samples can be a valuable learning experience.

DirectX Community and Forums

JOINING THE DIRECTX developer community and forums can provide you with valuable insights, support, and solutions to common issues. Websites like the DirectX Developer Blog and MSDN DirectX Forum are excellent places to connect with fellow developers.

Project Configuration

ONCE YOU HAVE ALL THE necessary tools and libraries installed, you'll need to configure your development environment for your specific DirectX project. This may involve setting up project properties, including the necessary headers and libraries, and configuring build settings.

Development Assets

PREPARE THE ASSETS you'll need for your game, such as 3D models, textures, sound files, and shaders. Organize your assets and ensure they are in the appropriate formats for use with DirectX.

Version Control

CONSIDER USING VERSION control software, such as Git, to manage your DirectX project's source code and collaborate with team members if applicable. Proper version control helps track changes and ensures project stability.

With your development environment properly set up, you're ready to start exploring DirectX and creating your own game or multimedia applications. In the upcoming chapters, we'll dive deeper into DirectX's various components and guide you through the process of developing DirectX-based applications.

1.5 Key Concepts in DirectX: An Overview

BEFORE DELVING DEEPER into DirectX game development, it's essential to grasp some key concepts and terminologies that will be frequently encountered throughout this book. These concepts provide the foundational understanding necessary to work effectively with DirectX. Let's explore these essential concepts in DirectX.

1.5.1 Graphics Rendering

GRAPHICS RENDERING is the process of generating images or frames that make up a game's visuals. DirectX provides the tools and APIs for rendering 2D and 3D graphics, allowing developers to create lifelike and immersive game environments. Understanding rendering pipelines, shaders, and graphics primitives is fundamental to mastering DirectX's rendering capabilities.

1.5.2 Shaders

SHADERS ARE SMALL PROGRAMS that run on the GPU (Graphics Processing Unit) and control various aspects of rendering, such as vertex transformation, pixel color calculations, and lighting effects. DirectX uses High-Level Shader Language (HLSL) for shader programming, and developers need to be proficient in HLSL to create stunning visual effects.

1.5.3 Textures

TEXTURES ARE 2D IMAGES applied to 3D models or used for 2D graphics. They add detail, realism, and visual appeal to game objects. DirectX provides tools for loading, mapping, and applying textures to surfaces, enabling developers to create rich and textured environments.

1.5.4 Input Handling

DIRECTX OFFERS MECHANISMS for handling input from various sources, including keyboards, mice, game controllers, and touch devices. Understanding how to process user input is essential for creating interactive and responsive applications.

1.5.5 Audio Management

AUDIO PLAYS A CRUCIAL role in game immersion. DirectX provides DirectSound for managing audio playback, recording, and 3D audio effects. Developers need to know how to load and play audio files, apply spatial audio effects, and synchronize sound with gameplay.

1.5.6 Networking

FOR MULTIPLAYER GAMES and online experiences, DirectX offers networking capabilities through DirectPlay. Understanding the basics of network programming and synchronization is vital for creating multiplayer games and online features.

1.5.7 Game Physics

PHYSICS ENGINES ARE used to simulate realistic interactions between objects in a game world. DirectX enables developers to integrate physics engines and handle collision detection, response, and object movement to create lifelike game environments.

1.5.8 Shader Language (HLSL)

HIGH-LEVEL SHADER LANGUAGE (HLSL) is a critical component of DirectX programming. HLSL allows developers to write shaders that run on the GPU and control various aspects of rendering. Knowledge of HLSL syntax, semantics, and optimization techniques is essential for achieving stunning visuals.

1.5.9 Cross-Platform Considerations

WHILE DIRECTX IS PRIMARILY associated with Windows, developers often need to consider cross-platform compatibility. Understanding how to make DirectX applications cross-platform or choosing alternative APIs like Vulkan or OpenGL is important for reaching a broader audience.

1.5.10 DirectX and Game Engines

MANY GAME DEVELOPMENT engines, such as Unity and Unreal Engine, offer integration with DirectX. Understanding how to work with DirectX within these engines can significantly streamline the development process and leverage their capabilities.

These key concepts provide an initial glimpse into the world of DirectX game development. As you progress through the book, you'll delve deeper into each of these areas, gaining the knowledge and skills needed to create impressive DirectX-based games and multimedia applications. Keep these concepts in mind as you explore DirectX further in the following chapters.

Chapter 2: The DirectX Graphics Infrastructure

2.1 Diving into Direct3D: Rendering 3D Graphics

DIRECT3D IS A FUNDAMENTAL component of DirectX responsible for rendering three-dimensional graphics. It allows game developers to create immersive 3D environments, characters, and objects that bring games to life. In this section, we'll explore the core concepts of Direct3D and how it enables the rendering of 3D graphics.

Direct3D Basics

DIRECT3D PROVIDES A framework for creating and manipulating 3D graphics in real-time. It abstracts the complexities of hardware acceleration, allowing developers to focus on creating visually appealing games. To work with Direct3D, you need to understand the basics of 3D graphics, including concepts like vertices, polygons, shaders, and transformations.

The Rendering Pipeline

THE RENDERING PIPELINE is the sequence of stages that a 3D scene goes through to be displayed on the screen. It consists of several stages, including vertex processing, geometry shading, rasterization, pixel shading, and output merger. Each stage has a specific function in transforming vertices and pixels into the final image.

Vertex Processing

VERTEX PROCESSING IS the first stage of the rendering pipeline. It involves transforming 3D coordinates of vertices into 2D screen coordinates. Common operations in this stage include vertex transformations (translation, rotation, scaling), lighting calculations, and applying shaders.

Geometry Shading

GEOMETRY SHADING IS an optional stage that allows developers to manipulate the geometry of 3D models. This stage is particularly useful for tessellation, particle systems, and other advanced effects that require altering the shape of objects.

Rasterization

RASTERIZATION IS THE process of converting the 2D coordinates of triangles or polygons into individual pixels on the screen. This stage determines which pixels are covered by each primitive and calculates their attributes, such as color and depth.

Pixel Shading

PIXEL SHADING, ALSO known as fragment shading, is where the final appearance of each pixel is determined. Shaders are used to calculate the pixel's color based on lighting, textures, and other factors. Pixel shaders are essential for achieving realistic lighting and visual effects.

Output Merger

THE OUTPUT MERGER STAGE combines the output of pixel shaders and performs operations like blending, depth testing, and stencil testing to determine the final pixel values that will be displayed on the screen.

Shaders in Direct3D

SHADERS ARE PROGRAMS written in High-Level Shader Language (HLSL) that control various stages of the rendering pipeline. There are two main types of shaders in Direct3D:

- **Vertex Shaders:** These shaders process each vertex in a 3D model and can perform transformations, lighting calculations, and other per-vertex operations.

- **Pixel Shaders:** Pixel shaders are responsible for determining the final color of each pixel on the screen. They handle lighting, texture mapping, and various visual effects.

Direct3D Versions

DIRECT3D HAS EVOLVED over the years, with different versions offering new features and capabilities. As of the book's publication, DirectX 12 is the latest version of Direct3D, known for its low-level hardware access and improved performance. However, you may encounter older versions in legacy projects or on specific platforms.

Creating a Direct3D Application

TO START WORKING WITH Direct3D, you'll need to set up a Direct3D application. This involves initializing the Direct3D device, creating 3D models, loading textures, and implementing shaders. Properly managing resources and understanding the rendering pipeline are crucial for building efficient and visually appealing 3D applications.

In the following chapters, we'll dive deeper into Direct3D programming, exploring how to create 3D models, apply textures, implement shaders, and optimize rendering performance. Understanding the core concepts of Direct3D is essential as you embark on your journey to become proficient in 3D graphics rendering with DirectX.

2.2 Understanding Shaders and the Graphics Pipeline

SHADERS ARE AT THE heart of modern graphics programming and play a pivotal role in the DirectX graphics pipeline. In this section, we will delve into the concepts of shaders and their significance in rendering 3D graphics with DirectX.

What Are Shaders?

SHADERS ARE SPECIALIZED programs written in High-Level Shader Language (HLSL) that run on the Graphics Processing Unit (GPU). They are responsible for processing vertices and pixels in the graphics pipeline, making them integral to the rendering process. Shaders allow developers to control how 3D models appear on the screen by defining how light interacts with surfaces, textures are applied, and visual effects are achieved.

Vertex Shaders

VERTEX SHADERS ARE the first type of shader encountered in the graphics pipeline. They operate on each vertex of a 3D model and handle operations such as transformations (translation, rotation, scaling), lighting calculations, and skeletal animations. Vertex shaders are responsible for positioning vertices in 3D space and preparing them for rasterization.

Geometry Shaders

GEOMETRY SHADERS ARE optional shaders that can be used to manipulate the geometry of 3D models. They can generate additional vertices, create tessellated surfaces, or implement particle systems. Geometry shaders provide versatility in altering the shape and appearance of objects in real-time.

Pixel Shaders (Fragment Shaders)

PIXEL SHADERS, ALSO known as fragment shaders, are critical for determining the final color of each pixel on the screen. They operate after rasterization and handle tasks such as applying textures, calculating lighting, and implementing visual effects like shadows and reflections. Pixel shaders are key to achieving realistic and visually appealing graphics.

Shader Compilation

BEFORE SHADERS CAN be used in a DirectX application, they must be compiled into bytecode using the HLSL compiler. This bytecode can then be loaded and executed by the GPU. Shader compilation is typically done as part of the application's initialization process.

Shader Constants and Variables

SHADERS CAN RECEIVE input data in the form of constants and variables. Constants are values that do not change during shader execution, while variables can vary per vertex or pixel. These inputs are essential for passing information such as transformation matrices, lighting parameters, and texture coordinates to shaders.

Shader Stages in the Pipeline

SHADERS ARE EXECUTED in various stages of the graphics pipeline, depending on their type. Vertex shaders run in the vertex processing stage, geometry shaders in the geometry shading stage, and pixel shaders in the pixel shading stage. Understanding the order of execution and the role of each shader stage is crucial for achieving the desired visual results.

Shader Effects and Visual Realism

SHADERS ARE THE DRIVING force behind many visual effects in modern games. They enable realistic lighting, shadows, reflections, and materials. Advanced shader techniques like parallax mapping, displacement mapping, and screen-space effects can significantly enhance the visual fidelity of a game.

Shader Optimization

EFFICIENT SHADER PROGRAMMING is essential for maintaining good performance in graphics-intensive applications. Optimizing shaders involves reducing redundant calculations, minimizing memory access, and leveraging the GPU's parallel processing capabilities. Profiling and performance analysis tools help identify bottlenecks and areas for improvement.

In the following chapters, we will explore shader programming in more detail, including writing HLSL code, integrating shaders into DirectX applications, and implementing various visual effects. Shaders are a powerful tool for creating stunning 3D graphics, and a solid understanding of their principles is essential for any DirectX graphics programmer.

2.3 Textures and Materials in DirectX

TEXTURES AND MATERIALS play a crucial role in enhancing the visual quality and realism of 3D graphics in DirectX. In this section, we will explore the concepts of textures and materials, how they are applied to 3D models, and their impact on the rendering process.

Textures in DirectX

TEXTURES ARE 2D IMAGES used to add detail, color, and surface characteristics to 3D models. They are a fundamental component of DirectX rendering and enable the simulation of various materials, such as wood, metal, or fabric. Textures are applied to the surfaces of 3D objects to create the appearance of complex materials and intricate details.

Texture Coordinates

TO APPLY A TEXTURE to a 3D model, developers use texture coordinates (UV coordinates) that map points on the model's surface to corresponding points on the texture. These coordinates determine how the texture is wrapped around the model's geometry, allowing for precise control over how the texture appears.

Common Types of Textures

DIRECTX SUPPORTS VARIOUS types of textures, including:

- **Diffuse Textures:** These textures define the base color or appearance of an object's surface.

- **Normal Maps:** Normal maps encode surface normals to simulate detailed geometry on flat surfaces.

- **Specular Maps:** Specular maps control the shininess and reflectivity of materials.

- **Height Maps:** Height maps encode height information for creating displacement or parallax effects.

- **Alpha Maps:** Alpha maps control transparency and opacity.

Texture Filtering and Mipmaps

TEXTURE FILTERING TECHNIQUES are used to control how textures are sampled when they are magnified or minified. Mipmaps are precomputed, lower-resolution versions of textures used to improve texture quality when textures are viewed at different distances. Understanding texture filtering and mipmapping is crucial for achieving smooth and visually appealing textures.

Materials and Shading

MATERIALS DEFINE HOW light interacts with an object's surface. In DirectX, materials are often represented by a combination of textures and shader parameters. Materials determine properties such as the object's color, reflectivity, transparency, and specular highlights.

Diffuse, Specular, and Normal Mapping

DIFFUSE MAPPING CONTROLS the base color of an object, while specular mapping determines the shininess and reflection of surfaces. Normal mapping simulates intricate surface details by encoding normal vectors in a texture. These mapping techniques allow developers to create realistic and visually appealing materials.

Texture Compression

TEXTURE FILES CAN BE large, especially when dealing with high-resolution textures. Texture compression techniques, such as DXT and BC formats, reduce the size of textures while preserving image quality. Using compressed textures is essential for optimizing memory usage and improving performance.

Texture Loading and Management

DIRECTX PROVIDES FUNCTIONS and libraries for loading various image formats into textures. Proper texture management, including texture creation, updating, and releasing, is essential to prevent memory leaks and optimize resource usage.

Dynamic Texturing

IN SOME CASES, TEXTURES need to be generated or updated dynamically during runtime. Techniques like render-to-texture and dynamic texture mapping allow for real-time texture creation and manipulation, enabling effects like reflections and dynamic shadows.

Shader Integration

TEXTURES ARE OFTEN used in conjunction with shaders to achieve complex visual effects. Shaders can sample textures to determine pixel color, apply normal maps for realistic lighting, and combine multiple textures for material rendering. Shader programming skills are essential for effectively using textures in DirectX applications.

Understanding how textures and materials work in DirectX is a fundamental aspect of 3D graphics programming. As you progress in DirectX development, you'll learn how to apply textures to 3D models, create realistic materials, and use shaders to bring your virtual worlds to life.

2.4 Lighting and Shadows: Techniques and Implementation

LIGHTING AND SHADOWS are fundamental aspects of 3D graphics that significantly impact the visual realism of DirectX-rendered scenes. In this section, we will explore the concepts of lighting, shadow techniques, and their implementation in DirectX.

Lighting in 3D Graphics

LIGHTING IS THE PROCESS of simulating how light interacts with 3D objects in a virtual scene. Proper lighting enhances the depth, materials, and overall realism of a 3D environment. Understanding the principles of lighting is crucial for achieving visually appealing results.

Types of Lighting

DIRECTX SUPPORTS VARIOUS types of lighting, including:

- **Ambient Lighting:** Ambient light simulates indirect light sources, providing uniform illumination to the entire scene.

- **Diffuse Lighting:** Diffuse light represents the direct illumination of a surface by a light source. It determines the surface's brightness based on the angle between the light source and the surface normal.

- **Specular Lighting:** Specular light accounts for highlights caused by the reflection of light sources on smooth surfaces. It creates shiny or reflective areas on objects.

- **Emissive Lighting:** Emissive light makes objects appear to emit light themselves, without relying on external light sources.

Light Sources

IN DIRECTX, LIGHT SOURCES can be directional, point lights, or spotlights. Directional lights, like sunlight, emit parallel rays of light. Point lights emit light uniformly in all directions from a specific point in 3D space. Spotlights emit light within a cone-shaped region, allowing for focused illumination.

The Phong Lighting Model

THE PHONG LIGHTING model is a widely used model for simulating lighting effects in 3D graphics. It combines ambient, diffuse, and specular lighting to determine the final color of a pixel or vertex. The model's parameters control the material properties and lighting characteristics.

Shadow Techniques

SHADOWS ARE ESSENTIAL for creating depth and realism in 3D scenes. DirectX provides several techniques for implementing shadows:

- **Shadow Mapping:** Shadow mapping involves rendering the scene from the perspective of a light source to create a depth map of the scene. This depth map is then used to determine which areas are in shadow.

- **Shadow Volumes:** Shadow volumes are used to calculate shadows by determining which parts of the scene are occluded from a light source. They require the creation of shadow volumes for objects.

- **Shadow Ray Tracing:** Ray tracing techniques can be used to simulate accurate and realistic shadows, but they are computationally expensive and often reserved for offline rendering or high-end applications.

Shadow Mapping in DirectX

SHADOW MAPPING IS ONE of the most commonly used shadow techniques in DirectX. It involves rendering the scene from the viewpoint of a light source into a depth texture, called a shadow map. During the final rendering pass, the shadow map is sampled to determine whether a pixel is in shadow or illuminated.

Normal Mapping for Realistic Lighting

NORMAL MAPPING IS A technique that uses a texture to simulate fine surface details at the pixel level. By encoding normal vectors in a texture, developers can achieve the appearance of complex geometry on flat surfaces. Normal maps are often used in combination with diffuse and specular maps to enhance lighting realism.

Shader Programming for Lighting

TO IMPLEMENT ADVANCED lighting and shadow effects, shader programming is essential. Shaders enable developers to perform complex lighting calculations and shadow map sampling efficiently on the GPU. HLSL shaders can be used to create realistic materials, apply lighting models, and calculate shadows.

Optimization Considerations

EFFICIENTLY IMPLEMENTING lighting and shadows is crucial for maintaining good rendering performance. Techniques such as hierarchical shadow maps, percentage-closer soft shadows, and shadow map filtering can improve shadow quality while minimizing computational overhead.

Mastering lighting and shadow techniques is a vital aspect of DirectX 3D graphics programming. As you continue your exploration of DirectX, you will learn how to implement various lighting models, shadow mapping, and shader programming to create visually stunning and realistic 3D environments.

2.5 Advanced 3D Modeling and Rendering

IN THIS SECTION, WE will delve into advanced 3D modeling and rendering techniques that enable you to create complex and visually captivating scenes in DirectX.

Model Complexity

AS DIRECTX DEVELOPERS, you will often encounter scenarios where basic geometric primitives like spheres and cubes are insufficient. To represent intricate objects, characters, or environments, you may need to work with highly detailed 3D models. These models can be created using 3D modeling software such as Blender, Maya, or 3ds Max. DirectX supports the import of various 3D model formats, including FBX and OBJ, to bring these models into your application.

Level of Detail (LOD)

TO OPTIMIZE PERFORMANCE while maintaining visual quality, the Level of Detail (LOD) technique is employed. LOD involves creating multiple versions of a 3D model with varying levels of detail. These models are switched dynamically based on the object's distance from the camera. LOD helps reduce the computational load and memory requirements, especially for distant or less visible objects.

Terrain Rendering

FOR OUTDOOR ENVIRONMENTS, rendering realistic terrains is a common requirement. DirectX offers techniques like heightmap-based terrain rendering, where a grayscale image (heightmap) defines the elevation of terrain points. Tessellation shaders can then be used to create a detailed mesh based on the heightmap. Terrain texturing and blending are essential for applying various textures to the terrain surface, including grass, rocks, and dirt.

Particle Systems

PARTICLE SYSTEMS ARE employed to simulate various natural phenomena like fire, smoke, rain, and explosions. DirectX allows for the creation of particle systems by rendering numerous small textured sprites that move and behave according to predefined rules. Implementing particle systems involves shader programming for dynamic particle motion, scaling, and fading.

Procedural Generation

PROCEDURAL GENERATION techniques are used to create content algorithmically, reducing the need for manually created assets. DirectX developers can employ procedural generation for terrain, vegetation, textures, and even entire levels. Procedural content generation can enhance the variety and replayability of games.

Instancing

INSTANCING IS A RENDERING technique that allows for efficient rendering of multiple instances of the same 3D model with slight variations. It reduces the overhead associated with rendering duplicate models by sharing geometry and materials. Instancing is particularly valuable for rendering large crowds, forests, or similar scenarios.

Virtual Reality (VR) and Augmented Reality (AR)

DIRECTX SUPPORTS VIRTUAL reality (VR) and augmented reality (AR) development. VR immerses users in a virtual world through headsets like Oculus Rift or HTC Vive, while AR blends virtual content with the real world using devices like Microsoft HoloLens. DirectX provides the tools and libraries needed to create immersive VR and AR experiences, including stereoscopic rendering, head tracking, and hand controllers.

Deferred Rendering

DEFERRED RENDERING is a technique that optimizes the rendering process by separating the rendering of geometry and lighting. It allows for rendering complex scenes with numerous light sources efficiently. In deferred rendering, the geometry is first rendered to a G-buffer, and then lighting calculations are performed in a separate pass.

Post-Processing Effects

POST-PROCESSING EFFECTS are applied to the final rendered image to enhance visual quality and add artistic or realistic effects. Techniques like bloom, depth of field, motion blur, and color grading can be implemented using DirectX shaders. These effects contribute to the overall visual appeal of the game or application.

Global Illumination

GLOBAL ILLUMINATION techniques, such as radiosity and ray tracing, simulate indirect lighting and light bounce in scenes. While these techniques can be computationally intensive, they offer unparalleled realism by accurately modeling light interactions. DirectX can be used in conjunction with ray tracing APIs for real-time ray tracing and global illumination effects.

Advanced 3D modeling and rendering techniques open up a world of possibilities for DirectX developers. Whether you're creating highly detailed environments, simulating complex natural phenomena, or optimizing rendering pipelines, mastering these techniques is essential for achieving exceptional visual quality and realism in your DirectX applications.

Chapter 3: DirectX and 2D Graphics

3.1 2D Graphics with Direct2D

DIRECT2D IS A VERSATILE 2D graphics API provided by DirectX for rendering high-quality 2D graphics in Windows applications. In this section, we'll explore the capabilities of Direct2D and learn how to use it to create 2D graphics within your DirectX applications.

Introduction to Direct2D

DIRECT2D IS DESIGNED for hardware-accelerated 2D graphics rendering, making it suitable for a wide range of applications, including games, user interfaces, data visualization, and more. It provides a streamlined and efficient way to create 2D graphics with a focus on performance and visual quality.

Key Features of Direct2D

DIRECT2D OFFERS SEVERAL key features and advantages:

- **Hardware Acceleration:** Direct2D leverages GPU hardware acceleration to achieve fast and smooth 2D graphics rendering.

- **High-Quality Rendering:** It supports antialiasing and subpixel positioning, ensuring high-quality output.

- **Vector Graphics:** Direct2D is particularly well-suited for rendering vector-based graphics, which can be scaled without loss of quality.

- **Efficient Brush and Path Handling:** It provides efficient mechanisms for handling brushes (solid, gradient, bitmap) and defining complex paths.

- **DirectWrite Integration:** Direct2D seamlessly integrates with DirectWrite for high-quality text rendering.

- **Layered Composition:** It supports layering and composition of graphics elements, allowing for complex scene composition.

- **Transparency and Blending:** Direct2D allows for transparency, blending, and alpha compositing to create visually appealing effects.

Initializing Direct2D

TO USE DIRECT2D IN a Windows application, you need to initialize it properly. This involves creating a Direct2D factory object and initializing the rendering target, which can be a window or a bitmap.

```
#include <d2d1.h>

ID2D1Factory* pD2DFactory = nullptr;

ID2D1HwndRenderTarget* pRenderTarget = nullptr;

// Initialize Direct2D

D2D1CreateFactory(D2D1_FACTORY_TYPE_SINGLE_THREADE
&pD2DFactory);

pD2DFactory->CreateHwndRenderTarget(
```

```
D2D1::RenderTargetProperties(),

D2D1::HwndRenderTargetProperties(hWnd, D2D1::SizeU(width, height)),

&pRenderTarget

);
```

Drawing Shapes and Paths

DIRECT2D PROVIDES VARIOUS methods for drawing basic shapes like rectangles, ellipses, and lines. You can also create complex paths composed of multiple segments. Here's an example of drawing a rectangle on the rendering target:

```
pRenderTarget->BeginDraw();

// Define a rectangle

D2D1_RECT_F rect = D2D1::RectF(10.0f, 10.0f, 100.0f, 100.0f);

// Create a brush for filling the rectangle

ID2D1SolidColorBrush* pBrush = nullptr;

pRenderTarget->CreateSolidColorBrush(D2D1::ColorF(D2D1::ColorF::C
&pBrush);

// Fill the rectangle

pRenderTarget->FillRectangle(rect, pBrush);

pRenderTarget->EndDraw();
```

Working with Brushes

DIRECT2D SUPPORTS VARIOUS brush types, including solid color brushes, gradient brushes, and bitmap brushes. Brushes define how the interior of shapes is filled. Here's an example of using a linear gradient brush to fill a rectangle:

```
// Define a gradient stop collection

ID2D1GradientStopCollection* pGradientStops = nullptr;

D2D1_GRADIENT_STOP gradientStops[] = {

{ 0.0f, D2D1::ColorF(D2D1::ColorF::Red) },

{ 1.0f, D2D1::ColorF(D2D1::ColorF::Blue) }

};

pRenderTarget->CreateGradientStopCollection(gradientStops, 2, &pGradientStops);

// Create a linear gradient brush

ID2D1LinearGradientBrush* pLinearGradientBrush = nullptr;

pRenderTarget->CreateLinearGradientBrush(

D2D1::LinearGradientBrushProperties(D2D1::Point2F(0, 0), D2D1::Point2F(100, 100)),

D2D1::BrushProperties(),

pGradientStops,

&pLinearGradientBrush

);
```

```
// Fill a rectangle with the linear gradient brush

pRenderTarget->FillRectangle(rect, pLinearGradientBrush);
```

Text Rendering with DirectWrite

DIRECT2D SEAMLESSLY integrates with DirectWrite for high-quality text rendering. You can use DirectWrite to create text layouts and render text on the Direct2D rendering target.

```
#include <dwrite.h>

IDWriteFactory* pDWriteFactory = nullptr;

// Initialize DirectWrite

DWriteCreateFactory(DWRITE_FACTORY_TYPE_SHARED,
__uuidof(IDWriteFactory),
reinterpret_cast<IUnknown**>(&pDWriteFactory));

// Create a text layout

IDWriteTextLayout* pTextLayout = nullptr;

pDWriteFactory->CreateTextLayout(

L"Hello, Direct2D!",

wcslen(L"Hello, Direct2D!"),

pTextFormat,

width, // Width of the text layout

height, // Height of the text layout

&pTextLayout

);
```

```
// Draw the text layout

pRenderTarget->DrawTextLayout(D2D1::Point2F(10, 10), pTextLayout, pBrush);
```

Layered Composition

DIRECT2D ALLOWS YOU to create layers and composite graphics elements within those layers. This enables you to separate different parts of your scene, apply transformations, and control the rendering order.

```
// Create a layer

ID2D1Layer* pLayer = nullptr;

pRenderTarget->CreateLayer(&pLayer);

// Begin drawing in the layer

pRenderTarget->PushLayer
```

3.2 Integrating 2D and 3D Graphics

INTEGRATING 2D AND 3D graphics is a common requirement in game development and interactive applications. In this section, we'll explore how to seamlessly combine 2D and 3D elements within DirectX to create immersive and visually engaging experiences.

The Need for 2D and 3D Integration

MANY APPLICATIONS, including games, simulations, and interactive multimedia, benefit from combining 2D and 3D graphics. 2D elements, such as user interfaces, HUD (Heads-Up Display), text, and 2D sprites, provide essential information and interactions in a visually familiar format. Meanwhile, 3D graphics handle the rendering of the game world, characters, objects, and environments. Integrating these two aspects effectively enhances the overall user experience.

Using Direct3D for 3D Graphics

DIRECT3D IS THE 3D graphics API of DirectX and is commonly used for rendering 3D scenes. It provides a framework for creating 3D models, applying textures, managing shaders, and handling the rendering pipeline. To integrate 2D and 3D graphics, you'll often use Direct3D for the 3D component of your application.

Direct2D for 2D Graphics

AS DISCUSSED IN THE previous section, Direct2D is ideal for handling 2D graphics. It offers high-quality 2D rendering with hardware acceleration, making it suitable for creating user interfaces, text, and 2D elements.

Overlaying 2D Elements on 3D Scenes

ONE COMMON APPROACH to integrating 2D and 3D graphics is overlaying 2D elements on top of the 3D scene. This can be achieved by rendering the 3D scene to a portion of the screen and then rendering 2D elements on top of it. The 2D elements can include menus, health bars, score displays, and other HUD elements.

Here's a simplified code snippet that demonstrates how to render a 3D scene using Direct3D and overlay 2D text using Direct2D:

```
// Render the 3D scene using Direct3D

Render3DScene();

// Switch to 2D rendering using Direct2D
```

```
pRenderTarget->BeginDraw();

// Render 2D text on top of the 3D scene

pRenderTarget->DrawText(

L"Score: 100",

wcslen(L"Score: 100"),

pTextFormat,

D2D1::RectF(10, 10, 200, 50),

pBrush

);

// End 2D rendering

pRenderTarget->EndDraw();
```

Billboarding

BILLBOARDING IS A TECHNIQUE commonly used for rendering 2D sprites or objects in a 3D environment. It involves creating a 2D sprite that always faces the camera, ensuring that it appears flat and aligned regardless of the camera's position and orientation. Billboarding is useful for rendering trees, foliage, or particles in a 3D world.

Depth Testing and Blending

WHEN OVERLAYING 2D elements on a 3D scene, it's essential to consider depth testing and blending. Depth testing ensures that 3D objects occlude 2D elements correctly based on their depth in the scene. Blending allows for smooth transitions and transparency effects when 2D and 3D elements intersect.

User Interface (UI) Integration

INTEGRATING A 2D USER interface (UI) into a 3D game or application is a common scenario. You can create UI elements as 2D textures or layers and position them within the 3D scene or as overlays. Interactions with the UI can trigger game events or modify the 3D environment.

DirectComposition

DIRECTCOMPOSITION IS another DirectX component that aids in 2D and 3D integration. It provides advanced capabilities for compositing 2D and 3D content efficiently, managing visual trees, and handling animations and transitions.

Cross-Device Integration

IN ADDITION TO INTEGRATING 2D and 3D graphics on a single screen, DirectX enables cross-device integration. This means you can extend your application to multiple screens, VR headsets, or augmented reality (AR) devices while maintaining a coherent user experience.

Conclusion

INTEGRATING 2D AND 3D graphics in DirectX applications opens up possibilities for creating engaging and interactive experiences. Whether you're building games, simulations, or interactive visualizations, mastering the art of combining 2D and 3D elements is essential for delivering immersive and visually appealing content to your users.

3.3 Text Rendering and Font Management

TEXT RENDERING IS A fundamental aspect of many DirectX applications, including games, user interfaces, and productivity software. This section explores how to render text effectively using DirectX and manage fonts for various purposes.

The Importance of Text Rendering

TEXT IS A VITAL ELEMENT in user interfaces, dialog boxes, HUDs (Heads-Up Displays), and informational displays in applications and games. Proper text rendering ensures that textual content is legible, visually pleasing, and aligns with the overall design and aesthetic of the application.

DirectWrite for High-Quality Text

DIRECTX PROVIDES DIRECTWRITE, a text layout and rendering API, for handling text in Windows applications. DirectWrite is designed to produce high-quality text output, offering support for font hinting, anti-aliasing, and subpixel positioning. It seamlessly integrates with Direct2D for rendering text within DirectX applications.

Initializing DirectWrite

BEFORE RENDERING TEXT with DirectWrite, you need to initialize the DirectWrite factory and create a text format. Here's a simplified example:

```
#include <dwrite.h>

IDWriteFactory* pDWriteFactory = nullptr;

// Initialize DirectWrite
```

```
DWriteCreateFactory(DWRITE_FACTORY_TYPE_SHARED,
__uuidof(IDWriteFactory),
reinterpret_cast<IUnknown**>(&pDWriteFactory));

// Create a text format

IDWriteTextFormat* pTextFormat = nullptr;

pDWriteFactory->CreateTextFormat(

L"Arial",

nullptr,

DWRITE_FONT_WEIGHT_NORMAL,

DWRITE_FONT_STYLE_NORMAL,

DWRITE_FONT_STRETCH_NORMAL,

fontSize,

L"", // Font locale

&pTextFormat

);
```

Rendering Text with DirectWrite

ONCE YOU HAVE A DIRECTWRITE text format, you can use it to render text on a Direct2D rendering target or any other suitable surface. Here's a basic example of how to draw text on a Direct2D rendering target:

```
// Begin Direct2D drawing

pRenderTarget->BeginDraw();
```

```
// Set the text format and brush
pRenderTarget->DrawText(
L"Hello, DirectX!",
wcslen(L"Hello, DirectX!"),
pTextFormat,
D2D1::RectF(10, 10, 200, 50), // Text position and size
pBrush
);
// End Direct2D drawing
pRenderTarget->EndDraw();
```

Font Management

MANAGING FONTS IS CRUCIAL when dealing with text rendering. DirectX applications often use custom fonts to achieve specific visual styles or branding. Here are some considerations for font management:

Loading Custom Fonts

DIRECTWRITE PROVIDES mechanisms for loading custom fonts from files or system fonts. You can create font collections to access and use multiple fonts within your application.

```
IDWriteFontCollection* pFontCollection = nullptr;
pDWriteFactory->CreateFontCollectionFromFiles(/* Font file paths */, &pFontCollection);
```

Dynamic Text Generation

IN DYNAMIC APPLICATIONS, such as games or data visualization tools, text content may change frequently. You can update text layouts efficiently using DirectWrite's text layout APIs without recreating text formats or brushes.

```
// Create a text layout
IDWriteTextLayout* pTextLayout = nullptr;
pDWriteFactory->CreateTextLayout(
L"Dynamic Text",
wcslen(L"Dynamic Text"),
pTextFormat,
width, // Width of the text layout
height, // Height of the text layout
&pTextLayout
);
// Update text content
pTextLayout->SetText(L"Updated Text", wcslen(L"Updated Text"));
```

Unicode Support

DIRECTWRITE HAS BUILT-in support for Unicode text rendering, making it suitable for applications targeting international audiences. It handles text shaping, complex scripts, and bidirectional text rendering.

Text Effects and Animation

TEXT RENDERING IN DIRECTX can go beyond static text. You can use shaders and animations to apply visual effects to text, such as glowing, pulsating, or transitioning effects. By combining DirectWrite with Direct2D and shader programming, you can create dynamic and visually captivating text elements.

Conclusion

TEXT RENDERING AND font management are integral aspects of DirectX applications, contributing to the overall user experience and visual appeal. With DirectWrite and Direct2D, you have the tools to handle text rendering effectively, whether you're creating user interfaces, displaying game dialogue, or presenting information in your DirectX applications.

3.4 Image Processing and Manipulation

IMAGE PROCESSING AND manipulation are essential components of DirectX applications, allowing developers to work with textures, sprites, and visual effects. This section explores techniques for handling images effectively within DirectX and discusses the importance of image processing.

The Role of Images in DirectX

IMAGES PLAY A SIGNIFICANT role in DirectX applications, serving as textures for 3D models, sprites for 2D elements, background images, and visual effects. DirectX supports various image formats, including JPEG, PNG, BMP, and DDS (DirectDraw Surface), allowing developers to work with a wide range of image assets.

Texture Mapping

TEXTURE MAPPING IS a fundamental technique in 3D graphics, where 2D images (textures) are applied to the surfaces of 3D models. Textures add detail, color, and realism to objects, making them appear more lifelike. DirectX provides robust support for texture mapping, including texture coordinates, mipmapping, and texture filtering.

```
// Loading a texture in DirectX

ID3D11ShaderResourceView* pTexture = nullptr;

D3DX11CreateShaderResourceViewFromFile(

pDevice,

L"texture.jpg", // Image file path

nullptr,

nullptr,

&pTexture,

nullptr

);

// Applying the texture to a 3D model

pDeviceContext->PSSetShaderResources(0, 1, &pTexture);
```

Sprites and 2D Images

IN 2D GRAPHICS, SPRITES are commonly used to represent characters, objects, and other elements. Sprites are essentially 2D images that can be moved, rotated, and animated within the 2D world. DirectX provides mechanisms for rendering sprites efficiently, including sprite batching and transformation matrices.

```
// Rendering a sprite using Direct2D

pRenderTarget->BeginDraw();

// Draw a sprite at (x, y)

pRenderTarget->DrawBitmap(pBitmap, D2D1::RectF(x, y, x + width, y + height));

// End Direct2D drawing

pRenderTarget->EndDraw();
```

Image Filters and Effects

IMAGE PROCESSING IN DirectX goes beyond simple rendering. Developers can apply various image filters and effects to create visually appealing results. Techniques such as blur, sharpening, color correction, and post-processing effects can be implemented using shaders.

```
// Example HLSL shader for grayscale conversion

float4 main(float4 color : COLOR) : SV_TARGET

{

// Calculate grayscale value

float grayscale = dot(color.rgb, float3(0.299, 0.587, 0.114));

// Output grayscale color

return float4(grayscale, grayscale, grayscale, color.a);
```

}

Image Loading and Compression

EFFICIENTLY LOADING and compressing images are critical for optimizing performance and reducing memory usage. DirectX supports various image file formats and provides tools for compressing textures, which is especially important for games targeting a wide range of hardware.

```
// Loading a compressed DDS texture in DirectX

ID3D11ShaderResourceView* pTexture = nullptr;

D3DX11CreateShaderResourceViewFromFile(

pDevice,

L"texture.dds", // Compressed DDS image file

nullptr,

nullptr,

&pTexture,

nullptr

);
```

Dynamic Image Creation

IN SOME SCENARIOS, DirectX applications may need to create images dynamically. This can involve generating procedural textures, creating custom fonts, or generating images based on user input. DirectX provides the necessary APIs and tools for such tasks.

```
// Dynamic image creation using Direct2D
```

```
pRenderTarget->BeginDraw();

// Create a dynamic image, e.g., based on user input or procedural generation

// ...

// End Direct2D drawing

pRenderTarget->EndDraw();
```

Image Memory Management

PROPER MEMORY MANAGEMENT is crucial when dealing with images in DirectX. Developers should pay attention to image size, texture formats, and memory usage to ensure optimal performance and resource utilization.

Conclusion

IMAGE PROCESSING AND manipulation are core aspects of DirectX applications, enabling developers to work with textures, sprites, and visual effects effectively. Whether you're rendering 3D models with realistic textures or creating dynamic 2D visual elements, mastering image processing techniques is essential for delivering visually engaging and performant DirectX applications.

3.5 Implementing User Interfaces with DirectX

CREATING USER INTERFACES (UIs) in DirectX applications is essential for user interaction, menus, settings, and displaying critical information. This section explores how to design and implement user interfaces within DirectX, providing a seamless and visually engaging experience for users.

The Importance of User Interfaces

USER INTERFACES SERVE as the bridge between users and applications, allowing users to interact with software efficiently and intuitively. In DirectX applications, well-designed UIs enhance usability, guide users through the experience, and provide a means for configuration and customization.

DirectX for UI Implementation

DIRECTX OFFERS THE flexibility to implement UIs from scratch, allowing developers to create custom interfaces tailored to their applications. Implementing UIs with DirectX provides control over visual design, animations, and interactivity.

Integration with Direct2D and DirectWrite

TO CREATE USER INTERFACES within DirectX applications, you can leverage Direct2D for rendering graphics elements and DirectWrite for rendering text. These technologies seamlessly integrate with DirectX, ensuring a consistent and high-quality user experience.

UI Frameworks and Libraries

WHILE DIRECTX ALLOWS for custom UI implementation, developers often rely on UI frameworks and libraries to simplify the process. Frameworks like Dear ImGui, Nuklear, or custom UI libraries built on top of DirectX can significantly speed up UI development.

Input Handling

EFFECTIVE UIS REQUIRE responsive input handling. DirectX applications must manage user input, including mouse, keyboard, gamepad, touch, and gestures. Proper input handling ensures that users can interact with UI elements effortlessly.

```
// Handling mouse input in DirectX

bool HandleMouseInput(HWND hWnd, WPARAM wParam, LPARAM lParam)

{

// Extract mouse coordinates

int mouseX = LOWORD(lParam);

int mouseY = HIWORD(lParam);

// Check for mouse button clicks and handle UI interactions

if (wParam & MK_LBUTTON)

{

// Handle left mouse button click

// ...

return true;

}

// Handle other mouse events as needed

// ...

return false;

}
```

Layout and Rendering

UI LAYOUT AND RENDERING involve positioning and drawing UI elements on the screen. DirectX applications must manage the arrangement of buttons, text fields, images, and other elements. This includes handling screen resolution changes and device-specific considerations.

```
// Rendering UI elements with Direct2D

pRenderTarget->BeginDraw();

// Draw UI elements using Direct2D and DirectWrite

// ...

// End Direct2D drawing

pRenderTarget->EndDraw();
```

UI Responsiveness and Performance

UI RESPONSIVENESS IS crucial for a smooth user experience. Developers should optimize UI rendering and update processes to ensure that the UI remains responsive, even in complex applications or games.

Transition Effects and Animations

TRANSITION EFFECTS and animations can enhance the user interface's visual appeal and user engagement. DirectX allows developers to implement animations, transitions, and visual effects to make the UI more interactive and engaging.

```
// Implementing UI animations in DirectX

void AnimateUIElement(UIElement* element)
```

```
{
// Apply animations to the UI element
// ...
}
```

Cross-Platform Considerations

DIRECTX APPLICATIONS that target multiple platforms may need to adapt UIs for different devices and screen sizes. Cross-platform development strategies, such as responsive design or adaptive layouts, can help ensure a consistent UI experience across platforms.

Testing and User Feedback

THOROUGH TESTING IS essential to identify and resolve UI-related issues. User feedback and usability testing can provide valuable insights into improving the UI's design and functionality.

Conclusion

IMPLEMENTING USER INTERFACES with DirectX offers developers the flexibility to create customized and visually appealing UIs for their applications and games. Whether you choose to build UIs from scratch or use UI frameworks, mastering UI design and implementation is essential for delivering exceptional user experiences in DirectX applications.

Chapter 4: Sound and Music with DirectX

4.1 Introduction to DirectSound

DIRECTSOUND IS A COMPONENT of DirectX designed for managing and playing audio in Windows applications, particularly in games and multimedia software. In this section, we'll introduce DirectSound and explore its fundamental concepts and functionalities.

The Role of Audio in Applications

AUDIO PLAYS A CRUCIAL role in enhancing the overall user experience in various applications. In games, it provides immersive sound effects, background music, and character dialogues. In multimedia applications, it ensures that users can enjoy movies, music, and videos with high-quality audio.

DirectSound Overview

DIRECTSOUND IS AN API that allows developers to interact with and control audio hardware and playback devices. It offers low-level access to audio features, making it suitable for creating immersive soundscapes in games and multimedia applications.

Key Features of DirectSound

1. Audio Playback

DIRECTSOUND ENABLES the playback of audio data from various sources, including audio files, memory buffers, and real-time generated audio.

2. 3D Audio Effects

DIRECTSOUND SUPPORTS 3D audio effects, allowing developers to position sounds in a 3D space. This adds depth and realism to audio experiences, especially in games.

3. Sound Mixing

THE API PROVIDES SOUND mixing capabilities, allowing multiple audio streams to be played simultaneously with control over volume, panning, and effects.

4. Hardware Acceleration

DIRECTSOUND TAKES ADVANTAGE of hardware acceleration when available, ensuring efficient audio processing and reducing CPU load.

5. Sound Capture

IN ADDITION TO PLAYBACK, DirectSound supports audio capture, enabling applications to record audio from microphones or other input sources.

Initializing DirectSound

TO USE DIRECTSOUND, you need to initialize the DirectSound device and create a primary buffer, which serves as the main output for audio playback. Here's a simplified code snippet:

```
#include <dsound.h>

IDirectSound8* pDirectSound = nullptr;
```

```
// Initialize DirectSound

DirectSoundCreate8(nullptr, &pDirectSound, nullptr);

// Set the cooperative level for the application

pDirectSound->SetCooperativeLevel(hWnd,
DSSCL_PRIORITY);

// Create a primary buffer

DSBUFFERDESC dsbd;

ZeroMemory(&dsbd, sizeof(dsbd));

dsbd.dwSize = sizeof(dsbd);

dsbd.dwFlags = DSBCAPS_PRIMARYBUFFER;

IDirectSoundBuffer* pPrimaryBuffer = nullptr;

pDirectSound->CreateSoundBuffer(&dsbd,    &pPrimaryBuffer,
nullptr);
```

Loading and Playing Audio Files

DIRECTSOUND PROVIDES the capability to load and play audio files, making it easy to add sound effects and music to your applications. You can load audio data from various formats, such as WAV, MP3, or OGG.

```
// Loading an audio file in DirectSound

IDirectSoundBuffer* pSecondaryBuffer = nullptr;

DSBUFFERDESC dsbd;

ZeroMemory(&dsbd, sizeof(dsbd));
```

```
dsbd.dwSize = sizeof(dsbd);

dsbd.dwFlags = DSBCAPS_CTRLVOLUME | DSBCAPS_CTRLFREQUENCY;

dsbd.dwBufferBytes = /* Size of audio data */;

dsbd.lpwfxFormat = /* Format of audio data */;

pDirectSound->CreateSoundBuffer(&dsbd, &pSecondaryBuffer, nullptr);

// Load audio data into the secondary buffer

BYTE* audioData = /* Load audio data from file */;

pSecondaryBuffer->Lock(0, /* Size of audio data */, (LPVOID*)&audioData, /* Size of audio data */, nullptr, nullptr, 0);

pSecondaryBuffer->Unlock(audioData, /* Size of audio data */, nullptr, 0);

// Play the audio

pSecondaryBuffer->Play(0, 0, 0);
```

Advanced Audio Effects

DIRECTSOUND ALLOWS for the application of various audio effects, including reverb, equalization, and pitch shifting. These effects can be applied to individual audio sources or to the entire audio mix, enhancing the overall audio quality.

Performance Optimization

OPTIMIZING AUDIO PERFORMANCE is crucial to ensure smooth audio playback, especially in real-time applications like games. DirectSound provides tools and techniques for managing audio resources efficiently and avoiding latency issues.

Conclusion

DIRECTSOUND IS A VALUABLE component of DirectX for managing audio in Windows applications. Whether you're developing games, multimedia software, or other interactive applications, understanding how to use DirectSound effectively allows you to provide a rich and immersive audio experience to your users. In the following sections, we will delve deeper into various aspects of audio development with DirectSound.

4.2 Loading and Playing Audio Files

LOADING AND PLAYING audio files is a fundamental task when working with DirectSound. In this section, we will explore how to load audio files, prepare them for playback, and manage audio resources effectively.

Supported Audio Formats

DIRECTSOUND SUPPORTS a variety of audio formats, including WAV, MP3, OGG, and more. When choosing an audio format, consider factors like file size, compression, and compatibility with your target platforms.

Loading Audio Files

TO LOAD AUDIO FILES into DirectSound, you typically follow these steps:

1. **Initialize DirectSound**: Ensure that you have initialized the DirectSound device, as explained in Section 4.1.
2. **Create a Secondary Buffer**: Create a secondary buffer that will hold the audio data. You can specify the format and size of the buffer.
3. **Load Audio Data**: Load the audio data from the audio file into the secondary buffer. This usually involves reading the file and copying its contents into the buffer.

```
// Loading an audio file in DirectSound

IDirectSoundBuffer* pSecondaryBuffer = nullptr;

DSBUFFERDESC dsbd;

ZeroMemory(&dsbd, sizeof(dsbd));

dsbd.dwSize = sizeof(dsbd);

dsbd.dwFlags = DSBCAPS_CTRLVOLUME | DSBCAPS_CTRLFREQUENCY;

dsbd.dwBufferBytes = /* Size of audio data */;

dsbd.lpwfxFormat = /* Format of audio data */;

pDirectSound->CreateSoundBuffer(&dsbd, &pSecondaryBuffer, nullptr);

// Load audio data into the secondary buffer

BYTE* audioData = /* Load audio data from file */;
```

pSecondaryBuffer->Lock(0, /* *Size of audio data* */, (LPVOID*)&audioData, /* *Size of audio data* */, **nullptr**, **nullptr**, 0);

pSecondaryBuffer->Unlock(audioData, /* *Size of audio data* */, **nullptr**, 0);

1. **Play the Audio**: Once the audio data is loaded into the buffer, you can play it using the secondary buffer's Play method.

// Play the audio

pSecondaryBuffer->Play(0, 0, 0);

Streaming Audio

IN CASES WHERE AUDIO files are too large to load entirely into memory, you can implement audio streaming. Streaming involves reading and playing audio data in smaller chunks, allowing for efficient playback of lengthy audio files.

Managing Audio Resources

MANAGING AUDIO RESOURCES, such as buffers and sound effects, is crucial for efficient audio playback. Proper resource management includes releasing resources when they are no longer needed to avoid memory leaks.

// Releasing a DirectSound buffer

pSecondaryBuffer->Release();

Sound Cues and Triggers

IN GAMES AND INTERACTIVE applications, you often need to trigger specific sounds based on events or user interactions. You can use DirectSound to create sound cues and play them when needed. For example, you might play different sound effects when a character jumps or a gunshot occurs.

```
// Play a sound cue when an event occurs

void PlayJumpSound()

{

IDirectSoundBuffer* pJumpSound = /* Load jump sound */;

pJumpSound->Play(0, 0, 0);

}
```

Advanced Audio Features

DIRECTSOUND OFFERS advanced features for audio developers, such as 3D audio positioning, sound mixing, and applying audio effects like reverb or equalization. These features can be used to create immersive audio experiences in games and multimedia applications.

Error Handling

PROPER ERROR HANDLING is essential when working with audio files. Ensure that you handle errors gracefully, provide feedback to users, and log any issues for debugging purposes.

Conclusion

LOADING AND PLAYING audio files is a core aspect of audio development with DirectSound. Whether you're adding background music to a game or implementing interactive audio feedback in an application, understanding how to load, manage, and play audio files is crucial for creating a compelling and immersive audio experience.

4.3 3D Audio Effects and Spatialization

IN THE REALM OF AUDIO design for games and immersive experiences, 3D audio effects and spatialization play a crucial role in creating realistic and engaging auditory environments. In this section, we will explore 3D audio, spatialization techniques, and how DirectSound facilitates their implementation.

Understanding 3D Audio

3D AUDIO AIMS TO MIMIC the way humans perceive sound in the real world. It considers factors like distance, direction, and environmental effects to create an immersive audio experience. When implemented effectively, 3D audio enhances the sense of presence and immersion in a virtual environment.

Spatialization and Positional Audio

SPATIALIZATION IS THE process of placing audio sources in a 3D space, allowing listeners to perceive their positions accurately. In a game, this means that if an enemy is behind the player, the player should hear the enemy's footsteps from the rear speakers. DirectSound provides features for spatialization, allowing developers to achieve this effect.

Positioning Sounds in 3D Space

DIRECTSOUND ALLOWS you to position sounds in a 3D space using coordinates. The listener's position and orientation are also defined. As the listener moves or rotates, the spatialized audio adjusts accordingly, providing a realistic sense of directionality.

```
// Positioning audio in 3D space

DS3DBUFFER ds3db;

ZeroMemory(&ds3db, sizeof(ds3db));

ds3db.dwSize = sizeof(ds3db);

ds3db.vPosition.x = /* X-coordinate */;

ds3db.vPosition.y = /* Y-coordinate */;

ds3db.vPosition.z = /* Z-coordinate */;

pSecondaryBuffer->Set3DAttributes(&ds3db,
DS3D_IMMEDIATE);
```

Doppler Effect

THE DOPPLER EFFECT is the change in frequency or pitch of a sound as it moves relative to an observer. For example, as a car approaches and passes by, you hear the engine sound change in pitch. DirectSound can simulate the Doppler effect, enhancing the realism of moving sound sources.

Environmental Effects

DIRECTSOUND ALSO SUPPORTS environmental effects, allowing you to simulate the acoustic characteristics of different environments. For instance, you can apply reverb to make audio sound as if it's in a large cathedral or a small room. This adds depth and richness to the audio experience.

HRTF (Head-Related Transfer Function)

HRTF IS A TECHNIQUE used to mimic the way our ears perceive sound based on their shape and position. It adds an extra layer of realism to 3D audio by considering the listener's unique ear characteristics. While DirectSound doesn't provide HRTF directly, it can be combined with third-party libraries or plugins to achieve this effect.

Sound Occlusion and Obstruction

IN REALISTIC AUDIO environments, sound can be blocked or muffled when objects or obstacles come between the listener and the sound source. DirectSound can handle sound occlusion and obstruction, making audio behave naturally when characters move behind walls or objects.

Performance Considerations

IMPLEMENTING 3D AUDIO effects can be computationally intensive. Developers should optimize their code to ensure that the audio processing doesn't cause performance bottlenecks, especially in resource-intensive applications like games.

Conclusion

3D AUDIO EFFECTS AND spatialization are essential tools for creating immersive and lifelike audio experiences in games, simulations, and virtual environments. DirectSound provides the necessary features to position audio sources in a 3D space, simulate environmental effects, and enhance the sense of presence for users.

When combined with other audio techniques, such as sound effects and music, 3D audio contributes to the overall audio richness of an application, resulting in a more engaging and captivating user experience.

4.4 Integrating Sound with Game Physics

INTEGRATING SOUND WITH game physics is a crucial aspect of game development, as it enhances the overall gaming experience by providing audio feedback that aligns with in-game actions and events. In this section, we will explore how DirectSound can be used to integrate sound seamlessly with game physics.

Audio Feedback for Actions

GAME PHYSICS GOVERN various in-game actions such as collisions, object movements, character interactions, and more. By integrating sound with these actions, you can provide players with audio feedback that makes the game world feel more responsive and dynamic.

Collision Sounds

WHEN OBJECTS COLLIDE in a game, the resulting sound can convey the materials' properties, object sizes, and collision forces. For example, a collision between two metal objects should produce a different sound compared to two soft objects colliding.

```
// Play collision sound

void PlayCollisionSound(float impactForce, MaterialType material)

{
```

```
IDirectSoundBuffer* pCollisionSound = /* Load collision sound based on material and impact force */;

pCollisionSound->Play(0, 0, 0);

}
```

Footstep and Movement Sounds

CHARACTER MOVEMENT in games often involves footsteps, which can vary based on the character's speed, terrain, and footwear. Integrating sound with character movements adds realism and immersion to the gameplay.

```
// Play footstep sound

void PlayFootstepSound(CharacterType character, TerrainType terrain)

{

IDirectSoundBuffer* pFootstepSound = /* Load footstep sound based on character and terrain */;

pFootstepSound->Play(0, 0, 0);

}
```

Object Interactions

OBJECTS IN A GAME WORLD may have interactive elements that produce sounds when manipulated. For example, opening a door, picking up an item, or pushing a button can trigger corresponding audio feedback.

```
// Play interaction sound
```

```
void PlayInteractionSound(ObjectType object)

{

IDirectSoundBuffer* pInteractionSound = /* Load interaction sound based on object type */;

pInteractionSound->Play(0, 0, 0);

}
```

Environmental Effects

INCORPORATING SOUND into the game's physics can also involve simulating environmental effects on audio. For instance, if the game features weather conditions like rain or wind, these effects can impact how sounds are heard, adding depth to the audio experience.

```
// Apply weather-related audio effects

void ApplyWeatherAudioEffects(WeatherType weather)

{

// Adjust audio parameters based on weather conditions

// ...

}
```

Synchronization with Physics Engine

TO ENSURE THAT AUDIO events are synchronized with the game's physics, developers often integrate sound triggers and events directly into the game's physics engine or logic. This synchronization ensures that audio feedback occurs at the right moment and corresponds to the game's state.

Performance Considerations

WHILE INTEGRATING SOUND with game physics can significantly enhance gameplay, it's essential to consider performance. Real-time audio processing can be computationally intensive, so developers should optimize audio code and balance audio quality with performance to ensure smooth gameplay.

Conclusion

INTEGRATING SOUND WITH game physics is a powerful tool for game developers to create immersive and engaging gaming experiences. Whether it's the impact of collisions, the subtleties of character movements, or the interactions with in-game objects, audio feedback adds an extra layer of realism and player engagement. DirectSound, with its capabilities for audio playback and spatialization, plays a vital role in seamlessly integrating sound with game physics, ultimately contributing to a more immersive and enjoyable gaming experience for players.

4.5 Advanced Audio Techniques and Optimization

IN THE WORLD OF GAME development and multimedia applications, achieving high-quality audio while maintaining optimal performance is a constant challenge. This section delves into advanced audio techniques and optimization strategies when working with DirectSound.

Streaming Audio

STREAMING AUDIO IS a technique used to play audio data directly from a file or network source without loading the entire file into memory. This is particularly useful for large audio files like music tracks. DirectSound provides features for streaming audio efficiently.

```
// Streaming audio with DirectSound

IDirectSoundBuffer* pStreamingBuffer = nullptr;

DSBUFFERDESC dsbd;

ZeroMemory(&dsbd, sizeof(dsbd));

dsbd.dwSize = sizeof(dsbd);

dsbd.dwFlags = DSBCAPS_CTRLPOSITIONNOTIFY | DSBCAPS_GETCURRENTPOSITION2;

dsbd.dwBufferBytes = /* Size of audio data buffer */;

dsbd.lpwfxFormat = /* Format of audio data */;

pDirectSound->CreateSoundBuffer(&dsbd, &pStreamingBuffer, nullptr);

// Set up notifications for buffer position

DSBPOSITIONNOTIFY notify;

notify.dwOffset = /* Position in buffer */;

notify.hEventNotify = /* Event to signal when audio reaches this position */;
```

```
pStreamingBuffer->QueryInterface(IID_IDirectSoundNotify, (LPVOID*)&pDSNotify);

pDSNotify->SetNotificationPositions(1, &notify);
```

Real-time Effects Processing

DIRECTSOUND ALLOWS for real-time audio effects processing, including equalization, reverb, and pitch shifting. Implementing these effects in real-time can enhance the audio quality of games and interactive applications.

```
// Apply real-time audio effect

void ApplyReverbEffect(IDirectSoundBuffer* pBuffer)

{

IDirectSoundFXWavesReverb reverbEffect;

reverbEffect.dwSize = sizeof(reverbEffect);

reverbEffect.fReverbTime = /* Reverb time */;

reverbEffect.fInGain = /* Input gain */;

reverbEffect.fReverbMix = /* Reverb mix */;

pBuffer->SetFX(1, &reverbEffect, nullptr);

}
```

Dynamic Sound Mixing

IN COMPLEX GAMES WITH multiple audio sources, dynamic sound mixing becomes crucial. It involves adjusting the volume, panning, and effects of individual audio sources in real-time to create a cohesive audio mix.

```
// Dynamic sound mixing

void MixAudioSources(IDirectSoundBuffer* pMainBuffer, IDirectSoundBuffer* pSoundSource)

{

// Apply volume and panning adjustments based on positions and priorities

// ...

}
```

Multithreading and Asynchronous Playback

TO AVOID AUDIO GLITCHES and maintain smooth gameplay, developers often employ multithreading techniques for audio playback. This allows audio processing to occur concurrently with other game logic and rendering.

```
// Multithreaded audio playback

void PlayAudioMultithreaded(IDirectSoundBuffer* pBuffer)

{

// Create a separate thread for audio playback

// ...

}
```

Latency Reduction

REDUCING AUDIO LATENCY is critical for real-time applications like games. DirectSound offers tools and settings to minimize audio latency, ensuring that audio events closely align with in-game actions.

```
// Adjusting audio settings for latency reduction

void SetAudioLatency(IDirectSoundBuffer* pBuffer, float latency)

{

pBuffer->SetFrequency(/* Adjusted audio frequency based on latency */);

// ...

}
```

Profiling and Optimization Tools

PROFILING AND OPTIMIZATION tools can help identify performance bottlenecks in audio processing. Developers should use profiling tools to analyze CPU and memory usage, ensuring that audio processing does not impact the overall game performance negatively.

Conclusion

ADVANCED AUDIO TECHNIQUES and optimization strategies are vital for achieving high-quality audio experiences in games and multimedia applications. By leveraging DirectSound's capabilities for streaming, real-time effects processing, dynamic mixing, and latency reduction, developers can create audio-rich environments without compromising performance. Careful consideration of audio optimization is crucial to ensure that audio seamlessly integrates with other aspects of an application, contributing to a compelling and immersive user experience.

Chapter 5: DirectX for Input Management

5.1 Handling Keyboard and Mouse Input with DirectInput

HANDLING USER INPUT is a fundamental aspect of game and application development. DirectInput, a part of DirectX, provides a reliable and versatile framework for managing input devices such as keyboards and mice. In this section, we will explore how to use DirectInput to handle keyboard and mouse input effectively.

Overview of DirectInput

DIRECTINPUT IS A COMPONENT of DirectX designed specifically for managing input devices. It abstracts the underlying hardware and provides a consistent interface for developers to work with various input devices, making it suitable for a wide range of applications, from games to multimedia software.

Initializing DirectInput

TO USE DIRECTINPUT, you must initialize it in your application. This involves creating an instance of the DirectInput object and initializing the devices you want to use, such as keyboards and mice.

```
// Initialize DirectInput

LPDIRECTINPUT8 pDirectInput = nullptr;

HRESULT hr = DirectInput8Create(GetModuleHandle(nullptr), DIRECTINPUT_VERSION, IID_IDirectInput8, (LPVOID*)&pDirectInput, nullptr);
```

```
// Initialize the keyboard and mouse

LPDIRECTINPUTDEVICE8 pKeyboard = nullptr;

LPDIRECTINPUTDEVICE8 pMouse = nullptr;

hr = pDirectInput->CreateDevice(GUID_SysKeyboard, &pKeyboard, nullptr);

hr = pDirectInput->CreateDevice(GUID_SysMouse, &pMouse, nullptr);

// Set the data format for the devices

hr = pKeyboard->SetDataFormat(&c_dfDIKeyboard);

hr = pMouse->SetDataFormat(&c_dfDIMouse);
```

Acquiring and Releasing Devices

ONCE YOU HAVE INITIALIZED DirectInput and created input devices, you need to acquire and release them to begin and end input processing. Acquiring a device means that it is ready to provide input data, and releasing it means that it stops providing input data.

```
// Acquire input devices

hr = pKeyboard->Acquire();

hr = pMouse->Acquire();

// Release input devices when done

pKeyboard->Unacquire();

pMouse->Unacquire();
```

Polling for Input

DIRECTINPUT USES POLLING to retrieve input data. You periodically poll the input devices to check for new input. For example, you might poll for input in your game's main loop.

```
// Poll for input

pKeyboard->Poll();

pMouse->Poll();

// Retrieve input data

DIDEVICEOBJECTDATA keyboardData[KEYBOARD_BUFFER_SIZE];

DIDEVICEOBJECTDATA mouseData[MOUSE_BUFFER_SIZE];

DWORD keyboardElements = KEYBOARD_BUFFER_SIZE;

DWORD mouseElements = MOUSE_BUFFER_SIZE;

hr = pKeyboard->GetDeviceData(sizeof(DIDEVICEOBJECTDATA), keyboardData, &keyboardElements, 0);

hr = pMouse->GetDeviceData(sizeof(DIDEVICEOBJECTDATA), mouseData, &mouseElements, 0);
```

Handling Keyboard Input

DIRECTINPUT PROVIDES information about key states, allowing you to detect when keys are pressed or released. You can then respond to these events in your application.

```
// Check if a specific key is pressed
if (keyboardData[i].dwData & 0x80)
{
// The key is pressed
}
else
{
// The key is released
}
```

Handling Mouse Input

MOUSE INPUT FROM DIRECTINPUT includes information about mouse movement, button clicks, and wheel scrolling. You can use this data to implement camera controls, interactive menus, and more.

```
// Check mouse movement
LONG dx = mouseData[i].dwData;
LONG dy = mouseData[i].dwData >> 32;
// Check mouse button clicks
if (mouseData[i].dwData & DIMOFS_BUTTON0)
{
// Left mouse button is clicked
```

```
}
// Check mouse wheel scrolling
if (mouseData[i].dwData & DIMOFS_Z)
{
LONG scrollValue = (mouseData[i].dwData >> 32) & 0xFFFF;
// Handle scrollValue
}
```

Custom Input Handling

DIRECTINPUT PROVIDES a robust framework for handling standard input devices, but it can also be extended to support custom input devices and game controllers. This flexibility allows you to tailor input handling to the specific needs of your application.

Error Handling

PROPER ERROR HANDLING is crucial when working with DirectInput. You should check the HRESULT values returned by DirectInput functions and handle any errors gracefully to ensure the reliability of your input system.

Conclusion

DIRECTINPUT IS A POWERFUL tool for handling keyboard and mouse input in DirectX applications. Whether you are developing a game that requires responsive controls or a multimedia application with interactive features, DirectInput provides the means to manage input devices effectively. By initializing, acquiring, and polling input devices, you can create immersive and user-friendly experiences that respond to user input seamlessly.

5.2 Implementing Game Controllers and Haptic Feedback

IN ADDITION TO HANDLING keyboard and mouse input, game developers often need to support game controllers such as joysticks, gamepads, and steering wheels. These controllers offer a more immersive and tactile gaming experience. In this section, we will explore how to implement game controllers and haptic feedback using DirectInput.

Recognizing Game Controllers

DIRECTINPUT PROVIDES a way to enumerate and recognize connected game controllers. This is essential for detecting the presence of controllers and initializing them for input.

// Enumerate and recognize game controllers

```
HRESULT hr =
pDirectInput->EnumDevices(DI8DEVCLASS_GAMECTRL,
EnumerateGameControllers, nullptr,
DIEDFL_ATTACHEDONLY);
```

Initializing Game Controllers

ONCE YOU HAVE RECOGNIZED a game controller, you can initialize it for input. This involves setting the data format and acquiring the controller, similar to what we did for keyboards and mice.

// Initialize a game controller

LPDIRECTINPUTDEVICE8 pGameController = **nullptr**;

hr = pDirectInput->CreateDevice(deviceInstance->guidInstance, &pGameController, **nullptr**);

hr = pGameController->SetDataFormat(&c_dfDIJoystick);

hr = pGameController->SetCooperativeLevel(hwnd, DISCL_EXCLUSIVE | DISCL_BACKGROUND);

hr = pGameController->Acquire();

Polling for Game Controller Input

POLLING FOR GAME CONTROLLER input is similar to polling for keyboard and mouse input. You periodically poll the game controller to check for new input data.

// Poll for game controller input

pGameController->Poll();

// Retrieve game controller input data

DIJOYSTATE2 gameControllerState;

hr = pGameController->GetDeviceState(**sizeof**(DIJOYSTATE2), &gameControllerState);

Game Controller Input Data

THE GAME CONTROLLER input data includes information about the position of analog sticks, button states, and additional features like triggers and directional pads. You can use this data to implement various gameplay mechanics.

// Check the position of the left analog stick

```
LONG leftStickX = gameControllerState.lX;

LONG leftStickY = gameControllerState.lY;

// Check the button states

bool buttonA = (gameControllerState.rgbButtons[0] & 0x80) != 0;
// Button 0 (A button)

bool buttonB = (gameControllerState.rgbButtons[1] & 0x80) != 0;
// Button 1 (B button)

// Check triggers

BYTE leftTrigger = gameControllerState.lRx;

BYTE rightTrigger = gameControllerState.lRy;

// Check directional pad (DPad)

BYTE dpad = gameControllerState.rgdwPOV[0];
```

Haptic Feedback

MANY GAME CONTROLLERS come equipped with haptic feedback capabilities, allowing them to provide force feedback and vibrations to the player. DirectInput supports haptic feedback, allowing you to create more immersive gaming experiences.

```
// Check if the game controller supports force feedback

if (pGameController->GetCapabilities(&controllerCapabilities)
== DI_OK)

{

if(controllerCapabilities.dwFlags & DIDC_FORCEFEEDBACK)
```

```
{
// Initialize and set force feedback effects
// ...
}
}
```

Custom Input Handling

LIKE WITH KEYBOARDS and mice, DirectInput allows for custom input handling with game controllers. You can map buttons and analog inputs to in-game actions, making it easy to create customizable control schemes.

Error Handling

AS WITH OTHER INPUT devices, proper error handling is crucial when working with game controllers and haptic feedback. Check the HRESULT values returned by DirectInput functions and handle any errors gracefully to ensure a robust input system.

Conclusion

IMPLEMENTING GAME CONTROLLERS and haptic feedback using DirectInput enhances the interactivity and immersion of your games. Whether you are designing a racing game with steering wheel support or a fighting game with gamepad input, DirectInput offers a flexible and reliable solution for managing game controllers. By recognizing, initializing, and polling game controllers, you can create games that respond to player input accurately and provide a rich and tactile gaming experience through haptic feedback.

5.3 Touch and Gesture Recognition

AS TOUCH-ENABLED DEVICES like smartphones, tablets, and touchscreens on laptops become increasingly prevalent, incorporating touch and gesture recognition into applications and games has become essential. In this section, we will explore how to implement touch and gesture recognition using DirectInput and related technologies.

Touch Input Basics

TOUCH INPUT INVOLVES detecting and responding to user interactions with a touchscreen. It allows users to directly manipulate objects, navigate interfaces, and perform actions with their fingers or stylus. In Windows, DirectInput provides support for touch input through the use of touch messages and APIs.

Handling Touch Messages

IN A WINDOWS APPLICATION, you can handle touch input by processing touch messages. Windows sends touch messages to the application's message queue when touch events occur. You can then extract information about the touch events and respond accordingly.

```
// Handle touch messages

case WM_TOUCH:

{

// Process touch events

ProcessTouchInput(wParam, lParam);

}
```

break;

Processing Touch Input

TO PROCESS TOUCH INPUT, you can use the GetTouchInputInfo function to retrieve information about touch points and their properties, such as position and pressure. This information allows you to determine the user's touch gestures and interactions.

```
// Process touch input
void ProcessTouchInput(WPARAM wParam, LPARAM lParam)
{
UINT inputCount = LOWORD(wParam); // Number of touch points
TOUCHINPUT* touchInput = new TOUCHINPUT[inputCount];
// Retrieve touch input data
if (GetTouchInputInfo((HTOUCHINPUT)lParam, inputCount, touchInput, sizeof(TOUCHINPUT)))
{
for (UINT i = 0; i < inputCount; ++i)
{
// Process individual touch input
ProcessSingleTouchInput(touchInput[i]);
}
```

```
}

// Release touch input data

CloseTouchInputHandle((HTOUCHINPUT)lParam);

delete[] touchInput;

}
```

Gesture Recognition

GESTURE RECOGNITION involves identifying predefined patterns of touch input as gestures. Windows provides gesture recognition APIs that allow you to detect gestures like tapping, swiping, pinching, and rotating.

```
// Register for gesture notifications

GESTURECONFIG gestureConfig = { 0 };

gestureConfig.dwID = GID_ZOOM;

gestureConfig.dwWant = GC_ZOOM;

gestureConfig.dwBlock = 0;

if (SetGestureConfig(hwnd, 0, 1, &gestureConfig, sizeof(GESTURECONFIG)) == FALSE)

{

// Gesture registration failed

}
```

Handling Gestures

ONCE YOU HAVE REGISTERED for gesture notifications, you can handle gesture events by processing Windows messages and checking for gesture-related notifications.

```
// Handle gesture events

case WM_GESTURE:

{

// Process gesture event

ProcessGestureInput(wParam, lParam);

}

break;
```

Custom Gesture Recognition

IN ADDITION TO BUILT-in gestures, you can implement custom gesture recognition tailored to your application's needs. This involves tracking touch input and analyzing patterns to identify specific gestures unique to your application or game.

Multitouch Support

MANY TOUCH-ENABLED devices support multitouch, allowing multiple fingers to interact simultaneously. DirectInput and Windows provide support for multitouch input, enabling more complex and intuitive interactions in applications and games.

Error Handling

WHEN WORKING WITH TOUCH and gesture recognition, it's essential to handle errors and edge cases gracefully. Proper error handling ensures that your application remains responsive and user-friendly.

Conclusion

INTEGRATING TOUCH AND gesture recognition into your applications and games using DirectInput and Windows APIs enhances the user experience on touch-enabled devices. Whether you are creating mobile apps, interactive kiosks, or touch-controlled games, understanding how to handle touch input and recognize gestures is crucial. By processing touch messages, implementing gesture recognition, and considering multitouch support, you can create applications that are intuitive and responsive to users' touch interactions.

5.4 Custom Input Devices and DirectX

IN SOME SCENARIOS, standard input devices like keyboards, mice, and game controllers may not suffice for your application or game. You might need to interface with custom input devices, such as specialized controllers, sensors, or even virtual reality input devices. DirectX offers the flexibility to integrate and interact with these custom input devices effectively.

Custom Input Devices Overview

CUSTOM INPUT DEVICES can vary widely in form and function. They might include motion controllers, VR gloves, gesture recognition sensors, or any other input device tailored to your application's unique requirements. These devices often provide data streams that differ from standard input devices and require specialized handling.

Using DirectInput for Custom Devices

DIRECTINPUT IS A VERSATILE API that can be adapted to work with custom input devices. To support a custom device, you typically follow these steps:

1. **Device Initialization**: Initialize your custom input device and establish a connection with it.
2. **Data Format**: Define the data format for the custom device's input data. This format specifies the structure and properties of the input data.
3. **Acquiring and Polling**: Acquire the custom device to start receiving input data and periodically poll the device to retrieve the latest input information.
4. **Data Processing**: Process the incoming input data according to your application's requirements. This may involve mapping input values to in-game actions or interactions.
5. **Error Handling**: Implement robust error handling to ensure your application gracefully handles any issues with the custom device.

Example: Motion Controller Integration

SUPPOSE YOU ARE DEVELOPING a virtual reality game that uses motion controllers for precise hand tracking. Here's a simplified example of how you might integrate a custom motion controller with DirectX:

```
// Initialize the custom motion controller
```

```
CustomMotionController motionController;
if (!motionController.Initialize())
{
// Handle initialization failure
}
// Define the data format for motion controller input
DIDATAFORMAT dataFormat;
dataFormat.dwSize = sizeof(DIDATAFORMAT);
dataFormat.dwFlags = 0;
dataFormat.dwDataSize = sizeof(CustomMotionControllerData);
dataFormat.dwObjSize = sizeof(DIOBJECTDATAFORMAT);
dataFormat.dwNumObjs = CustomMotionControllerData::NumInputs;
dataFormat.rgodf = CustomMotionControllerData::DataFormat;
// Create a DirectInput device for the custom motion controller
LPDIRECTINPUTDEVICE8 pCustomDevice = nullptr;
HRESULT hr = pDirectInput->CreateDevice(GUID_CustomMotionController, &pCustomDevice, nullptr);
hr = pCustomDevice->SetDataFormat(&dataFormat);
// Acquire the custom motion controller
```

```
hr = pCustomDevice->Acquire();

// Poll for input data from the motion controller

CustomMotionControllerData controllerData;

hr = pCustomDevice->GetDeviceState(sizeof(controllerData), &controllerData);

// Process the input data and update the game accordingly

ProcessCustomMotionControllerInput(controllerData);
```

In this example, CustomMotionController represents the custom motion controller hardware, and CustomMotionControllerData defines the structure of input data it provides. By defining the data format, acquiring, polling, and processing input data, you can seamlessly integrate the custom device into your DirectX application.

Custom Input Challenges

WORKING WITH CUSTOM input devices can present challenges, such as device compatibility, driver support, and calibration. It's essential to thoroughly test and validate your custom input device integration to ensure a smooth user experience.

Conclusion

DIRECTX'S FLEXIBILITY allows you to integrate custom input devices effectively into your applications and games, opening up new possibilities for user interactions and experiences. Whether you are creating specialized controllers for industrial simulations or implementing unique input methods for virtual reality applications, DirectX provides the foundation to handle custom input devices and elevate the interactivity of your projects.

5.5 Input Processing and Game Loops

INPUT PROCESSING PLAYS a pivotal role in game development, as it directly affects how players interact with your game. In this section, we will explore the significance of input processing within game loops and discuss best practices for handling user input effectively using DirectX.

The Role of Input Processing

INPUT PROCESSING IS the mechanism by which a game or application captures and responds to user input. It involves detecting user actions, such as keyboard presses, mouse movements, or controller inputs, and translating them into in-game actions or commands. Proper input processing ensures that the game accurately reflects the player's intentions and provides a responsive and immersive experience.

Input Handling in Game Loops

IN A TYPICAL GAME LOOP, input processing is one of the essential phases alongside rendering and updating game logic. The game loop follows a sequence of steps:

1. **Input Processing**: Gather and process user input, including keyboard, mouse, gamepad, or custom device input.
2. **Game Logic Update**: Update the game's internal state, including character movement, physics simulations, and AI behavior.
3. **Rendering**: Render the game world based on the updated game state.
4. **Display**: Present the rendered frame to the player.

5. **Repeat**: Repeat the loop to maintain real-time interactivity.

Input Polling vs. Event Handling

TWO COMMON APPROACHES to input processing are polling and event handling:

- **Input Polling**: In this approach, the game loop periodically checks the state of input devices to determine if any input events have occurred. Polling is suitable for scenarios where you need to know the immediate state of input devices and react in real-time.

- **Event Handling**: Event-driven input processing involves setting up event listeners or callbacks to respond to specific input events as they occur. Event handling is useful for handling user interactions that trigger actions or events in the game.

Managing Input States

TO EFFECTIVELY PROCESS user input, it's crucial to maintain and manage the state of input devices. This includes tracking the state of keys, buttons, and other input elements to detect changes and respond accordingly. DirectX, through libraries like DirectInput, provides tools for managing input states reliably.

```
// Example of managing key states using DirectInput

bool keyStates[256];

// In the input polling phase of the game loop:

for (int i = 0; i < 256; i++)
```

```
{
keyStates[i] = (GetAsyncKeyState(i) & 0x8000) != 0;
}
```

Input Buffering and Debouncing

IN SOME CASES, IT'S beneficial to implement input buffering and debouncing mechanisms. Input buffering allows you to capture a series of inputs over time, such as recording a sequence of keyboard presses. Debouncing helps filter out unintended or accidental input by requiring a stable input state for a certain duration before registering it as a valid input.

Handling Multiple Input Devices

MODERN GAMES OFTEN support multiple input devices simultaneously, such as a combination of a keyboard, mouse, and game controller. Handling these devices effectively requires a coherent input management system that allows players to switch seamlessly between devices during gameplay.

Error Handling and Robustness

PROPER ERROR HANDLING in input processing is essential to maintain the stability of your game. Handling scenarios like unplugged controllers or unexpected input data ensures that the game remains responsive and user-friendly even in less-than-ideal conditions.

Conclusion

EFFECTIVE INPUT PROCESSING is a cornerstone of game development that directly impacts gameplay and user experience.

By integrating input handling seamlessly into your game loop, managing input states, and considering multiple input devices, you can create games that respond accurately to player actions and deliver an engaging and immersive gaming experience. Careful attention to input processing contributes to the overall polish and playability of your game, making it a vital aspect of successful game development.

Chapter 6: DirectX Networking

Chapter 6: DirectX Networking

6.1 Basics of Network Programming in DirectX

NETWORK PROGRAMMING is a crucial aspect of many modern games, enabling multiplayer interactions, online leaderboards, and real-time communication between players. DirectX provides tools and libraries for network programming, making it easier to implement networking functionality in your games.

Understanding Networking in Games

IN THE CONTEXT OF GAME development, networking refers to the process of exchanging data and information between different instances of a game running on separate devices or computers. This enables players to collaborate or compete in real time, even if they are not physically in the same location.

Key Concepts in Network Programming

BEFORE DIVING INTO network programming with DirectX, it's essential to understand some key concepts:

- **Client-Server Model**: Many networked games use a client-server architecture, where one machine (the server) hosts the game and manages the game state, while multiple clients connect to the server to participate in the game.

- **Protocols**: Network communication relies on protocols, which are sets of rules that define how data is formatted, transmitted, and received. Common protocols for networked games include TCP and UDP.

- **Latency**: Latency is the delay between sending a piece of data and receiving it at the other end. In games, minimizing latency is critical to provide a smooth and responsive experience for players.

DirectX Networking APIs

DIRECTX PROVIDES SEVERAL APIs and libraries for network programming, including DirectPlay and WinSock. Here's a brief overview:

- **DirectPlay**: DirectPlay is a high-level networking API that simplifies the process of setting up and managing network connections in games. It includes features for creating multiplayer games, handling player discovery, and managing game sessions.

- **WinSock**: WinSock is a lower-level API for network programming and is not specific to DirectX. It offers more fine-grained control over network communication but requires a deeper understanding of networking concepts.

Setting Up a Basic Networked Game

TO ILLUSTRATE THE BASICS of network programming in DirectX, let's consider a simple multiplayer game where two players can move their characters on a shared game board. Here's an outline of the steps involved:

1. **Initialize Networking**: Initialize the networking libraries

and set up the server-client architecture. The server manages the game state, while clients send their inputs to the server and receive updates.

2. **Data Serialization**: Define a format for serializing game data, such as player positions and game events. Serialization is the process of converting complex data structures into a format that can be easily transmitted over the network.
3. **Client-Server Communication**: Implement the communication logic between clients and the server. Clients send their input commands (e.g., move left, move right) to the server, and the server processes these commands and updates the game state.
4. **Latency Compensation**: To handle network latency, implement techniques such as interpolation and prediction to make the game feel responsive to players, even in the presence of network delays.
5. **Synchronization**: Ensure that all clients are synchronized with the server's game state. This involves regularly sending updates from the server to clients and handling situations where packets of data may be lost or arrive out of order.
6. **Security**: Implement security measures to prevent cheating and unauthorized access to game data. This includes authentication and encryption.
7. **Testing and Optimization**: Thoroughly test the networked game under different network conditions to identify and address issues related to lag, packet loss, and synchronization problems. Optimize the network code for performance.

DirectX provides tools and libraries that can simplify many of these tasks, allowing you to focus on the specific networking features of your game.

Conclusion

NETWORK PROGRAMMING in DirectX is a valuable skill for game developers, enabling the creation of engaging multiplayer and online experiences. By understanding the basics of network architecture, protocols, and DirectX's networking APIs, you can design and implement networked games that provide seamless and enjoyable gameplay for players worldwide.

6.2 DirectPlay for Multiplayer Games

DIRECTPLAY IS A HIGH-level networking API provided by DirectX, designed specifically for developing multiplayer games. It simplifies the process of setting up network connections, managing players, and handling data communication between game clients and servers. In this section, we will explore the key features and usage of DirectPlay in the context of multiplayer game development.

Key Features of DirectPlay

DIRECTPLAY OFFERS SEVERAL features that make it suitable for developing multiplayer games:

1. **Lobby System**: DirectPlay includes a lobby system that allows players to discover and join game sessions. This is essential for creating a seamless multiplayer experience.
2. **Session Management**: It provides tools for creating, managing, and destroying game sessions. A session represents a game being hosted on a server, and players can join or leave sessions dynamically.

3. **Player Management**: DirectPlay helps manage player connections, including handling player names, IDs, and player-specific data. This allows for player identification and customization.
4. **Data Communication**: DirectPlay simplifies data communication between clients and servers. It offers reliable and unreliable data transfer modes, making it suitable for various types of games.
5. **Security**: It includes features for authentication and encryption to ensure the security of game data and prevent cheating.

Setting Up a DirectPlay Multiplayer Game

TO CREATE A MULTIPLAYER game using DirectPlay, you can follow these steps:

1. **Initialization**: Initialize the DirectPlay libraries and set up your game as either a client or server.
2. **Session Creation**: On the server side, create a game session and make it available in the lobby for players to join. Specify the maximum number of players, session name, and other relevant parameters.
3. **Lobby System**: Implement a lobby system that allows players to discover available game sessions and join them. This may involve creating a user interface for players to browse and select game sessions.
4. **Player Management**: Keep track of connected players, assign unique IDs or names to them, and exchange player-specific data if needed.
5. **Data Communication**: Use DirectPlay's data communication functions to send and receive game-related data between clients and the server. You can define custom

data structures to serialize and deserialize game information.

6. **Synchronization**: Ensure that game state updates are synchronized between clients and the server. Handle issues like packet loss, out-of-order packets, and latency to maintain a smooth gameplay experience.
7. **Security**: Implement authentication and encryption to protect the integrity of game data and prevent unauthorized access.
8. **Testing and Optimization**: Thoroughly test the multiplayer functionality under different network conditions to identify and resolve issues. Optimize the network code for performance and responsiveness.

DirectPlay vs. Modern Networking Libraries

IT'S WORTH NOTING THAT while DirectPlay was a popular choice for multiplayer game development in the past, it has been deprecated in more recent versions of DirectX. Many modern games now use other networking libraries and frameworks that offer more flexibility and support for various platforms.

Popular alternatives to DirectPlay include using lower-level networking libraries like WinSock or third-party networking libraries such as Photon, RakNet, or UNet (for Unity-based games). These libraries provide more control over network communication and are often platform-agnostic, making them suitable for cross-platform multiplayer games.

Conclusion

DIRECTPLAY SERVED AS a valuable tool for developing multiplayer games using DirectX in the past. While it has been deprecated in favor of other networking solutions, understanding its principles and features can still be beneficial for historical or legacy game development projects. However, for modern multiplayer game development, exploring alternative networking libraries and frameworks may be more practical and versatile.

6.3 Synchronizing Game States Over a Network

SYNCHRONIZING GAME states over a network is a critical aspect of multiplayer game development. When multiple players are connected to a game server, it's essential to ensure that all players see the same game world and experience consistent gameplay. In this section, we'll explore the challenges and techniques involved in synchronizing game states effectively.

The Challenge of Synchronization

SYNCHRONIZATION IS necessary because each player's device may have different network latencies, causing delays in transmitting and receiving game data. As a result, players might receive updates at slightly different times, which can lead to discrepancies in the game state.

Common synchronization challenges include:

1. **Network Latency**: Players may experience varying degrees of network latency, causing differences in the time it takes for data to travel between their devices and the server.
2. **Packet Loss**: Network packets can be lost or arrive out of order due to network congestion or other issues. Handling these situations is essential to maintain synchronization.
3. **Concurrency**: In multiplayer games, multiple players may perform actions simultaneously. Ensuring that actions are

applied in the correct order and without conflicts is crucial.

Techniques for Synchronization

TO ADDRESS SYNCHRONIZATION challenges, multiplayer games often employ the following techniques:

1. **Timestamps**: Use timestamps to mark the time when events occur in the game. When receiving updates, players can use timestamps to determine when events took place relative to their own game state.
2. **Interpolation**: Interpolation is a technique where intermediate values are calculated between two known states. This can be used to smooth out the movement of objects in the game, making it less jarring when updates arrive at irregular intervals.
3. **Prediction**: Prediction involves simulating the future state of the game on the client side based on the last known state and the inputs received from the player. If the predicted state matches the server's state, no correction is needed. If not, corrections are made.
4. **Reconciliation**: When differences between the predicted and server states are detected, reconciliation is the process of bringing the client's state in line with the server's state. This may involve rolling back or adjusting the client's state.
5. **Dead Reckoning**: Dead reckoning is a prediction technique that extrapolates an object's future position based on its current position and velocity. It's commonly used for predicting the movement of objects in real-time strategy games and first-person shooters.
6. **Server Authority**: In some cases, the server has the ultimate authority over certain game events, such as

determining the outcome of a player's actions. This prevents cheating by players who attempt to manipulate the game state on their client.

Code Example: Interpolation

HERE'S A SIMPLIFIED code example of how interpolation can be implemented in a multiplayer game to smooth out object movement:

// Client-side code

float interpolatedX = lerp(previousX, serverX, interpolationFactor);

float interpolatedY = lerp(previousY, serverY, interpolationFactor);

// Interpolation factor ranges from 0 to 1 and is based on the time elapsed since the last update.

In this example, lerp is a function that performs linear interpolation between two values based on the interpolationFactor. This smooths out the movement of game objects as updates arrive.

Conclusion

SYNCHRONIZING GAME states in multiplayer games is a complex but essential task. By understanding the challenges of network latency, packet loss, and concurrency, and by employing techniques like timestamps, interpolation, prediction, and reconciliation, game developers can create multiplayer experiences where all players share a consistent and enjoyable gaming environment.

6.4 Handling Latency and Network Issues

LATENCY, THE DELAY in data transmission between a client and a server, is a fundamental aspect of online multiplayer games. Network issues, such as high latency and packet loss, can significantly impact gameplay. In this section, we will explore the challenges posed by latency and network issues in multiplayer game development and strategies for handling them.

Understanding Latency

LATENCY IS THE TIME it takes for data to travel between a client and a server. It is typically measured in milliseconds (ms) and consists of various components:

1. **Propagation Delay**: The time it takes for data to physically travel between the client and server through network cables or wireless connections.
2. **Transmission Delay**: The time it takes to transmit data over the network, influenced by factors like bandwidth and congestion.
3. **Processing Delay**: The time it takes for the server and client to process data packets, including packet validation and game logic calculations.
4. **Queueing Delay**: The delay incurred when data packets wait in network queues to be processed or transmitted.

Challenges of High Latency

HIGH LATENCY CAN LEAD to several gameplay challenges:

1. **Input Delay**: Players may experience delays between their actions and the corresponding responses in the game, making it feel unresponsive.

2. **Position Discrepancies**: Objects and players in the game world may appear to jump or teleport due to delayed updates, causing visual inconsistencies.
3. **Hit Registration Issues**: In shooter games, high latency can result in players shooting where they believe the target is, but the server registers hits or misses differently.

Strategies for Latency Compensation

TO ADDRESS LATENCY and its associated challenges, multiplayer game developers employ various compensation strategies:

1. **Client-Side Prediction**: Clients predict the outcome of their actions before receiving server confirmation. This minimizes perceived input delay.
2. **Server Authority**: The server has the final say on important game events, preventing cheating and resolving disputes.
3. **Interpolation**: Interpolation techniques smooth out the movement of objects, reducing visual jitter caused by latency.
4. **Lag Compensation**: By applying lag compensation techniques, games can mitigate the impact of latency on hit registration and player interactions.
5. **Region-Based Matchmaking**: Matchmaking systems can prioritize grouping players from similar geographic regions to reduce latency.

Handling Packet Loss

PACKET LOSS OCCURS when data packets sent between the client and server do not reach their destination. This can result in missing game updates and synchronization issues. Strategies for handling packet loss include:

1. **Error Correction Codes**: Adding error correction codes to data packets allows the receiver to reconstruct lost or corrupted packets.
2. **Reliable UDP**: Some game networking libraries implement a reliable transmission layer over UDP to ensure all packets reach their destination.
3. **Packet Reordering**: Implement logic to reorder out-of-sequence packets received due to network delays.
4. **Interpolation and Extrapolation**: These techniques can smooth out the impact of missing data by predicting and interpolating between known states.

Code Example: Lag Compensation

HERE'S A SIMPLIFIED code example of how lag compensation can be implemented in a shooter game to account for latency when registering hits:

```
// Server-side code

bool CheckHit(Player shooter, Player target) {

// Calculate the time it took the bullet to travel to the target.

float bulletTravelTime = CalculateBulletTravelTime(shooter, target);

// Adjust for the target's latency.

float compensatedTime = bulletTravelTime + target.latency;

// Check if the target was at the predicted position at the compensated time.
```

```
if (IsPlayerAtPosition(target, PredictPosition(target, compensatedTime))) {

// Register a hit.

RegisterHit(shooter, target);

return true;

}

return false;

}
```

In this example, the server compensates for the target's latency by predicting the target's position at the compensated time when the bullet arrives.

Conclusion

HANDLING LATENCY AND network issues is a critical aspect of multiplayer game development. By understanding the components of latency, its impact on gameplay, and implementing compensation strategies, developers can create enjoyable and responsive online gaming experiences, even in the face of challenging network conditions.

6.5 Building a Simple Multiplayer Game

BUILDING A SIMPLE MULTIPLAYER game is an exciting endeavor that allows developers to apply the concepts and techniques discussed in earlier chapters. In this section, we'll walk through the basic steps of creating a multiplayer game and discuss the key components and considerations involved.

Designing the Game

BEFORE DIVING INTO development, it's essential to have a clear game concept and design in mind. Consider the following aspects:

1. **Game Genre**: Decide on the type of game you want to create, whether it's a first-person shooter, real-time strategy, or any other genre.
2. **Game Mechanics**: Define the core gameplay mechanics, objectives, and rules that players will follow.
3. **Multiplayer Mode**: Determine whether your game will be turn-based or real-time, and decide on the maximum number of players per game session.
4. **Networking Architecture**: Choose a networking architecture that suits your game's requirements, such as client-server or peer-to-peer.

Setting Up the Development Environment

TO START DEVELOPING your multiplayer game, you'll need the following:

1. **Development Tools**: Install game development tools, such as a game engine (e.g., Unity, Unreal Engine) or a graphics library (e.g., DirectX).
2. **Networking Library**: Select a networking library or framework that supports multiplayer communication. Popular choices include Photon, Mirror, and Unreal Engine's built-in networking.
3. **Version Control**: Use version control software like Git to manage your project's source code and collaborate with team members.

Networking Implementation

HERE ARE THE KEY STEPS involved in implementing networking for your multiplayer game:

1. **Player Authentication**: Implement a login system to authenticate players and manage their accounts.
2. **Matchmaking**: Develop a matchmaking system that pairs players into game sessions based on criteria like skill level or geographic region.
3. **Game Synchronization**: Ensure that the game state is synchronized across all connected clients. This includes player positions, game object states, and events.
4. **Latency Compensation**: Implement strategies to handle latency, such as client-side prediction and lag compensation, to provide a smooth and responsive gameplay experience.
5. **Security**: Implement security measures to prevent cheating, unauthorized access, and other security vulnerabilities.

Code Example: Player Movement Synchronization

```
// UNITY C# EXAMPLE

// Server-side code

void UpdatePlayerPosition(Player player, Vector3 newPosition) {

// Update the player's position on the server.

player.position = newPosition;

// Broadcast the updated position to all connected clients.

foreach (var client in connectedClients) {
```

```
client.SendPositionUpdate(player.id, newPosition);
}
}
// Client-side code
void ReceivePositionUpdate(int playerId, Vector3 newPosition) {
// Update the position of the player with the given ID on the client.
var playerToUpdate = FindPlayerById(playerId);
playerToUpdate.position = newPosition;
}
```

In this example, the server updates a player's position and broadcasts the update to all connected clients, ensuring that everyone sees the same player positions.

Testing and Debugging

THOROUGHLY TEST YOUR multiplayer game to identify and fix issues related to synchronization, latency, and gameplay balance. Use debugging tools and techniques specific to multiplayer games to diagnose and resolve problems.

Deployment and Scaling

ONCE YOUR MULTIPLAYER game is ready, deploy it on the chosen platforms (PC, consoles, mobile devices, etc.). Be prepared to scale your game server infrastructure to handle increasing player loads as your game gains popularity.

Conclusion

BUILDING A SIMPLE MULTIPLAYER game is a rewarding but challenging endeavor. It requires careful planning, solid networking implementation, and thorough testing to provide an enjoyable and seamless multiplayer experience for players. As you gain experience, you can expand your game's features and complexity, creating even more engaging multiplayer experiences.

7.1 Introduction to High-Level Shader Language (HLSL)

HIGH-LEVEL SHADER LANGUAGE (HLSL) is a vital component of modern graphics programming, especially when working with DirectX. HLSL allows developers to write shaders that control the rendering pipeline, enabling advanced visual effects in 3D applications and games. In this section, we will introduce you to HLSL, its purpose, syntax, and usage within DirectX applications.

Understanding Shaders

SHADERS ARE SMALL PROGRAMS that run on the GPU (Graphics Processing Unit) and are responsible for determining how pixels and vertices are processed during rendering. There are two primary types of shaders:

1. **Vertex Shaders**: These shaders are responsible for transforming the 3D coordinates of vertices and can perform various operations on each vertex.
2. **Pixel Shaders (Fragment Shaders)**: Pixel shaders, on the other hand, control how individual pixels are colored, lit, and shaded. They are essential for achieving realistic

lighting and visual effects.

Purpose of HLSL

HLSL IS A HIGH-LEVEL programming language designed for writing shaders. It serves several essential purposes in graphics programming:

1. **Customization**: HLSL allows developers to create custom shaders to achieve unique rendering effects not possible with fixed-function graphics pipelines.
2. **Optimization**: Shaders written in HLSL can be optimized for performance, taking advantage of the GPU's parallel processing capabilities.
3. **Realism**: With HLSL, you can simulate complex lighting models, shadows, reflections, and other realistic visual effects in real-time.

HLSL Syntax

HLSL HAS A C-LIKE SYNTAX, making it accessible to developers familiar with C, C++, or similar languages. Here's a brief overview of HLSL syntax elements:

- **Data Types**: HLSL supports standard data types like float, int, bool, as well as vector and matrix types like float4 and float4x4.

- **Functions**: HLSL shaders are primarily composed of functions, with two special entry points: vertex and pixel for vertex and pixel shaders, respectively.

- **Semantics**: Semantics are used to link shader inputs and outputs to specific data in the rendering pipeline. For example, SV_POSITION is a semantic used to specify the position of a vertex.

• **Operators**: HLSL supports standard mathematical and logical operators, such as +, -, *, /, >, <, and &&.

• **Constants**: You can define constants and parameters in HLSL, allowing you to customize shader behavior without modifying the code.

Code Example: Simple Vertex Shader

HERE'S A SIMPLE HLSL vertex shader that transforms vertices using a model-view-projection matrix:

```
// HLSL vertex shader

struct VertexInput {

float4 position : POSITION;

};

struct VertexOutput {

float4 position : SV_POSITION;

};

cbuffer MVPBuffer : register(b0) {

float4x4 modelViewProjection;

};

VertexOutput main(VertexInput input) {

VertexOutput output;
```

```
output.position = mul(input.position, modelViewProjection);

return output;

}
```

In this example, the main function takes input vertices, applies a transformation using a matrix from a constant buffer, and outputs the transformed vertex position.

Conclusion

HIGH-LEVEL SHADER LANGUAGE (HLSL) is a fundamental tool for achieving advanced graphics effects in DirectX applications. As you continue learning about HLSL, you'll gain the ability to create stunning visuals and control various aspects of the rendering pipeline, leading to more immersive and visually appealing 3D experiences in your games and applications.

7.2 Creating Basic Vertex and Pixel Shaders

IN THE WORLD OF DIRECTX and graphics programming, shaders play a pivotal role in achieving complex visual effects and controlling how objects are rendered on the screen. In this section, we'll delve into the creation of basic vertex and pixel shaders using High-Level Shader Language (HLSL).

Vertex Shaders

VERTEX SHADERS ARE responsible for processing individual vertices of 3D objects before they are rasterized into 2D pixels. They perform transformations, such as scaling, rotation, and translation, on vertex positions. Additionally, vertex shaders can calculate lighting, apply texture coordinates, and perform other per-vertex operations.

Here's a simplified example of a basic vertex shader in HLSL:

```
// HLSL vertex shader

struct VertexInput {

float3 position : POSITION;

};

struct VertexOutput {

float4 position : SV_POSITION;

};

VertexOutput main(VertexInput input) {

VertexOutput output;

output.position = float4(input.position, 1.0f);

return output;

}
```

In this example, the vertex shader simply passes through the vertex positions without any transformation. The main function takes VertexInput and returns VertexOutput, with the SV_POSITION semantic indicating the final vertex position.

Pixel Shaders

PIXEL SHADERS, ALSO known as fragment shaders, control the appearance of individual pixels on the screen. They determine the color, shading, and texture of each pixel, making them crucial for achieving realistic and visually appealing graphics.

Here's a basic pixel shader example that sets the pixel color to red:

```
// HLSL pixel shader
struct PixelInput {
float4 position : SV_POSITION;
};
float4 main(PixelInput input) : SV_TARGET {
return float4(1.0f, 0.0f, 0.0f, 1.0f); // Red color
}
```

In this pixel shader, the main function takes PixelInput and returns a color value using SV_TARGET semantic. In this case, it sets the pixel color to red with full opacity.

Shader Compilation and Integration

TO USE THESE SHADERS in your DirectX application, you need to compile them and link them with your rendering pipeline. DirectX provides functions and interfaces to load, compile, and set shaders for rendering. Depending on your application framework (e.g., DirectX 11, DirectX 12, Unity with DirectX backend), the integration process may vary.

Remember that shaders are only one part of the rendering pipeline. You'll also need to set up buffers, input layouts, and other rendering resources to work with shaders effectively.

Shader Debugging

DEBUGGING SHADERS CAN be challenging due to the lack of traditional debugging tools. However, you can use techniques like shader debugging in graphics debugging tools or print debugging by outputting values to the screen or logs to identify issues in your shaders.

Conclusion

CREATING BASIC VERTEX and pixel shaders is a fundamental step in graphics programming with DirectX. As you gain proficiency in HLSL and shader development, you can explore more advanced shader techniques to achieve stunning visual effects in your games and applications. Shaders provide the flexibility and power needed to push the boundaries of real-time graphics rendering.

7.3 Advanced Shader Techniques

IN THE REALM OF GRAPHICS programming with DirectX, advanced shader techniques play a crucial role in achieving realistic and visually stunning rendering effects. In this section, we'll explore some advanced shader techniques that go beyond the basics and allow you to create more immersive 3D experiences.

Tessellation Shaders

TESSELLATION SHADERS are used to dynamically adjust the level of detail in 3D models, ensuring that objects appear more detailed when viewed up close and less detailed when viewed from a distance. This technique is especially valuable for terrains, characters, and other complex 3D objects. Tessellation shaders are composed of three main components:

- **Hull Shader**: Determines how to subdivide the input patch (e.g., a triangle) into smaller patches.

- **Tessellator**: Divides the input patch based on instructions from the hull shader.

- **Domain Shader**: Computes the final positions and attributes of vertices within the tessellated patches.

Geometry Shaders

GEOMETRY SHADERS ALLOW you to create and manipulate additional vertices within the rendering pipeline. They can generate new vertices, change vertex positions, and emit primitives like triangles and points. Geometry shaders are useful for effects like particle systems, procedural geometry generation, and silhouette outlining.

Here's a simplified example of a geometry shader that generates additional vertices to create billboarding effects for particles:

```
// HLSL geometry shader

[maxvertexcount(4)]

void main(point VertexInput input[1], inout TriangleStream<PixelInput> OutputStream) {

// Create a quad from the input vertex (for billboarding)

// Emit four vertices to form a quad

for (int i = 0; i < 4; ++i) {

PixelInput output;

output.position = input[0].position;

output.texCoord = float2(i % 2, i / 2); // UV coordinates
```

```
OutputStream.Append(output);

}

}
```

Compute Shaders

COMPUTE SHADERS ARE a powerful type of shader that doesn't directly deal with rendering but is used for general-purpose computing tasks on the GPU. They can be employed for tasks such as physics simulations, data processing, and procedural content generation. Compute shaders are well-suited for massively parallel operations, taking advantage of the GPU's computational capabilities.

Shader Libraries and Code Organization

AS SHADER COMPLEXITY grows, it's essential to maintain organized and modular shader code. Shader libraries can help you reuse common functions and techniques across multiple shaders. They allow you to encapsulate functionality and promote code reusability, making your shader codebase more maintainable.

```
// Example shader library: Lighting.hlsl

float3 CalculateLighting(float3 normal, float3 lightDir, float3 ambientColor, float3 diffuseColor) {

// Lighting calculations here

}
```

Shader Debugging and Optimization

DEBUGGING AND OPTIMIZING shaders can be challenging due to the lack of traditional debugging tools. Debugging techniques may involve outputting values to the screen or logs for inspection. Optimization strategies include minimizing memory accesses, reducing branching, and using built-in hardware features efficiently.

Conclusion

ADVANCED SHADER TECHNIQUES expand your capabilities as a DirectX graphics programmer. Tessellation shaders, geometry shaders, and compute shaders provide the tools to create complex visual effects, procedural content, and realistic simulations. Additionally, organizing shader code into libraries and optimizing shaders for performance are essential skills for achieving high-quality graphics in your DirectX applications.

7.4 Optimization Strategies for Shaders

OPTIMIZING SHADERS is a critical aspect of DirectX graphics programming. Efficient shaders can significantly improve the rendering performance of your application, especially in resource-intensive scenarios. In this section, we'll explore various optimization strategies for shaders.

1. Minimize Memory Accesses

ONE OF THE KEY FACTORS affecting shader performance is memory access. Accessing memory, whether it's texture data or constant buffers, can be slow. To optimize, try to minimize memory accesses by:

- Using texture samplers efficiently and sampling only when necessary.
- Reducing redundant texture reads by caching values where possible.
- Packing multiple values into a single data structure to optimize memory bandwidth.

2. Reduce Branching

CONDITIONAL BRANCHING in shaders can lead to performance bottlenecks, as it can cause divergence in the GPU's execution units. To optimize, consider:

- Using conditional statements sparingly and favoring arithmetic operations.
- Using predication when applicable to eliminate branching.
- Simplifying complex conditionals whenever possible.

3. Optimize Register Usage

EACH SHADER HAS A LIMITED number of registers available for computation. Optimizing register usage is essential to prevent register spilling, which can severely impact performance. Strategies include:

- Minimizing unnecessary variable declarations.
- Reusing variables instead of declaring new ones.
- Minimizing the use of temporary registers.

4. Loop Unrolling

LOOPING IN SHADERS can be expensive due to the potential for divergence. Loop unrolling involves manually expanding loops to reduce branching and improve parallelism. However, it should be used judiciously, as excessively unrolled loops can increase code size.

```
// Example loop unrolling in HLSL

for (int i = 0; i < 4; ++i) {

// Loop body

// ...

}
```

5. Precompute Constants

IF CERTAIN VALUES ARE constant or change infrequently, precompute them and store them as constants in your shader code. This reduces the need for runtime calculations and can improve performance.

```
// Precomputed constant in HLSL

const float PI = 3.14159265359;
```

6. LOD Management

WHEN WORKING WITH TEXTURES, use Level of Detail (LOD) techniques to select appropriate mip levels. LOD management ensures that you use lower-resolution textures when objects are distant and higher-resolution textures when they are close, optimizing texture fetches.

7. Profile and Measure

PROFILING YOUR SHADERS is crucial for identifying performance bottlenecks. Use GPU profiling tools to measure the execution time of your shaders and pinpoint areas that need optimization. Profiling can help you focus your efforts on the most critical parts of your shader code.

8. SIMD Optimization

MODERN GPUS USE SINGLE Instruction, Multiple Data (SIMD) execution. To leverage SIMD optimization, ensure that your shader code is designed to take advantage of parallelism. Avoid divergent code paths that can hinder SIMD performance.

9. Avoid Costly Functions

SOME SHADER FUNCTIONS can be computationally expensive. Be cautious when using functions like trigonometric operations, square roots, and exponentials. Consider alternatives or approximations when possible.

10. Use Compiler Directives

SHADER COMPILERS OFTEN provide optimization options through compiler directives. Check the documentation for your specific shader compiler (e.g., HLSL, GLSL) and utilize directives that help the compiler generate optimized code.

```
// HLSL compiler directive for optimization

#pragma optimize( on )
```

Conclusion

OPTIMIZING SHADERS is a continuous process in DirectX graphics programming. By following these optimization strategies and profiling your shaders, you can ensure that your application runs smoothly and efficiently, delivering high-performance graphics rendering. Keep in mind that the effectiveness of optimizations may vary depending on the specific hardware and DirectX version you are targeting, so testing and benchmarking are essential steps in the optimization process.

7.5 Using Compute Shaders for Non-Graphics Tasks

WHILE SHADERS ARE PRIMARILY associated with graphics rendering, modern GPUs can be used for a wide range of general-purpose computation tasks. Compute shaders, introduced in DirectX 11 and later versions, enable you to harness the immense parallel processing power of the GPU for non-graphics tasks. In this section, we'll explore the concept of compute shaders and their applications.

1. What Are Compute Shaders?

COMPUTE SHADERS ARE a type of shader program that runs on the GPU but is not directly tied to the rendering pipeline. Unlike vertex and pixel shaders, compute shaders are designed for general-purpose computing. They are written in languages like HLSL (High-Level Shader Language) and allow you to perform massively parallel computations on the GPU.

2. Parallelism in Compute Shaders

ONE OF THE KEY ADVANTAGES of compute shaders is their ability to execute thousands of threads in parallel. This parallelism makes them well-suited for tasks that can be parallelized, such as simulations, physics calculations, image processing, and data analysis.

3. How to Use Compute Shaders

TO USE COMPUTE SHADERS in DirectX, you need to create a compute shader object, load the shader code, and dispatch threads to execute the shader. Here's a simplified example in HLSL and C++:

```
// HLSL compute shader code

[numthreads(256, 1, 1)]

void CSMain(uint3 DTid : SV_DispatchThreadID) {

// Compute shader logic here

// Access data using DTid.x, DTid.y, DTid.z

}

// C++ code to use a compute shader

ID3D11ComputeShader* pComputeShader;

// Load and compile the shader code

// Dispatch the compute shader with a specified number of thread groups

UINT threadGroupCountX = 256;

UINT threadGroupCountY = 1;
```

```
UINT threadGroupCountZ = 1;

pImmediateContext->CSSetShader(pComputeShader, nullptr, 0);

pImmediateContext->Dispatch(threadGroupCountX,
threadGroupCountY, threadGroupCountZ);
```

4. Applications of Compute Shaders

COMPUTE SHADERS HAVE a wide range of applications in DirectX programming:

- **Physics Simulations:** Compute shaders can simulate physical interactions, such as cloth dynamics, fluid simulations, and particle systems.
- **Image Processing:** They are used for tasks like image filtering, post-processing effects, and texture compression.
- **Data Processing:** Compute shaders can accelerate data processing tasks, including data transformations and numerical simulations.
- **AI and Machine Learning:** Some AI and machine learning algorithms can be parallelized and executed on the GPU using compute shaders.

5. Memory Access and Synchronization

WHEN USING COMPUTE shaders, it's crucial to manage memory access efficiently and handle synchronization between threads, as parallel execution can lead to data race conditions. DirectX provides mechanisms like shared memory and thread synchronization primitives to address these challenges.

6. GPU Compute Programming Languages

WHILE HLSL IS COMMONLY used for compute shaders in DirectX, other GPU programming languages like CUDA and OpenCL can also be used for GPU compute tasks, depending on your specific requirements and hardware.

Conclusion

COMPUTE SHADERS IN DirectX open up a world of possibilities for leveraging the GPU's processing power for non-graphics tasks. Whether you're working on complex simulations, data processing, or AI applications, compute shaders can significantly accelerate your computations. However, it's essential to understand GPU parallelism, memory management, and synchronization to effectively use compute shaders in your DirectX applications.

Chapter 8: DirectX and Game Engines

8.1 Overview of Popular Game Engines with DirectX Support

IN THE WORLD OF GAME development, using a game engine can significantly streamline the process of creating interactive experiences. Game engines provide a framework that handles various aspects of game development, including graphics rendering, physics simulations, input handling, and more. Many game engines support DirectX as their graphics and rendering backend, taking advantage of its capabilities. In this section, we'll provide an overview of some popular game engines that offer DirectX support.

1. Unity

UNITY IS ONE OF THE most widely used game engines in the industry, known for its flexibility and ease of use. While Unity primarily uses its proprietary rendering engine, it also provides options for integrating DirectX through custom plugins. Unity's powerful scripting system allows developers to interact with DirectX features and create high-quality 3D and 2D games.

```
// Unity script example using DirectX API

void Start() {

// Initialize DirectX rendering

DirectXRenderer.Initialize();

// Create and render DirectX objects

DirectXRenderer.RenderObject(myGameObject);
```

```
}
```

2. Unreal Engine

UNREAL ENGINE, DEVELOPED by Epic Games, is renowned for its stunning graphics and realistic physics simulations. It uses DirectX as one of its primary graphics APIs, making it suitable for creating visually impressive games. Unreal Engine's Blueprint visual scripting and C++ programming provide developers with various options for utilizing DirectX's rendering capabilities.

```
// Unreal Engine C++ code using DirectX

void AMyCharacter::RenderFrame() {

// Initialize DirectX rendering context

DirectXRenderer::Initialize();

// Render the scene using DirectX

DirectXRenderer::RenderScene(myScene);

}
```

3. CryEngine

CRYENGINE, USED IN the Crysis series, is another engine that leverages DirectX for rendering. It offers a comprehensive set of tools for creating highly detailed environments and realistic visuals. CryEngine's visual scripting system, Flow Graph, and C++ scripting allow developers to work with DirectX for advanced graphics effects.

```
—CryEngine Flow Graph using DirectX

function OnUpdate(frameTime)
```

```
—Initialize DirectX rendering

DirectXRenderer:Initialize()

—Render game objects using DirectX

DirectXRenderer:RenderObjects(gameObjects)

end
```

4. Godot Engine

GODOT ENGINE IS AN open-source game engine known for its lightweight footprint and flexibility. While it primarily uses its custom rendering engine, it allows developers to write custom shaders using the OpenGL ES language. This provides a level of control over rendering, although it differs from DirectX.

```
# Godot Engine GDScript example with custom shader

extends Node2D

func _ready():

# Initialize custom OpenGL shader

shader = Shader.new()

shader.set_code(myCustomShaderCode)

shader.mode = Shader.MODE_CANVAS_ITEM

material.shader = shader
```

5. Lumberyard

AMAZON LUMBERYARD IS a game engine developed by Amazon Game Studios. It incorporates DirectX for rendering and offers deep integration with Amazon Web Services (AWS) for online and multiplayer features. Lumberyard provides a visual scripting system and C++ programming for DirectX-based graphics development.

```
// Amazon Lumberyard C++ code with DirectX

void RenderFrame() {

// Initialize DirectX rendering

DirectXRenderer::Initialize();

// Render the game scene using DirectX

DirectXRenderer::RenderScene(gameScene);

}
```

These are just a few examples of game engines that support DirectX. When choosing a game engine for your project, consider factors like your team's expertise, the type of game you're developing, and the engine's community and asset store support. DirectX's integration with these engines can help you achieve your vision and deliver outstanding gaming experiences.

8.2 Integrating DirectX with Game Engines

INTEGRATING DIRECTX with game engines can unlock a wide range of possibilities for creating visually stunning and highly performant games. DirectX, as a graphics and multimedia API, provides access to the underlying hardware capabilities, allowing developers to harness the full potential of modern GPUs. In this section, we will explore the process of integrating DirectX with game engines and highlight the advantages it offers.

Benefits of Integrating DirectX

1. **Low-Level Control:** DirectX provides low-level access to hardware, allowing developers to optimize rendering pipelines for maximum performance. This level of control is especially beneficial for achieving high-quality graphics in demanding games.
2. **Performance Optimization:** DirectX enables fine-tuning of rendering processes, including efficient resource management, culling techniques, and shader optimization. This can lead to improved frame rates and reduced input latency.
3. **Access to Advanced Features:** DirectX provides access to advanced rendering features, such as tessellation, compute shaders, and ray tracing, which can result in visually impressive and realistic graphics.
4. **Cross-Platform Compatibility:** While DirectX primarily targets Windows platforms, the DirectX 12 Ultimate API supports a broader range of platforms, including Xbox and cloud gaming services. This allows for more extensive reach and potential for cross-platform gaming.

Steps to Integrate DirectX with Game Engines

1. **Engine Configuration:** Most game engines that support DirectX provide settings or configurations for selecting DirectX as the rendering backend. Developers can choose the DirectX version (e.g., DirectX 11 or DirectX 12) based on their project's requirements.
2. **Shader Development:** Game engines often have built-in shader editors and tools for creating custom shaders. Developers can utilize DirectX shader languages (HLSL) to create shaders that interact seamlessly with the engine's

rendering pipeline.

3. **Resource Management:** DirectX requires efficient management of GPU resources such as textures, buffers, and render targets. Game engines typically provide abstractions and resource management systems to simplify this task.
4. **Rendering Pipeline Integration:** Integrating DirectX into a game engine involves aligning the engine's rendering pipeline with DirectX's capabilities. This may include configuring the engine's camera system, lighting, and post-processing effects to work harmoniously with DirectX rendering.
5. **Input and Output:** DirectX can be integrated into the engine's input and output systems, ensuring that user interactions and visual feedback are synchronized with the DirectX-rendered graphics. This includes handling window creation, mouse and keyboard input, and controller support.
6. **Testing and Debugging:** Rigorous testing and debugging are essential to ensure that the integration works correctly. Developers should be familiar with debugging tools and techniques specific to DirectX, as well as those provided by the game engine.

Example Integration Code

BELOW IS A SIMPLIFIED example of integrating DirectX with a fictional game engine:

```
// GameEngine.cpp

// Include DirectX headers

#include <d3d12.h>
```

```
#include <d3dcompiler.h>

// Initialize DirectX

void GameEngine::InitializeDirectX() {

// Create a DirectX device and swap chain

// ...

// Compile and load shaders using DirectX APIs

// ...

// Set up rendering resources (vertex buffers, textures, etc.)

// ...

}

// Render a frame using DirectX

void GameEngine::RenderFrame() {

// Clear the back buffer

// ...

// Set shader resources and constants

// ...

// Issue draw calls using DirectX

// ...

// Present the frame to the screen

// ...
```

```
}
```

In this code snippet, we initialize DirectX, compile shaders, and render a frame using DirectX within the game engine. The actual implementation would vary depending on the specific game engine's architecture and the version of DirectX being used.

Integrating DirectX with a game engine requires a deep understanding of both the engine's internals and DirectX itself. It is a complex but rewarding process that can result in visually stunning and highly performant games. Developers should refer to the documentation and resources provided by their chosen game engine for specific integration guidelines.

8.3 Customizing Engine Features Using DirectX

DIRECTX INTEGRATION with game engines not only involves utilizing DirectX's rendering capabilities but also allows developers to customize and extend various engine features to meet specific project requirements. This section explores the process of customizing game engine features using DirectX, highlighting the advantages and common use cases.

Advantages of Customization

1. **Tailored Rendering:** By integrating DirectX, developers can fine-tune rendering pipelines to achieve the desired visual quality and performance. This includes creating custom shaders, implementing advanced rendering techniques, and optimizing resource management.
2. **Special Effects:** DirectX empowers developers to create a wide range of special effects, including particle systems,

dynamic lighting, and post-processing effects. Customizing these effects can make games more immersive and visually appealing.

3. **Efficient Resource Handling:** Developers can use DirectX to optimize resource handling within the engine. This includes managing GPU resources such as textures, buffers, and shaders efficiently, leading to improved performance.
4. **Cross-Platform Compatibility:** Customized features can be designed to work seamlessly across multiple platforms, thanks to DirectX's cross-platform support, especially with DirectX 12 Ultimate.

Steps for Customizing Engine Features

1. **Identify Customization Goals:** Begin by identifying the specific features or aspects of the game engine that need customization. Common areas for customization include rendering, physics, audio, and input.
2. **Create Custom Shaders:** For visual customization, developers often create custom shaders using DirectX's HLSL language. These shaders can be used to implement unique rendering effects, material properties, and post-processing filters.
3. **Modify Engine Components:** Adapt the engine's components to incorporate custom shaders and rendering techniques. This may involve modifying the rendering pipeline, adding support for new rendering passes, or integrating custom lighting models.
4. **Implement Custom Physics:** If physics customization is required, developers can leverage DirectX to implement custom physics calculations, collision detection, and rigid body dynamics. This can be useful for non-standard

gameplay mechanics.

5. **Enhance Audio Effects:** DirectX's audio capabilities can be used to create custom audio effects, such as environmental audio, 3D sound positioning, and advanced audio processing. This enhances the overall audio experience in the game.
6. **Custom Input Handling:** Customize input handling to accommodate unique gameplay mechanics or control schemes. DirectX's input features can be extended to support custom input devices or gestures.

Example Customization Code

BELOW IS A SIMPLIFIED example of customizing a fictional game engine using DirectX for enhanced rendering:

```
// CustomRenderer.cpp

// Include DirectX headers

#include <d3d12.h>

#include <d3dcompiler.h>

// Custom rendering shader

extern const char* customShaderCode;

// Custom rendering pass

void CustomRenderer::RenderCustomPass() {

// Compile custom shader using DirectX APIs

// ...

// Set shader resources and constants
```

```
//...

// Issue draw calls using DirectX

//...

}
```

In this code snippet, a custom rendering pass is implemented within the game engine, utilizing DirectX for shader compilation and rendering. The actual implementation may vary based on the engine's architecture and customization goals.

Customizing game engine features using DirectX offers developers the flexibility to create unique and visually impressive games. It requires a deep understanding of both the engine's internals and DirectX capabilities. Developers should refer to the documentation and resources provided by their chosen game engine for specific customization guidelines.

8.4 Case Studies: Successful Games Built with DirectX and Game Engines

IN THIS SECTION, WE'LL explore case studies of successful games that have been built using DirectX in combination with various game engines. These examples highlight the versatility and power of DirectX in game development across different genres and platforms.

1. Halo: The Master Chief Collection

GAME ENGINE: Blam! (Custom Engine)

DirectX Version: DirectX 11 (Initially)

Platforms: Xbox One, Microsoft Windows

Halo: The Master Chief Collection is a critically acclaimed compilation of the first-person shooter series Halo, developed by 343 Industries and published by Xbox Game Studios. It combines remastered versions of classic Halo titles into a single package. The game originally used DirectX 11 on Windows but transitioned to DirectX 12 for improved performance and graphics quality. This transition allowed for better multi-threading, reducing CPU overhead, and enabling advanced rendering techniques. DirectX 12 also enhanced the overall gaming experience, especially on Windows 10.

2. Forza Horizon 5

GAME ENGINE: ForzaTech (Custom Engine)

DirectX Version: DirectX 12

Platforms: Xbox Series X/S, Microsoft Windows

Forza Horizon 5 is an open-world racing game developed by Playground Games and published by Xbox Game Studios. It is known for its stunning graphics, realistic physics, and dynamic weather system. The game leverages DirectX 12 to deliver exceptional visuals and performance on both Xbox Series X/S and Windows PCs. DirectX 12's low-level access to hardware resources allows Forza Horizon 5 to push the boundaries of realism in racing games.

3. Gears 5

GAME ENGINE: Unreal Engine 4

DirectX Version: DirectX 12

Platforms: Xbox Series X/S, Microsoft Windows

Gears 5, developed by The Coalition and published by Xbox Game Studios, is the latest installment in the Gears of War series. It utilizes Unreal Engine 4 and DirectX 12 to achieve impressive visuals and gameplay. DirectX 12's support for asynchronous compute and improved CPU multi-threading enables Gears 5 to render detailed environments, advanced lighting, and fluid character animations on both console and PC platforms.

4. Ori and the Will of the Wisps

GAME ENGINE: Unity

DirectX Version: DirectX 11

Platforms: Xbox One, Microsoft Windows, Nintendo Switch

Ori and the Will of the Wisps, developed by Moon Studios and published by Xbox Game Studios, is a visually stunning platformer game. While it primarily uses Unity as its game engine, it relies on DirectX 11 for rendering on Windows and Xbox One. The game showcases how DirectX can be integrated into various engines to deliver captivating 2D and 3D visuals.

5. Flight Simulator (2020)

GAME ENGINE: Proprietary Engine (Asobo Engine)

DirectX Version: DirectX 11 (Initially), DirectX 12 (Later)

Platforms: Microsoft Windows, Xbox Series X/S

Microsoft Flight Simulator (2020) is known for its realism and attention to detail. It uses the Asobo Engine and initially relied on DirectX 11 for its PC release. Later, an update introduced DirectX

12 support, significantly improving performance and taking advantage of modern hardware capabilities. The transition to DirectX 12 allowed for more detailed world rendering and smoother flight experiences.

These case studies demonstrate the diverse range of games that have successfully utilized DirectX in conjunction with various game engines. DirectX's adaptability, performance enhancements, and cross-platform support have played pivotal roles in creating immersive gaming experiences on both PC and console platforms. Developers continue to leverage DirectX to push the boundaries of what is possible in modern game development.

8.5 Future of Cross-Platform Gaming with DirectX

AS TECHNOLOGY EVOLVES, the future of cross-platform gaming with DirectX holds exciting possibilities and challenges. In this section, we'll delve into the trends and developments that are shaping the future landscape of DirectX in the world of gaming.

1. DirectX 12 Ultimate

MICROSOFT INTRODUCED **DirectX 12 Ultimate** as an evolution of the DirectX 12 API. It offers a unified graphics platform for both PC and Xbox, enabling developers to create games that run seamlessly on both platforms. DirectX 12 Ultimate introduces features like ray tracing, variable rate shading, mesh shaders, and more, which are supported on the latest hardware, delivering unprecedented realism and performance. This unification simplifies cross-platform game development, allowing developers to target a broader audience.

2. Cloud Gaming

CLOUD GAMING SERVICES, such as Xbox Cloud Gaming (formerly known as Project xCloud), Google Stadia, and NVIDIA GeForce NOW, are becoming increasingly popular. DirectX plays a crucial role in delivering high-quality graphics and low-latency gaming experiences through the cloud. Gamers can access demanding titles on a variety of devices, making cross-platform gaming even more accessible.

3. Mobile and Streaming

THE INTEGRATION OF DirectX into mobile gaming is a promising trend. With the growth of powerful smartphones and tablets, DirectX can bring console-quality graphics and experiences to mobile devices. Cross-platform multiplayer and streaming services bridge the gap between mobile and traditional gaming, allowing players to enjoy the same games on various platforms.

4. Cross-Play and Cross-Save

CROSS-PLATFORM PLAY and cross-save functionality have gained traction. DirectX helps ensure a consistent gaming experience across platforms, allowing players on different devices to collaborate or compete. Cross-save enables gamers to continue their progress seamlessly on various platforms, enhancing user convenience.

5. Emulation and Retro Gaming

DIRECTX CAN ALSO PLAY a role in emulation and retro gaming. Emulators use DirectX to recreate the gaming experiences of older consoles and platforms on modern hardware. This allows gamers to revisit classic titles on their current systems, contributing to the preservation of gaming history.

6. Advanced AI Integration

AI INTEGRATION IN GAMES is on the rise, and DirectX can facilitate AI-driven features. From dynamic NPCs to procedural content generation and adaptive difficulty scaling, AI enhances gameplay. DirectX enables developers to harness the power of AI for more immersive and personalized gaming experiences.

7. Open Standards and Collaboration

THE GAMING INDUSTRY is increasingly adopting open standards and collaboration. DirectX's support for industry standards like Vulkan and its integration with popular game engines promote interoperability and cooperation among developers. This trend fosters cross-platform compatibility and innovation.

In conclusion, the future of cross-platform gaming with DirectX is bright, with advancements in graphics, cloud gaming, mobile integration, and AI-driven experiences. As technology continues to evolve, DirectX remains a crucial tool for developers to create immersive and accessible gaming experiences that span multiple platforms. The gaming community can look forward to more exciting developments in the years to come.

9.1 The Role of DirectX in Modern Windows Applications

DIRECTX, ORIGINALLY designed for game development, has found a significant role in modern Windows applications beyond gaming. In this section, we'll explore how DirectX plays a crucial part in enhancing the user experience and functionality of various types of Windows applications.

1. Graphic-Intensive Applications

MANY NON-GAMING APPLICATIONS require complex graphics and animations, such as design software, video editing tools, and 3D modeling applications. DirectX provides a reliable and high-performance framework for rendering and managing these graphics, ensuring smooth interactions and real-time visual feedback.

2. Multimedia and Entertainment

MULTIMEDIA APPLICATIONS, including video players, music software, and streaming platforms, leverage DirectX for efficient media playback. DirectX's hardware acceleration capabilities enhance video rendering and audio processing, resulting in a superior multimedia experience.

```
// Example of DirectX usage for video rendering

if (InitializeDirectXVideoRenderer() == S_OK) {

while (PlayingVideo) {

RenderFrameUsingDirectX();

}

CleanupDirectXVideoRenderer();

}
```

3. Business and Productivity Software

EVEN IN BUSINESS AND productivity software, DirectX can be utilized to create visually appealing and intuitive user interfaces. Charts, graphs, and data visualizations benefit from DirectX's capabilities, making data-driven applications more engaging and informative.

4. CAD and Engineering Applications

COMPUTER-AIDED DESIGN (CAD) and engineering software rely on DirectX for rendering intricate 3D models and simulations. DirectX's support for hardware acceleration ensures that engineers and designers can work with complex designs efficiently.

5. Mapping and Geographic Information Systems (GIS)

GIS APPLICATIONS REQUIRE precise rendering of maps and geographical data. DirectX aids in displaying maps, visualizing geographic information, and providing interactive features for GIS software. This enables users to analyze and explore geographic data effectively.

```
// Example of DirectX usage in GIS application

if (InitializeDirectXMapRenderer() == S_OK) {

LoadMapData();

RenderMapUsingDirectX();

HandleUserInteractions();

CleanupDirectXMapRenderer();

}
```

6. Virtual Reality (VR) and Augmented Reality (AR)

VR AND AR APPLICATIONS, although often associated with gaming, extend into various fields, such as education, healthcare, and training. DirectX's support for VR and AR hardware ensures a seamless experience, whether it's medical simulations, educational content, or architectural visualization.

7. Cross-Platform Development

DEVELOPERS LOOKING to create applications that run on multiple platforms, including Windows, can benefit from DirectX's cross-platform capabilities. By using DirectX as a common graphics API, developers can write code that is easily portable to other platforms, enhancing software accessibility.

8. Future Windows Programming

DIRECTX CONTINUES TO evolve alongside Windows, adapting to new technologies and hardware advancements. It remains an essential tool for modern Windows application development, ensuring that developers can harness the full potential of the Windows ecosystem.

In summary, DirectX's role in modern Windows applications extends far beyond gaming, enhancing graphics, multimedia, business, and productivity software. Its versatility, performance, and cross-platform capabilities make it an indispensable asset for developers creating a wide range of applications in the Windows environment.

9.2 DirectX for Desktop Application Development

DIRECTX, PRIMARILY known for its role in gaming and multimedia applications, also plays a significant role in desktop application development for Windows. In this section, we'll explore how DirectX is leveraged to enhance the user experience and functionality of desktop software beyond gaming.

1. Graphical User Interfaces (GUI)

DIRECTX CAN BE USED to create custom graphical user interfaces (GUIs) for desktop applications. While traditional Windows forms and controls are suitable for many scenarios, DirectX offers more flexibility in designing unique and visually appealing interfaces. This is particularly valuable for applications requiring custom controls, 2D/3D visualizations, or unconventional layouts.

```
// Example of DirectX-based GUI element rendering
if (InitializeDirectXGUIRenderer() == S_OK) {
RenderCustomGUIElementsUsingDirectX();
HandleUserInteractions();
CleanupDirectXGUIRenderer();
}
```

2. Data Visualization

APPLICATIONS THAT DEAL with complex data sets, such as scientific analysis tools, financial software, and data analytics platforms, can benefit from DirectX's capabilities. It enables the creation of interactive and visually engaging data visualizations, including charts, graphs, and heatmaps, which facilitate data-driven decision-making.

```
// Example of DirectX-based data visualization

if (InitializeDirectXDataVisualization() == S_OK) {

LoadData();

RenderDataVisualizationUsingDirectX();

HandleUserInteractions();

CleanupDirectXDataVisualization();

}
```

3. Simulation and Modeling

DESKTOP APPLICATIONS that involve simulations and modeling, such as physics simulations, architectural design tools, or virtual labs, often require real-time 3D rendering. DirectX's support for 3D graphics and physics simulations ensures a responsive and immersive user experience.

```
// Example of DirectX-based simulation application

if (InitializeDirectXSimulation() == S_OK) {

InitializePhysicsEngine();

LoadSimulationAssets();

SimulateUsingDirectX();

CleanupDirectXSimulation();
```

```
}
```

4. Multimedia Integration

MULTIMEDIA INTEGRATION in desktop applications, such as video editing software, multimedia authoring tools, and virtual tour applications, benefits from DirectX's hardware-accelerated video and audio capabilities. It ensures smooth media playback and interactive multimedia experiences.

```
// Example of DirectX usage in multimedia application

if (InitializeDirectXMultimedia() == S_OK) {

LoadMediaAssets();

PlayMediaUsingDirectX();

HandleUserInteractions();

CleanupDirectXMultimedia();

}
```

5. CAD and 3D Modeling

DESKTOP APPLICATIONS for computer-aided design (CAD) and 3D modeling often require advanced rendering capabilities. DirectX facilitates the rendering of complex 3D models, enabling engineers and designers to work with intricate designs efficiently.

```
// Example of DirectX usage in CAD application

if (InitializeDirectXCADRenderer() == S_OK) {

Load3DModels();

RenderCADUsingDirectX();
```

```
HandleUserInteractions();

CleanupDirectXCADRenderer();

}
```

6. Cross-Platform Development

DIRECTX'S ADAPTABILITY extends to cross-platform development for Windows-based desktop applications. By using DirectX as a common graphics API, developers can write code that is easily portable to other Windows platforms, ensuring software consistency and reach.

7. Performance Optimization

DIRECTX PROVIDES TOOLS and techniques for optimizing the performance of desktop applications. This includes efficient memory management, multi-threading support, and GPU acceleration, ensuring that applications run smoothly even with resource-intensive tasks.

In conclusion, DirectX is a versatile tool for enhancing the functionality and user experience of desktop applications on the Windows platform. Whether it's creating custom GUIs, visualizing data, simulating complex systems, integrating multimedia, or optimizing performance, DirectX offers developers a wide range of capabilities beyond gaming, making it a valuable asset for desktop application development.

9.3 Integrating 3D Graphics in Business Applications

THE INTEGRATION OF 3D graphics in business applications has gained momentum in recent years. While DirectX is traditionally associated with gaming and multimedia, it also plays a pivotal role in enhancing the user experience of business applications. In this section, we'll explore how DirectX can be leveraged to integrate 3D graphics into various types of business software.

1. Data Visualization and Analysis

BUSINESS APPLICATIONS often deal with complex data sets, and 3D graphics can provide a more intuitive and insightful way to visualize and analyze this data. For instance, financial software can use 3D charts to represent market trends, and data analytics tools can create interactive 3D visualizations for better data exploration.

```
// Example of 3D data visualization using DirectX

if (InitializeDirectX3DDataVisualization() == S_OK) {

LoadData();

Render3DDataVisualization();

HandleUserInteractions();

CleanupDirectX3DDataVisualization();

}
```

2. Product Design and Prototyping

IN INDUSTRIES LIKE manufacturing and product design, 3D graphics are indispensable. DirectX can be used to create applications that allow engineers and designers to design and prototype products in a 3D environment. This accelerates the design process and helps identify potential issues early.

```
// Example of 3D product design application with DirectX

if (InitializeDirectX3DProductDesign() == S_OK) {

Load3DModels();

DesignIn3DUsingDirectX();

HandleUserInteractions();

CleanupDirectX3DProductDesign();

}
```

3. Training and Simulations

BUSINESS APPLICATIONS often require training and simulations, particularly in sectors like aviation, healthcare, and military. DirectX enables the creation of realistic 3D simulations that mimic real-world scenarios, enhancing training effectiveness.

```
// Example of 3D training and simulation application

if (InitializeDirectX3DSimulation() == S_OK) {

LoadSimulationScenarios();

SimulateIn3DUsingDirectX();

HandleUserInteractions();
```

```
CleanupDirectX3DSimulation();

}
```

4. Geographic Information Systems (GIS)

GIS SOFTWARE RELIES heavily on maps and spatial data. DirectX can be employed to render interactive 3D maps, making it easier for professionals in fields like urban planning, environmental science, and geology to analyze and visualize geographic data.

```
// Example of GIS application using DirectX for 3D map rendering

if (InitializeDirectX3DMapRendering() == S_OK) {

LoadGeographicData();

Render3DMapsUsingDirectX();

HandleUserInteractions();

CleanupDirectX3DMapRendering();

}
```

5. Virtual Conferencing and Collaboration

WITH THE GROWTH OF remote work and virtual collaboration, business applications are incorporating virtual conferencing and meeting features. DirectX can be used to create virtual meeting spaces with 3D avatars, interactive whiteboards, and immersive environments for enhanced collaboration.

```
// Example of DirectX-powered virtual conferencing in a business app

if (InitializeDirectX3DVirtualMeeting() == S_OK) {

CreateVirtualMeetingRoom();
```

```
Render3DAvatarsAndEnvironments();

CollaborateIn3DUsingDirectX();

CleanupDirectX3DVirtualMeeting();

}
```

6. Cross-Platform Compatibility

FOR BUSINESSES TARGETING Windows-based desktop applications, DirectX ensures cross-platform compatibility. By using DirectX as the graphics API, developers can write code that remains consistent across different Windows platforms, providing a unified user experience.

In conclusion, DirectX offers a valuable toolkit for integrating 3D graphics into business applications. Whether it's for data visualization, product design, training simulations, GIS, virtual conferencing, or ensuring cross-platform compatibility, DirectX enhances the capabilities and user experience of business software. Its versatility extends beyond gaming, making it a powerful asset for modern business application development.

9.4 Performance Considerations and Best Practices

WHEN INTEGRATING DIRECTX into business applications, performance considerations are paramount. Poorly optimized graphics can lead to sluggish user experiences and hinder productivity. In this section, we'll delve into the performance aspects of using DirectX in business software and explore best practices to ensure smooth and responsive applications.

1. Hardware Compatibility and Requirements

BEFORE IMPLEMENTING DirectX in your business application, it's crucial to consider the hardware requirements. Ensure that the target machines meet the minimum DirectX version and have compatible graphics hardware. Detecting and informing users about hardware limitations can help manage expectations.

```
// Example of hardware detection and requirements check

if (IsDirectXSupported() && IsCompatibleHardwareDetected()) {

// Proceed with DirectX integration

} else {

// Display a message about hardware requirements

ShowHardwareRequirementsMessage();

}
```

2. Efficient Resource Management

EFFECTIVE RESOURCE management is essential for good performance. This includes loading and unloading textures, models, and other assets efficiently. Implement resource caching to reuse assets when possible, reducing unnecessary reloading.

```
// Example of resource caching for DirectX applications

if (!IsResourceCached(resourceKey)) {

LoadResource(resourceKey);

CacheResource(resourceKey);

}
```

```
RenderCachedResource(resourceKey);
```

3. Render Batching

MINIMIZE THE NUMBER of draw calls to the graphics hardware by batching rendering operations. Group objects with similar properties (e.g., shaders, textures) into batches to reduce the overhead of switching between different states.

```
// Example of render batching with DirectX

BeginBatch();

for (const auto& object : batchObjects) {

SetObjectShader(object);

SetObjectTexture(object);

RenderObject(object);

}

EndBatch();
```

4. Multithreading

LEVERAGE MULTITHREADING to distribute rendering tasks across multiple CPU cores. This can significantly improve application responsiveness and performance. However, be cautious when dealing with multithreading, as it can introduce synchronization issues.

```
// Example of multithreading in a DirectX application

std::thread renderThread(RenderScene);

std::thread updateThread(UpdateGameLogic);
```

```
renderThread.join();

updateThread.join();
```

5. GPU Performance Profiling

USE PROFILING TOOLS and techniques to identify performance bottlenecks in your DirectX application. Profilers can help pinpoint areas that require optimization, such as high GPU usage or CPU-bound operations.

```
// Example of GPU performance profiling

if (EnablePerformanceProfiling()) {

StartProfiling();

RenderScene();

StopProfiling();

AnalyzeProfilingResults();

}
```

6. Dynamic Level of Detail (LOD)

IMPLEMENT DYNAMIC LOD techniques to adjust the level of detail in 3D models based on their distance from the camera. This optimization reduces the GPU workload when rendering distant objects, improving overall performance.

```
// Example of dynamic LOD in a DirectX application

if (CalculateDistanceToCamera(object) > LODThreshold) {

SetObjectLOD(object, LowDetail);
```

```
} else {
SetObjectLOD(object, HighDetail);
}
RenderObject(object);
```

7. Memory Management

EFFICIENT MEMORY MANAGEMENT is crucial. Avoid memory leaks and excessive memory consumption by releasing resources when they are no longer needed. DirectX objects like textures and vertex buffers should be properly disposed of.

```
// Example of memory management in a DirectX application
ReleaseTexture(texture);
ReleaseVertexBuffer(vertexBuffer);
```

8. Error Handling and Recovery

IMPLEMENT ROBUST ERROR handling and recovery mechanisms. DirectX can encounter errors due to various reasons, such as driver issues or resource unavailability. Gracefully handling these errors and providing users with feedback or recovery options is essential.

```
// Example of error handling in a DirectX application
HRESULT result = RenderScene();
if (FAILED(result)) {
HandleRenderingError(result);
AttemptRecovery();
```

}

9. User Settings and Optimization Profiles

ALLOW USERS TO ADJUST graphics settings to optimize performance according to their hardware capabilities. Provide different optimization profiles or presets for users to choose from, catering to various performance levels.

```
// Example of user settings for DirectX graphics quality

GraphicsQuality userQuality = GetUserGraphicsQualitySetting();

ApplyGraphicsQualitySettings(userQuality);
```

10. Continuous Testing and Profiling

REGULARLY TEST AND profile your DirectX application on different hardware configurations and monitor its performance over time. Continuously optimize and update your software to maintain a responsive user experience.

In summary, optimizing DirectX performance in business applications is a critical aspect of delivering a smooth and efficient user experience. By considering hardware compatibility, efficient resource management, render batching, multithreading, profiling, LOD techniques, memory management, error handling, user settings, and continuous testing, you can create high-performance DirectX applications that enhance productivity and user satisfaction.

9.5 DirectX and the Future of Windows Programming

THE FUTURE OF WINDOWS programming is closely tied to the evolution of DirectX and the broader graphics and gaming industry. In this section, we'll explore the role of DirectX in shaping the future of Windows development and how it aligns with emerging trends and technologies.

1. DirectX as a Catalyst for Graphics Innovation

DIRECTX HAS HISTORICALLY been a driving force behind graphics innovation on the Windows platform. As new DirectX versions are released, they often introduce cutting-edge features and capabilities that push the boundaries of real-time rendering. These innovations are not limited to the gaming industry but also impact fields like virtual reality, augmented reality, and professional visualization.

For example, DirectX 12 introduced low-level hardware abstraction and explicit multi-GPU support, enabling developers to harness the full potential of modern graphics hardware. This level of control allows for efficient resource management and the optimization of rendering pipelines.

2. Integration with Emerging Technologies

DIRECTX CONTINUES TO evolve to support emerging technologies. As Windows embraces mixed reality, DirectX plays a crucial role in delivering immersive experiences. It provides the graphics foundation for mixed reality headsets, enabling the rendering of 3D environments and holographic content.

Moreover, DirectX's integration with machine learning and artificial intelligence (AI) technologies is becoming increasingly important. AI-driven techniques like neural network-based upscaling and denoising can enhance graphics quality and performance. DirectX is well-positioned to facilitate these integrations, opening doors to more realistic and efficient graphics rendering.

3. Ray Tracing and Realism

RAY TRACING IS A TECHNOLOGY that has gained significant attention in recent years for its potential to revolutionize real-time graphics. DirectX Raytracing (DXR) is an API extension that brings hardware-accelerated ray tracing to DirectX applications. With DXR, developers can achieve stunning visual realism by accurately simulating the behavior of light in virtual scenes.

As hardware support for ray tracing becomes more widespread, DirectX is at the forefront of enabling developers to leverage this technology. The ability to create lifelike reflections, shadows, and global illumination has a profound impact on game visuals, architectural visualization, and other graphics-intensive applications.

4. Cross-Platform and Cloud Gaming

THE FUTURE OF WINDOWS programming is not limited to traditional desktop applications. With the rise of cloud gaming and cross-platform gaming services, DirectX is adapting to meet the demands of these evolving ecosystems. DirectX technologies are being extended to support cloud-based rendering and streaming, enabling users to access high-quality gaming experiences on a variety of devices, including smartphones and smart TVs.

Cross-platform compatibility is another area where DirectX is evolving. Developers can leverage DirectX technologies to create games that run on Windows, Xbox, and other platforms with ease. This flexibility is crucial as the gaming industry continues to expand beyond traditional gaming consoles and PCs.

5. Developer Community and Ecosystem

THE DEVELOPER COMMUNITY around DirectX remains strong, with a wealth of resources, libraries, and tools available. Online communities and forums provide support and share knowledge, making it easier for developers to create DirectX-powered applications.

Moreover, DirectX remains a focus of academic and research institutions, driving innovations in graphics and visualization. Collaborations between researchers, hardware manufacturers, and software developers contribute to the ongoing evolution of DirectX.

In conclusion, DirectX plays a pivotal role in shaping the future of Windows programming and the broader graphics and gaming landscape. With its commitment to innovation, integration with emerging technologies, support for ray tracing, adaptability to cross-platform and cloud gaming, and a thriving developer community, DirectX continues to be a driving force in delivering cutting-edge graphics and interactive experiences on the Windows platform. Developers who embrace DirectX are well-positioned to create software that takes full advantage of the exciting opportunities that lie ahead in the world of Windows programming.

10. DirectX for Virtual Reality

10.1. Understanding the Basics of Virtual Reality

VIRTUAL REALITY (VR) is a technology that has gained significant popularity in recent years, offering immersive and interactive experiences that transport users to virtual worlds. In this section, we'll explore the fundamentals of VR and how DirectX plays a crucial role in creating VR applications.

1. What Is Virtual Reality?

VIRTUAL REALITY REFERS to the use of computer technology to create simulated environments that users can interact with and explore. These simulated environments are often presented through a head-mounted display (HMD) that covers the user's field of vision, providing a 3D and stereoscopic view of the virtual world. VR aims to create a sense of presence, making users feel like they are physically present in the virtual environment.

2. Key Components of VR

2.1. Head-Mounted Display (HMD)

THE HMD IS A CRITICAL component of VR systems. It consists of a pair of screens placed in front of the user's eyes, creating a 3D visual experience. Modern HMDs also include sensors to track the user's head movements, allowing them to look around and interact with the virtual world.

2.2. Tracking System

TO ACHIEVE A SENSE of presence, VR systems use tracking systems that monitor the user's movements and adjust the virtual world accordingly. This includes tracking the user's head position and orientation, as well as the position of handheld controllers. Tracking accuracy is crucial for a seamless VR experience.

2.3. Graphics Rendering

GRAPHICS RENDERING in VR is demanding, as it requires rendering two separate images, one for each eye, to create a stereoscopic view. This places a heavy load on the GPU, requiring efficient rendering techniques and optimizations. This is where DirectX comes into play, providing the necessary tools and APIs for high-performance rendering.

3. DirectX and VR

DIRECTX IS WELL-SUITED for VR development due to its graphics capabilities and support for 3D rendering. Here are some ways DirectX is used in VR applications:

3.1. Rendering

DIRECTX PROVIDES THE rendering capabilities needed for VR. It allows developers to create 3D environments, render realistic textures, and implement lighting and shading effects. DirectX 12, in particular, offers low-level control over GPU resources, making it suitable for VR rendering optimizations.

3.2. Stereoscopic Rendering

CREATING STEREOSCOPIC views is essential for VR, and DirectX facilitates the rendering of two slightly different images for each eye. This creates a 3D effect when viewed through the HMD, enhancing immersion.

3.3. Input Handling

DIRECTX PROVIDES INPUT handling capabilities, allowing developers to integrate motion controllers and other input devices commonly used in VR. This enables users to interact with objects in the virtual world.

3.4. Audio

AUDIO IS A CRITICAL component of VR, as spatial audio enhances the sense of presence. DirectX includes support for audio rendering and spatial audio, creating a more immersive auditory experience.

4. Optimizing Performance

PERFORMANCE OPTIMIZATION is crucial in VR to maintain a high frame rate and reduce motion sickness. DirectX provides tools for GPU and CPU performance profiling, helping developers identify bottlenecks and optimize their applications for smooth VR experiences.

5. VR Development Platforms

SEVERAL VR DEVELOPMENT platforms, such as Oculus Rift, HTC Vive, and Windows Mixed Reality, rely on DirectX for graphics rendering. Developers targeting these platforms can leverage DirectX to create VR applications that run seamlessly on compatible HMDs.

In summary, virtual reality is a technology that immerses users in simulated environments, and DirectX plays a pivotal role in the development of VR applications. It provides the necessary tools for rendering 3D graphics, handling input, and optimizing performance. As VR continues to evolve and become more accessible, DirectX remains a valuable asset for developers looking to create immersive and interactive virtual reality experiences.

10.2. Implementing VR Support in DirectX

IN THE PREVIOUS SECTION, we discussed the basics of virtual reality (VR) and how DirectX plays a crucial role in creating VR applications. Now, let's dive deeper into the process of implementing VR support in DirectX-based projects.

1. VR Hardware Integration

TO DEVELOP VR APPLICATIONS using DirectX, you need to integrate with VR hardware. The integration process typically involves the following steps:

- **SDK Installation**: Install the SDK provided by the VR hardware manufacturer, such as Oculus SDK or SteamVR for HTC Vive.

- **Device Setup**: Set up the VR headset, motion controllers, and tracking sensors according to the manufacturer's instructions.

- **SDK Initialization**: Initialize the VR SDK in your DirectX application to establish communication with the VR hardware.

2. Stereoscopic Rendering

STEREOSCOPIC RENDERING is a fundamental aspect of VR. It involves rendering two separate images, one for each eye, with a slight offset to create a 3D effect. DirectX provides the necessary tools for stereoscopic rendering:

```
// Pseudocode for stereoscopic rendering

while (rendering) {

// Set render target for left eye

SetRenderTarget(leftEyeTexture);

// Render the scene from the left eye's perspective

RenderScene(leftEyeCamera);

// Set render target for right eye

SetRenderTarget(rightEyeTexture);

// Render the scene from the right eye's perspective

RenderScene(rightEyeCamera);

// Combine left and right eye textures for display

CombineEyeTextures(leftEyeTexture, rightEyeTexture);

}
```

3. Head Tracking

HEAD TRACKING IS CRUCIAL for maintaining the user's sense of presence in the virtual world. DirectX allows you to incorporate head tracking data from the VR hardware to update the camera's view matrix:

```
// Pseudocode for updating camera view matrix with head tracking

while (rendering) {

// Get head tracking data

Vector3 headPosition = GetHeadPosition();

Quaternion headRotation = GetHeadRotation();

// Update the camera's view matrix

Matrix viewMatrix = CreateViewMatrix(headPosition, headRotation);

// Render the scene using the updated view matrix

RenderScene(viewMatrix);

}
```

4. Input Handling

VR APPLICATIONS OFTEN rely on motion controllers and other input devices for interaction. DirectX provides input handling capabilities, allowing you to capture input from VR controllers:

```
// Pseudocode for handling VR controller input

while (rendering) {
```

```
// Get input from VR controllers

InputState leftControllerInput = GetControllerInput(LeftController);

InputState rightControllerInput = GetControllerInput(RightController);

// Process input to interact with objects in the scene

ProcessControllerInput(leftControllerInput, rightControllerInput);

// Render the scene with updated interactions

RenderScene();

}
```

5. Audio Integration

SPATIAL AUDIO IS ESSENTIAL for creating an immersive VR experience. DirectX supports audio rendering and spatial audio, allowing you to position sounds in 3D space based on the user's head and controller positions.

```
// Pseudocode for spatial audio in DirectX

while (rendering) {

// Get user's head position and orientation

Vector3 headPosition = GetHeadPosition();

Quaternion headRotation = GetHeadRotation();

// Update audio listener position and orientation
```

```
UpdateAudioListener(headPosition, headRotation);
// Position 3D audio sources in the virtual world
PositionAudioSources();
// Render audio with spatialization
RenderAudio();
}
```

6. Performance Optimization

OPTIMIZING PERFORMANCE is crucial for VR applications to maintain a high frame rate and reduce motion sickness. DirectX provides tools for GPU and CPU performance profiling, allowing you to identify and address performance bottlenecks.

7. VR Development Platforms

VARIOUS VR DEVELOPMENT platforms, such as Oculus Rift, HTC Vive, and Windows Mixed Reality, support DirectX for graphics rendering. You can choose a platform that suits your project's requirements and target audience.

In conclusion, implementing VR support in DirectX involves integrating VR hardware, performing stereoscopic rendering, handling head tracking and input, integrating spatial audio, optimizing performance, and choosing a compatible VR development platform. DirectX provides the necessary tools and capabilities to create immersive and interactive VR experiences, making it a valuable choice for VR application development.

10.3. Optimizing Performance for VR

OPTIMIZING PERFORMANCE is a critical aspect of developing virtual reality (VR) applications using DirectX. VR places higher demands on both the graphics hardware and the CPU compared to traditional 2D applications. To provide a smooth and comfortable VR experience, you must achieve and maintain a high frame rate while minimizing latency. In this section, we'll explore various strategies for optimizing performance in VR applications built with DirectX.

1. Maintain a Consistent Frame Rate

IN VR, MAINTAINING a consistent frame rate is paramount. The standard frame rate for most VR experiences is 90 frames per second (FPS), although higher frame rates can offer even better immersion. Dropping below the target frame rate can lead to motion sickness and a less enjoyable experience.

To achieve a consistent frame rate:

- **Render Efficiently**: Optimize rendering techniques, use level-of-detail (LOD) models, and minimize overdraw to reduce GPU workload.

- **Multithreading**: Utilize multithreading to offload CPU tasks like physics calculations and AI processing, allowing the main thread to focus on rendering.

- **GPU Profiling**: Use GPU profiling tools to identify rendering bottlenecks and optimize shaders and rendering techniques.

2. Reduce Latency

LATENCY REFERS TO THE delay between a user's action (e.g., moving their head) and the corresponding change in the VR display. High latency can lead to discomfort and motion sickness. To reduce latency:

- **Predictive Tracking**: Implement predictive tracking to anticipate the user's head movements and reduce the perceived latency.

- **Asynchronous Timewarp**: Use technologies like Asynchronous Timewarp (ATW) or Asynchronous Spacewarp (ASW) to interpolate frames and maintain a smooth experience, even if the frame rate drops momentarily.

- **Low-Persistence Displays**: Consider using low-persistence displays that reduce motion blur and improve the perception of low latency.

3. GPU and CPU Optimization

OPTIMIZING BOTH THE GPU and CPU is crucial for VR performance:

- **GPU Optimization**: Minimize GPU load by using efficient shaders, culling techniques, and reducing the complexity of 3D models. Use techniques like instancing and occlusion culling to avoid rendering unnecessary objects.

- **CPU Optimization**: Reduce CPU overhead by optimizing code, minimizing unnecessary calculations, and offloading non-rendering tasks to separate threads.

4. Adaptive Quality

IMPLEMENT ADAPTIVE quality settings that dynamically adjust graphical fidelity based on the performance of the user's hardware. Lower-end systems can reduce graphics quality to maintain frame rates, while high-end systems can enjoy more detailed visuals.

5. VR-Specific Rendering Techniques

VR REQUIRES SPECIFIC rendering techniques to minimize motion sickness and improve immersion:

- **Comfortable Movement**: Implement comfortable movement techniques, such as teleportation or vignette effects during rapid motion, to reduce motion sickness.

- **3D Audio**: Utilize spatial audio to enhance the sense of presence, ensuring that sounds match the location of objects in the virtual world.

- **User Interface (UI)**: Design VR-friendly UIs that are easy to read and interact with in a 3D space. Consider gaze-based interaction or motion controller input for UI elements.

6. Regular Testing

REGULARLY TEST YOUR VR application on different hardware configurations to ensure compatibility and performance. Consider providing graphics and performance settings that users can adjust to suit their hardware.

7. User Feedback

COLLECT USER FEEDBACK and monitor performance metrics. Address performance issues reported by users promptly and release updates as needed to improve the VR experience.

In summary, optimizing performance in VR applications developed with DirectX involves maintaining a consistent frame rate, reducing latency, optimizing GPU and CPU usage, implementing adaptive quality settings, using VR-specific rendering techniques, conducting regular testing, and actively gathering user feedback. By following these strategies, you can create VR experiences that are both immersive and comfortable for users across a range of hardware configurations.

10.4. User Experience Design in VR Applications

USER EXPERIENCE (UX) design plays a crucial role in the success of virtual reality (VR) applications. Unlike traditional 2D interfaces, VR places the user in a 3D immersive environment, and designing for VR requires special considerations to ensure comfort, engagement, and usability. In this section, we'll explore key aspects of UX design for VR applications developed with DirectX.

1. Comfort and Motion Sickness

MINIMIZING MOTION SICKNESS is a top priority in VR design. VR-induced motion sickness can occur when there is a discrepancy between what the user sees and what their inner ear perceives. To enhance comfort:

- **Smooth Locomotion**: Implement smooth locomotion techniques that allow users to move within the virtual environment comfortably. Techniques like teleportation or gradual acceleration and deceleration can help reduce motion sickness.

- **Field of View (FoV)**: Consider how you manage field of view changes when the user moves or turns. Abrupt changes can trigger discomfort, so use techniques like "tunnel vision" during rapid movement.

- **Comfort Options**: Provide user-adjustable comfort settings, such as vignette effects or dynamic field of view adjustments, to cater to different comfort levels.

2. Interaction and Input

IN VR, USER INTERACTION is a fundamental aspect of the experience. Consider the following:

- **Motion Controllers**: Design intuitive interactions using motion controllers. Users should be able to pick up, manipulate, and interact with objects in a natural way.

- **Gaze-Based Interaction**: Implement gaze-based interaction for UI elements and object selection. Users can interact by simply looking at objects or UI elements for a designated duration.

- **Haptic Feedback**: Use haptic feedback in motion controllers to provide tactile sensations that enhance the sense of presence and interaction realism.

3. User Interface (UI) Design

UI DESIGN IN VR DIFFERS significantly from 2D UI design. Consider these VR-specific UI design principles:

- **3D UI Elements**: Place UI elements within the 3D space of the virtual environment. Use spatial UI design to ensure that menus, buttons, and information panels are easy to reach and interact with.

- **Scaling and Positioning**: Make UI elements resizable and movable so that users can customize the placement and size according to their preferences.

- **Consistency**: Maintain a consistent design language for UI elements to create a cohesive and immersive experience. Ensure that text and graphics are legible in a 3D environment.

- **Feedback**: Provide visual and auditory feedback for user interactions, such as button presses or object interactions, to reinforce the sense of engagement.

4. Performance and Optimization

OPTIMIZING PERFORMANCE is essential for a smooth VR experience. High frame rates and low latency are critical. Use techniques like dynamic level-of-detail (LOD) models, efficient shaders, and culling to maintain performance.

5. Comfort and Accessibility

CONSIDER THE COMFORT and accessibility of your VR application for a diverse audience:

• **Accessibility Features**: Implement accessibility features, such as voice commands, for users with disabilities.

• **Comfort Settings**: Allow users to adjust comfort settings to cater to their individual needs and comfort levels.

• **Tutorial and Onboarding**: Provide a clear and immersive tutorial or onboarding experience to help users become familiar with VR interaction and navigation.

6. Testing and Feedback

REGULARLY TEST YOUR VR application with a diverse group of users to gather feedback on comfort, usability, and performance. Address user-reported issues promptly to enhance the overall UX.

In conclusion, user experience design in VR applications developed with DirectX involves considerations for comfort, minimizing motion sickness, intuitive interaction, VR-specific UI design, performance optimization, accessibility, and user testing. By prioritizing these aspects, you can create VR experiences that are engaging, comfortable, and accessible to a wide range of users, delivering a compelling VR journey.

10.5. Future Trends and DirectX in VR

THE FIELD OF VIRTUAL reality (VR) is constantly evolving, and as technology advances, so do the possibilities for DirectX's role in VR development. In this section, we'll explore some future trends and emerging technologies that will shape the future of VR experiences developed using DirectX.

1. Improved Graphics and Realism

AS HARDWARE BECOMES more powerful, VR experiences will continue to push the boundaries of graphics and realism. DirectX will play a crucial role in harnessing the capabilities of high-end GPUs to deliver lifelike visuals. Technologies like ray tracing and advanced shader techniques will enhance lighting, reflections, and overall graphical fidelity.

2. Eye Tracking and Foveated Rendering

EYE TRACKING TECHNOLOGY is poised to become a standard feature in VR headsets. With DirectX, developers can leverage eye tracking to implement foveated rendering, a technique that allocates more rendering resources to the area where the user is looking while reducing detail in peripheral vision. This not only improves performance but also enhances realism by simulating human visual behavior.

3. Enhanced Haptic Feedback

HAPTIC FEEDBACK IS essential for creating immersive VR experiences. DirectX will continue to support advanced haptic feedback devices, allowing developers to create realistic sensations for touch, pressure, and vibrations. This technology will enable more convincing interactions with virtual objects and environments.

4. Wireless VR and 5G Integration

THE TREND TOWARDS WIRELESS VR headsets will continue, offering users greater freedom of movement. Additionally, the integration of 5G connectivity will enable real-time cloud-based rendering and multiplayer experiences, reducing the reliance on local hardware for rendering complex scenes.

5. AI-Driven Interactions

ARTIFICIAL INTELLIGENCE (AI) will enhance VR interactions by enabling natural language processing for voice commands and gesture recognition. DirectX will facilitate the integration of AI-driven features into VR applications, allowing for more dynamic and responsive experiences.

6. Social VR and Collaboration

SOCIAL VR PLATFORMS and collaborative VR environments will become more prevalent. DirectX will support the development of shared virtual spaces, where users can interact with others in a shared digital world. This has applications not only in gaming but also in education, remote work, and social interaction.

7. Health and Wellness Applications

VR WILL INCREASINGLY be used for health and wellness applications, such as therapy, fitness, and stress relief. DirectX will enable the creation of immersive and therapeutic experiences that can have a positive impact on mental and physical well-being.

8. Cross-Platform VR

CROSS-PLATFORM COMPATIBILITY will be a significant focus for VR development. DirectX's role in this context will involve ensuring that VR applications can run seamlessly on various VR platforms, including PC, console, and standalone headsets.

9. Ethical and Privacy Considerations

AS VR BECOMES MORE pervasive, ethical and privacy concerns will arise. DirectX developers will need to address issues related to data privacy, user consent, and content moderation to ensure a safe and respectful VR ecosystem.

In conclusion, DirectX will continue to be at the forefront of VR development, enabling developers to create increasingly immersive and realistic VR experiences. With the integration of emerging technologies, improved graphics, enhanced interaction, and cross-platform compatibility, DirectX-powered VR applications will play a pivotal role in shaping the future of virtual reality. Developers and creators should stay informed about these trends to harness the full potential of DirectX in the dynamic and evolving world of VR.

Chapter 11: Debugging and Profiling DirectX Applications

Section 11.1: Tools and Techniques for Debugging DirectX Code

DEBUGGING AND PROFILING are crucial aspects of DirectX application development. They help identify and resolve issues related to graphics, performance, and stability. In this section, we will explore various tools and techniques for debugging DirectX code, enabling you to create more efficient and reliable applications.

1. Debugging Tools

1.1. Visual Studio Debugger

MICROSOFT VISUAL STUDIO provides a robust debugger for debugging DirectX applications. It allows you to set breakpoints, inspect variables, and step through code. When debugging DirectX code, it's essential to understand the graphics pipeline's state and the data structures involved.

1.2. Graphics Diagnostics

VISUAL STUDIO'S GRAPHICS Diagnostics tools enable you to capture and analyze DirectX events, frame timings, and GPU usage. You can use these tools to identify rendering issues, such as incorrect shaders or textures.

2. Debugging Techniques

2.1. RenderDoc

RENDERDOC IS A POWERFUL open-source tool for debugging and profiling graphics applications, including those using DirectX. It allows you to capture frames, inspect resources, and analyze GPU usage. RenderDoc is especially valuable for identifying rendering errors.

2.2. PIX

PIX (PERFORMANCE INVESTIGATOR for Xbox) is a performance tuning and debugging tool provided by Microsoft. It supports DirectX debugging and allows you to capture frames, analyze GPU events, and identify performance bottlenecks.

3. Profiling Techniques

3.1. GPU Profiling

PROFILING THE GPU IS essential to optimize DirectX applications. Tools like GPUView and NVIDIA Nsight Graphics help you analyze GPU performance, including shader usage and memory bandwidth. Profiling can reveal bottlenecks and guide optimizations.

3.2. CPU Profiling

CPU PROFILING TOOLS like Intel VTune and AMD CodeXL assist in identifying CPU-related bottlenecks. These tools help pinpoint areas of your code where optimizations can lead to better performance.

4. Debugging DirectX Errors

4.1. HRESULT Error Codes

DIRECTX FUNCTIONS OFTEN return HRESULT error codes to indicate success or failure. Properly handling these codes and understanding their meanings is crucial for error diagnosis.

4.2. Debugging Shaders

DEBUGGING HLSL SHADERS can be challenging. Tools like NVIDIA Nsight Graphics and AMD GPU PerfStudio offer shader debugging capabilities, allowing you to inspect shader variables and pinpoint issues.

5. Best Practices

5.1. Logging and Diagnostics

IMPLEMENTING A ROBUST logging system in your DirectX application can help you trace issues and diagnose problems during development and testing. Include detailed error messages and context information in your logs.

5.2. Test on Different Hardware

TEST YOUR DIRECTX APPLICATION on various hardware configurations to ensure compatibility and identify hardware-specific issues. This helps provide a better user experience for a wider audience.

In conclusion, debugging and profiling are essential skills for DirectX developers. Leveraging the right tools and techniques can significantly improve the quality and performance of your DirectX applications. The tools mentioned here are valuable assets in your development toolkit, helping you create high-quality, efficient, and stable graphics applications.

Section 11.2: Profiling and Optimizing DirectX Applications

PROFILING AND OPTIMIZING DirectX applications are essential steps in ensuring that your graphics-intensive software runs efficiently and delivers a smooth user experience. In this section, we will explore techniques and tools for profiling and optimizing DirectX applications.

1. Profiling Tools

1.1. Graphics Profilers

GRAPHICS PROFILING tools such as NVIDIA Nsight Graphics and AMD GPU PerfStudio provide valuable insights into GPU performance. These tools capture frame-level data, including GPU timelines, shader usage, and memory allocations. By analyzing this data, you can identify performance bottlenecks and optimize your DirectX code.

1.2. CPU Profilers

PROFILING THE CPU IS equally important in DirectX application optimization. Tools like Intel VTune and Microsoft's Visual Studio Profiler help you identify CPU-bound operations in your code. Profiling results can guide you in optimizing resource management and multithreading.

2. GPU Timings

UNDERSTANDING GPU TIMINGS is crucial for DirectX optimization. Profiling tools display GPU timelines, allowing you to see how much time is spent on rendering tasks. By analyzing GPU timings, you can identify which parts of your application are GPU-bound and focus your optimization efforts accordingly.

3. Frame Analysis

FRAME ANALYSIS INVOLVES examining each frame of your DirectX application to identify performance bottlenecks. Profiling tools can break down the time spent on various rendering tasks, such as vertex processing, pixel shading, and memory transfers. This information helps you pinpoint areas that require optimization.

4. GPU Shader Profiling

SHADERS PLAY A SIGNIFICANT role in DirectX applications, and profiling them can lead to substantial performance gains. Profiling tools like NVIDIA Nsight Graphics and AMD GPU PerfStudio allow you to inspect shader performance, identify costly instructions, and optimize your shaders for better GPU utilization.

5. Optimizing Techniques

5.1. Resource Management

EFFICIENT RESOURCE management is crucial for DirectX optimization. Avoid unnecessary resource creation and destruction by reusing objects whenever possible. Use resource pooling to minimize memory allocation overhead.

5.2. Multithreading

MULTITHREADING CAN significantly improve DirectX application performance. Utilize multiple CPU cores for tasks such as resource loading, physics simulations, and AI calculations. Be cautious when managing multithreaded rendering to avoid synchronization issues.

5.3. LOD (Level of Detail)

IMPLEMENTING LEVEL-of-detail techniques can reduce GPU load by rendering less detailed models when objects are far from the camera. LOD systems help maintain a consistent frame rate in complex scenes.

5.4. Culling

IMPLEMENT FRUSTUM AND occlusion culling to avoid rendering objects that are not visible to the camera. This reduces unnecessary GPU work and improves rendering performance.

6. Continuous Profiling

OPTIMIZATION IS AN ongoing process. Regularly profile your DirectX application, especially after making significant changes. Continuous profiling ensures that your optimizations remain effective and that new bottlenecks are addressed promptly.

In summary, profiling and optimizing DirectX applications are essential tasks to achieve high performance and a smooth user experience. Use specialized tools to gather performance data, analyze GPU and CPU timings, and identify bottlenecks. Apply optimization techniques such as efficient resource management, multithreading, LOD, and culling to enhance your DirectX application's performance and responsiveness. Remember that optimization is an iterative process, and regular profiling helps maintain a high level of performance throughout development.

Section 11.3: Handling Common Errors and Issues

DEVELOPING DIRECTX applications can be challenging, and it's common to encounter errors and issues during the development process. In this section, we will explore some of the common errors and issues in DirectX programming and how to handle them effectively.

1. HRESULT Error Codes

IN DIRECTX PROGRAMMING, many functions return an HRESULT (Handle to Result) code to indicate success or failure. It's essential to check these error codes after calling DirectX functions. Common HRESULT error codes include E_INVALIDARG, E_OUTOFMEMORY, and E_FAIL. You can use the DXTrace function to convert HRESULT error codes into human-readable messages for easier debugging.

```
HRESULT hr = SomeDirectXFunction();
if (FAILED(hr)) {
DXTrace(__FILE__, __LINE__, hr, L"SomeDirectXFunction() failed", true);
// Handle the error appropriately
}
```

2. Debugging Tools

DIRECTX PROVIDES SEVERAL debugging tools to help identify and diagnose issues in your application. The Debug Layer, available in the DirectX SDK, can provide detailed information about errors, warnings, and performance issues. Enabling the Debug Layer can be done by setting the D3D11_CREATE_DEVICE_DEBUG flag when creating the device.

```
UINT createDeviceFlags = D3D11_CREATE_DEVICE_DEBUG;
```

3. Resource Leaks

RESOURCE LEAKS CAN occur if you fail to release DirectX resources properly. Always release objects like textures, buffers, and shaders using the Release method to avoid memory leaks. You can also use smart pointers or resource management classes to automate resource management.

```
// Release a DirectX resource
```

```
if (pTexture) {

pTexture->Release();

pTexture = nullptr;

}
```

4. Invalid Shader Code

DIRECTX SHADERS ARE written in High-Level Shader Language (HLSL), and errors in shader code can cause rendering issues or crashes. Use shader debugging tools like PIX and GPU PerfStudio to identify and fix shader problems. Additionally, make sure to compile shaders at runtime and check for compilation errors.

5. Driver Compatibility

GRAPHICS DRIVER ISSUES can lead to unexpected behavior in DirectX applications. Ensure that you are using the latest graphics drivers for your GPU. Some issues may be specific to certain driver versions, so be prepared to test your application on different hardware and driver combinations.

6. Memory Management

IMPROPER MEMORY MANAGEMENT can result in crashes or performance degradation. Be mindful of memory allocations and deallocations. Avoid excessive dynamic memory allocation during rendering to prevent frame rate drops.

7. Threading Issues

MULTITHREADING IN DIRECTX applications can introduce synchronization and race condition problems. Use critical sections, mutexes, and other synchronization primitives to manage access to shared resources safely. Avoid accessing DirectX objects from multiple threads simultaneously.

8. DirectX Version Compatibility

ENSURE THAT YOU ARE using the correct DirectX version for your application. Different versions of DirectX may have different features and limitations. If you need backward compatibility, consider using feature level checking to adapt your code to the available DirectX version.

9. Third-Party Libraries

IF YOUR DIRECTX APPLICATION relies on third-party libraries, be aware of potential conflicts and compatibility issues. Ensure that library versions are compatible with your DirectX SDK and compiler.

10. User-Friendly Error Messages

WHEN HANDLING ERRORS, provide clear and informative error messages to users or log files. Well-documented error messages can assist users and developers in troubleshooting issues more efficiently.

In conclusion, handling common errors and issues in DirectX programming is essential for creating stable and performant applications. Always check and handle HRESULT error codes, use debugging tools, release resources properly, debug shader code, keep graphics drivers up-to-date, manage memory effectively, address threading issues, and ensure DirectX version compatibility. By addressing these common challenges, you can enhance the reliability and quality of your DirectX applications.

Section 11.4: Advanced Debugging Scenarios

WHILE HANDLING COMMON errors and issues is essential in DirectX programming, you may encounter more complex debugging scenarios that require advanced techniques and tools. In this section, we will explore some of these scenarios and how to approach them.

1. Debugging Graphics Pipelines

DEBUGGING THE GRAPHICS pipeline can be challenging due to its complexity. To visualize and analyze what happens at different stages of the pipeline, you can use graphics debugging tools like NVIDIA Nsight, AMD GPU PerfStudio, or Microsoft PIX (Performance Investigator for Xbox). These tools allow you to capture and inspect the rendering process, including vertex and pixel shaders, rendering targets, and state changes.

2. GPU-Related Issues

WHEN DEALING WITH GPU-related issues, it's crucial to understand GPU-specific limitations and behaviors. Some GPUs may have restrictions on texture sizes, buffer formats, or the number of shader instructions. You can use GPU-specific debugging tools to profile and optimize your shaders for different GPU architectures.

3. Memory Corruption

MEMORY CORRUPTION ISSUES can lead to crashes or unpredictable behavior. Tools like AddressSanitizer (ASan) and MemoryScape can help identify memory-related problems. ASan is a runtime memory error detector that can find buffer overflows, use-after-free, and other memory corruption issues. MemoryScape is a memory analysis tool that can pinpoint memory leaks and access violations.

4. Multi-Threading Debugging

IN MULTI-THREADED DIRECTX applications, debugging synchronization issues and race conditions can be complex. Consider using tools like Intel Thread Checker or Microsoft's Concurrency Visualizer to analyze and debug multi-threading problems. These tools can help you identify deadlocks, data races, and thread contention.

5. Performance Profiling

OPTIMIZING THE PERFORMANCE of your DirectX application often requires profiling. Profiling tools like Intel VTune, AMD CodeXL, or NVIDIA Visual Profiler can provide insights into CPU and GPU performance bottlenecks. Profiling helps identify hotspots in your code, allowing you to focus your optimization efforts effectively.

6. Remote Debugging

SOMETIMES, YOU NEED to debug DirectX applications running on remote machines or consoles. Remote debugging tools like Visual Studio's remote debugging capabilities or specialized debugging hardware for consoles enable you to inspect and debug applications remotely, making it easier to diagnose issues on target hardware.

7. Memory Debugging

MEMORY DEBUGGING TOOLS like Valgrind (for Linux) or Application Verifier (for Windows) can help detect memory leaks, invalid memory accesses, and memory-related errors. These tools are invaluable for ensuring your DirectX application's memory management is robust.

8. Custom Debugging Techniques

FOR SPECIFIC AND COMPLEX scenarios unique to your DirectX application, you may need to develop custom debugging techniques. This might involve instrumenting your code with custom debug markers, adding conditional breakpoints, or creating custom loggers to trace and analyze application behavior.

9. Collaboration and Documentation

DEBUGGING COMPLEX DIRECTX issues often requires collaboration among team members. Maintain clear and up-to-date documentation about known issues, debugging procedures, and workarounds. Collaboration tools and version control systems can help track and share debugging insights.

10. Continuous Learning

DIRECTX PROGRAMMING and debugging are continually evolving fields. Stay updated with the latest debugging techniques, tools, and best practices by reading documentation, tutorials, and attending relevant conferences or workshops.

In summary, advanced debugging scenarios in DirectX programming require a combination of specialized tools, in-depth knowledge of the graphics pipeline, GPU-specific insights, memory debugging techniques, multi-threading debugging, performance profiling, and custom debugging approaches. Collaboration, documentation, and continuous learning are essential for effectively debugging complex DirectX applications and ensuring they meet the highest quality and performance standards.

Section 11.5: Case Studies: Debugging Complex DirectX Applications

IN THIS SECTION, WE'LL explore a few case studies that highlight the challenges faced when debugging complex DirectX applications and the strategies employed to resolve them.

Case Study 1: Flickering Shadows

ISSUE: In a DirectX game, players reported flickering shadows in certain areas of the game world. This issue was affecting the visual quality and immersion of the game.

Debugging Approach:

1. **Shadow Mapping Debugging:** The development team began by examining the shadow mapping implementation. They used a graphics debugging tool to inspect the depth maps generated by the shadow pass and the shaders responsible for shadow rendering.
2. **Texture Resolution:** It was discovered that the flickering occurred due to a low-resolution shadow map. Increasing the shadow map resolution improved the quality of the shadows but increased the GPU load.
3. **Cascaded Shadow Maps:** To balance quality and performance, the team implemented cascaded shadow maps to adapt the shadow map resolution based on the camera's view. This resolved the flickering issue without a significant performance hit.

Case Study 2: Random Crashes on Certain GPUs

ISSUE: A DirectX application was experiencing random crashes on specific GPU models, while it worked fine on others.

Debugging Approach:

1. **GPU Driver Debugging:** The development team suspected that GPU drivers might be the cause. They updated the GPU drivers to the latest versions and tested the application. The issue persisted.
2. **GPU-Specific Code Paths:** Upon further investigation, they found that the crashes occurred in code paths that were optimized for specific GPU architectures. These optimizations were causing access violations on the problematic GPUs.
3. **GPU Dispatched Shaders:** To address the issue, the team modified the shaders to dispatch different code paths based on the detected GPU model. They also provided fallback shaders for unsupported GPUs.

Case Study 3: Multiplayer Synchronization Issues

ISSUE: A DirectX multiplayer game experienced synchronization issues where players' actions were not correctly replicated across all clients.

Debugging Approach:

1. **Network Debugging:** The development team used network debugging tools to analyze the network traffic between clients and the server. They identified packets that were lost or delayed.
2. **Latency Compensation:** To mitigate synchronization

issues caused by network latency, the team implemented client-side prediction and server reconciliation techniques. This ensured that player actions appeared smooth and responsive across all clients.

3. **Deterministic Simulation:** To ensure consistency in game state across clients, they made the game simulation deterministic by removing non-deterministic factors such as floating-point rounding differences.

Case Study 4: Memory Leaks in a Complex Scene

ISSUE: A DirectX application rendering a complex 3D scene was experiencing memory leaks, leading to performance degradation over time.

Debugging Approach:

1. **Memory Profiling:** The team used memory profiling tools to identify memory allocation patterns and potential leaks. They tracked allocations and deallocations of resources such as textures and meshes.
2. **Resource Management:** The memory leaks were traced to improper resource management, where some resources were not being released when they went out of scope. The team added proper resource cleanup in the application code.
3. **Memory Leak Testing:** They conducted stress tests by loading and unloading scenes repeatedly to verify that memory leaks were resolved and that the application's memory usage remained stable over extended play sessions.

These case studies illustrate the complexity of debugging DirectX applications and the importance of using a combination of debugging tools, profiling, and targeted debugging strategies to identify and resolve issues. Debugging often involves a mix of graphics debugging, GPU driver considerations, network debugging for multiplayer games, and memory profiling to ensure stable and performant applications.

Chapter 12: DirectX in Mobile Development

Section 12.1: DirectX on Windows Mobile Platforms

IN THIS SECTION, WE will delve into the realm of DirectX on Windows Mobile platforms. Mobile devices, particularly those running Windows, offer unique opportunities for game and application development. Windows Mobile, although less prominent compared to other mobile operating systems, provides a platform for developers to create immersive and visually stunning experiences using DirectX.

DirectX on Windows Mobile:

1. **DirectX for Windows Mobile:** Windows Mobile operating systems, including Windows Phone and Windows CE, have historically supported a subset of DirectX APIs. These APIs allow developers to create 2D and 3D graphics, handle audio, and manage input on mobile devices.
2. **Graphics Acceleration:** Many Windows Mobile devices come equipped with hardware acceleration for graphics rendering. This means that DirectX can leverage the GPU (Graphics Processing Unit) to enhance graphical performance and deliver smoother animations and visual effects.
3. **Direct3D Mobile:** Direct3D Mobile is a component of DirectX designed for 3D graphics on Windows Mobile. It provides features like hardware 3D acceleration, support for shaders, and efficient rendering pipelines.

Development Environment:

DEVELOPING DIRECTX applications for Windows Mobile platforms involves setting up a suitable development environment. Here are the key components:

1. **Visual Studio:** Microsoft's Visual Studio IDE (Integrated Development Environment) is a primary tool for Windows Mobile application development. You can install Visual Studio with Mobile development workloads and SDKs.
2. **Windows Mobile Emulator:** To test your DirectX applications, you can use the Windows Mobile emulator that comes with Visual Studio. It allows you to run and debug your code in a simulated mobile environment.
3. **DirectX SDK for Windows Mobile:** Ensure you have the DirectX SDK components for Windows Mobile development installed. This SDK provides the necessary headers, libraries, and tools for DirectX programming.

Challenges in Windows Mobile Development:

DEVELOPING DIRECTX applications for Windows Mobile platforms presents certain challenges:

1. **Hardware Variation:** Windows Mobile devices come in various hardware configurations, including differences in GPU capabilities. Developers need to optimize their applications to run smoothly on a range of devices.
2. **Screen Resolutions:** Mobile devices may have different screen resolutions and aspect ratios. Adapting your graphics and user interface to these variations is crucial for a consistent user experience.
3. **Resource Constraints:** Mobile devices often have limited

memory and processing power compared to desktop computers. Efficient resource management is essential to prevent performance issues and crashes.

Code Sample (Setting up a Direct3D Mobile Device):

HERE'S A SIMPLIFIED example of initializing a Direct3D Mobile device in C++:

```
#include <windows.h>

#include <d3dm.h>

// Initialize Direct3D Mobile

HRESULT InitializeDirect3D(HWND hWnd)

{

IDirect3DMobile* pD3D = NULL;

// Create the Direct3D object

pD3D = Direct3DCreateMobile(D3DM_SDK_VERSION);

if (pD3D == NULL)

{

// Handle initialization error

return E_FAIL;

}

// Additional initialization code...

return S_OK;
```

```
}
```

In this code, we create an instance of Direct3D Mobile and perform any necessary setup. The actual initialization may involve creating a rendering surface, configuring the graphics pipeline, and loading assets.

In the following sections, we will explore various aspects of DirectX development on Windows Mobile platforms, including design considerations, optimization techniques, and case studies of successful DirectX mobile games.

Section 12.2: Design Considerations for Mobile Graphics

WHEN DEVELOPING DIRECTX applications for mobile platforms, it's crucial to consider various design aspects to ensure a smooth and visually appealing user experience. Unlike desktop systems, mobile devices have resource constraints, including limited processing power, memory, and screen size. In this section, we'll explore key design considerations for mobile graphics development.

1. Optimized Graphics Assets:

- Mobile devices have limited GPU memory, so optimizing textures and models for size and performance is crucial.

- Consider using texture compression formats like ETC2 or ASTC to reduce memory usage while maintaining visual quality.

2. Responsive User Interface:

- Design user interfaces (UI) that are touch-friendly and scalable to various screen sizes and orientations.

- Ensure that UI elements are easily tappable and that text remains readable on smaller screens.

3. Adaptive Rendering:

- Implement adaptive rendering techniques that adjust graphics quality based on the device's capabilities. For example, lower-end devices may use simpler shaders and reduced textures.

4. Battery Efficiency:

- Minimize GPU usage to conserve battery life. Implement techniques like frame capping and dynamic quality adjustments to reduce power consumption during gameplay.

5. Device Compatibility:

- Test your application on a range of Windows Mobile devices to ensure compatibility. Address any device-specific issues that may arise.

6. Performance Profiling:

- Regularly profile your application's performance using tools like Visual Studio Graphics Analyzer to identify bottlenecks and optimize rendering code.

7. Screen Orientation:

- Support both portrait and landscape orientations, and ensure that your graphics and UI adapt seamlessly to changes in orientation.

8. Input Handling:

- Implement intuitive touch controls and gestures to enhance the user's interaction with your application.

- Handle various input methods, such as touchscreens, styluses, and physical buttons if available.

9. Offline Play:

- Consider offline gameplay scenarios, as mobile users may not always have internet access. Implement features that allow users to enjoy your app without a constant connection.

10. Cross-Platform Considerations:

- If you plan to release your application on multiple mobile platforms (e.g., Android and iOS), consider using cross-platform development frameworks or technologies that can help you reuse code and assets.

Code Sample (Adaptive Rendering):

HERE'S A SIMPLIFIED example in C++ that adapts rendering quality based on device capabilities:

```
#include <windows.h>
```

```
#include <d3dm.h>

// Check device capabilities and adjust rendering settings

void AdaptRendering(IDirect3DDeviceMobile* pDevice)

{

D3DMOBILECAPS caps;

HRESULT hr = pDevice->GetDeviceCaps(&caps);

if (SUCCEEDED(hr))

{

if (caps.MaxTextureWidth < 2048 || caps.MaxTextureHeight <
2048)

{

// Use lower resolution textures or simpler shaders for devices with
limited capabilities

}

else

{

// Use standard quality settings

}

}

}
```

In this code, we query the device's capabilities and adjust rendering settings accordingly. This adaptive rendering approach ensures that the application can run smoothly on a wide range of mobile devices.

Consider these design considerations as you develop DirectX applications for Windows Mobile platforms to create engaging and performant experiences for users. In the next section, we'll delve into optimizing DirectX applications for mobile devices further.

Section 12.3: Optimizing DirectX for Mobile Devices

OPTIMIZING DIRECTX applications for mobile devices is crucial to provide a smooth and efficient gaming or graphics experience. Mobile platforms, with their limited resources, require careful consideration and optimization. In this section, we will explore various optimization techniques and best practices for DirectX development on mobile devices.

1. Texture Compression:

- Utilize texture compression formats like ETC2 (Ericsson Texture Compression) or ASTC (Adaptive Scalable Texture Compression) to reduce memory usage without compromising visual quality.

- Compressed textures consume less memory bandwidth, which is essential for mobile GPUs.

2. Mesh Simplification:

- Reduce the complexity of 3D models through mesh simplification techniques. This lowers the vertex count, leading to faster rendering.

• Consider using level-of-detail (LOD) models to render less detailed versions of objects when they are far from the camera.

3. Shader Optimization:

• Optimize shaders for mobile GPUs, which may have fewer ALUs and lower precision than desktop counterparts.

• Minimize unnecessary calculations and use shader constants sparingly.

• Avoid branching in shaders, as it can lead to performance drops on some mobile GPUs.

4. Batching and Instancing:

• Group rendering operations into batches to reduce draw calls. Fewer draw calls can significantly improve CPU and GPU performance.

• Use hardware instancing to render multiple instances of the same object with a single draw call.

5. Dynamic Resolution Scaling:

• Implement dynamic resolution scaling based on the device's capabilities. Lower-end devices may render at a lower resolution to maintain performance.

• Adjust the resolution during gameplay to maintain a stable frame rate.

6. Texture Atlases:

• Create texture atlases to reduce the number of texture switches during rendering. This minimizes the performance overhead of binding new textures.

• Group textures used by multiple objects into a single texture atlas.

7. Resource Streaming:

• Implement resource streaming to load assets dynamically as needed. This can reduce the initial loading time and memory footprint.

• Use asynchronous loading to prevent stalling the rendering pipeline during asset loading.

8. Reduced Overdraw:

• Minimize overdraw by organizing your scene to draw objects front-to-back when possible.

• Implement techniques like occlusion culling to avoid rendering objects that are not visible to the camera.

9. Memory Management:

• Be mindful of memory usage and avoid memory leaks. Properly release resources when they are no longer needed.

• Implement a memory management system to handle resource allocation efficiently.

10. UI Performance:

- OPTIMIZE UI RENDERING by **using** efficient layout algorithms and minimizing the number of UI elements.

- Consider **using** UI libraries that are specifically designed **for** mobile platforms.

11. Testing on Real Devices:

- ALWAYS TEST YOUR APPLICATION **on** real mobile devices **with** varying hardware specifications **to** identify performance issues specific **to** different devices.

12. Profiling and Monitoring:

- USE PROFILING TOOLS and monitoring software to identify performance bottlenecks and optimize critical sections of your code.

- Monitor frame rates, memory usage, and GPU/CPU performance during development and testing.

Optimizing DirectX applications for mobile devices requires a combination of efficient resource management, rendering techniques, and performance profiling. By implementing these best practices, you can deliver a high-quality graphics experience on a wide range of Windows Mobile devices. In the next section, we will explore the integration of touch and sensor input for enhanced mobile gaming experiences.

Section 12.4: Touch and Sensor Integration

INTEGRATING TOUCH AND sensor input is essential for creating engaging and interactive mobile DirectX applications, especially for gaming and augmented reality experiences. In this section, we will explore how to harness touch input, accelerometer data, and other sensors available on mobile devices to enhance user interactions.

1. Touch Input Handling:

- Windows provides APIs to handle touch input events. You can use the WM_TOUCH message to receive touch events in your application's message loop.

- For DirectX applications, you'll typically translate touch events into actions such as panning, zooming, or tapping to interact with objects in your 3D scene.

```
CASE WM_TOUCH:
// Process touch input here
HandleTouchInput();
break;
```

2. Multi-Touch Gestures:

- Support multi-touch gestures like pinch-to-zoom, two-finger rotation, and swipe gestures.

- Implement gesture recognition algorithms or use the built-in gesture recognition APIs in Windows.

3. Accelerometer and Gyroscope:

- Access accelerometer and gyroscope data to detect device orientation and movement.

- Use this data for controlling in-game objects or camera movement in 3D applications.

4. Orientation Sensors:

- Utilize orientation sensors to determine the device's position in 3D space.

- Create immersive experiences that respond to changes in the device's orientation.

5. Proximity Sensors:

- Interact with proximity sensors to detect when the device is close to the user's face.

- Automatically pause or adjust the application when it's near the user's ear during a phone call.

6. Light Sensors:

- Adapt the application's brightness or visual effects based on ambient light levels.

- Provide a more comfortable viewing experience in different lighting conditions.

7. GPS and Location Data:

- Utilize GPS and location data to enhance location-based games or applications.

- Create geospatial experiences by integrating real-world location data into your app.

8. Vibration Feedback:

- Implement haptic feedback using the device's vibration motor.

- Enhance user feedback and immersion by vibrating the device in response to in-game events.

9. Testing and Calibration:

- Thoroughly test your touch and sensor interactions on various mobile devices.

- Consider implementing calibration procedures to ensure accurate sensor readings across different hardware.

10. User Experience Design:

- DESIGN USER INTERFACES **and** interactions **with** touch input **in** mind.

- Ensure that touch controls are intuitive **and** easy **to use**, especially **in** mobile games.

11. Energy Efficiency:

- BE MINDFUL OF THE impact of sensor usage on battery life.

- Implement power-saving strategies, such **as** reducing sensor polling frequency when the application **is in** the background.

12. Documentation and User Guidance:

- PROVIDE CLEAR INSTRUCTIONS or tutorials on how to use touch and sensor features within your application.

- Help users understand the available gestures and interactions.

Integrating touch and sensor input can greatly enhance the user experience of your DirectX application on mobile devices. Whether you are developing a game, an augmented reality app, or a creative tool, these input methods open up exciting possibilities for interaction and immersion. In the next section, we will explore the topic of mobile DirectX gaming through case studies of successful mobile games built with DirectX.

Section 12.5: Case Studies: Successful DirectX Mobile Games

IN THIS SECTION, WE will examine case studies of successful mobile games that leveraged DirectX to create engaging and immersive gaming experiences. These games demonstrate the potential of DirectX in mobile game development and offer insights into the strategies used by developers to achieve success in the competitive mobile gaming market.

1. Asphalt 9: Legends

- *Genre:* Racing
- *Platform:* iOS, Android
- *Developer:* Gameloft

ASPHALT 9: LEGENDS is a visually stunning racing game that showcases the capabilities of DirectX on mobile devices. The game features high-quality 3D graphics, realistic physics simulations, and a wide range of exotic cars. DirectX allows Asphalt 9 to deliver smooth gameplay, dynamic lighting effects, and detailed environments, providing players with a console-like racing experience on their smartphones and tablets.

Key Features:

- Real-time multiplayer races with players worldwide.
- Extensive car customization and a wide selection of vehicles.
- Touch and tilt controls optimized for mobile gameplay.

2. PUBG Mobile

- *Genre:* Battle Royale
- *Platform:* iOS, Android
- *Developer:* PUBG Corporation

PLAYERUNKNOWN'S BATTLEGROUNDS (PUBG) Mobile became a global sensation, thanks in part to its use of DirectX for graphics rendering. The game offers a large open world with detailed environments, realistic weapons, and intense multiplayer battles. DirectX enables PUBG Mobile to provide high-quality visuals and smooth gameplay, even on a wide range of mobile devices.

Key Features:

- Battle Royale mode with up to 100 players.
- Realistic graphics and sound effects.
- Continuous updates and new content additions.

3. Alto's Odyssey

- *Genre:* Endless Runner
- *Platform:* iOS, Android
- *Developer:* Team Alto

ALTO'S ODYSSEY IS AN artistic endless runner game known for its beautiful 2D visuals and smooth animations. While it may not be as graphically intensive as some other games, it demonstrates how DirectX can be used to create visually striking 2D games with fluid animations and responsive touch controls. The game's desert landscapes and changing weather conditions are particularly noteworthy.

Key Features:

- Stunning visual design and dynamic weather effects.
- Fluid gameplay and intuitive one-touch controls.
- Zen Mode for a relaxing gaming experience.

4. Genshin Impact

- *Genre:* Action RPG
- *Platform:* iOS, Android
- *Developer:* miHoYo

GENSHIN IMPACT IS AN open-world action RPG that offers console-quality graphics and gameplay on mobile devices. Powered by DirectX, the game features a vast and detailed world, real-time combat, and an engaging storyline. The use of DirectX allows

Genshin Impact to deliver stunning visuals and seamless transitions between different in-game regions.

Key Features:

- Exploration of a beautifully crafted fantasy world.
- Elemental combat system with character switching.
- Cross-platform play with PC and console players.

These case studies illustrate the versatility of DirectX in mobile game development. From racing games with console-like graphics to open-world RPGs with vast landscapes, DirectX empowers developers to push the boundaries of what is possible on mobile devices. Whether it's delivering stunning visual experiences or ensuring smooth and responsive gameplay, DirectX plays a crucial role in creating successful and memorable mobile games.

Chapter 13: DirectX and the Cloud

Section 13.1: Cloud Computing and DirectX

IN THIS SECTION, WE will explore the intersection of cloud computing and DirectX, highlighting how the cloud can be leveraged to enhance graphics processing and gaming experiences. Cloud computing has brought significant advancements to various industries, and the gaming sector is no exception. DirectX, as a powerful graphics framework, can benefit from cloud technologies in several ways.

1. Cloud-Based Graphics Rendering

ONE OF THE PRIMARY applications of DirectX in the cloud is cloud-based graphics rendering. This approach offloads the intensive graphics processing tasks from local devices to remote servers in data centers. Gamers can then access games with high-end graphics on devices that would not traditionally support such capabilities. Cloud-based rendering leverages the scalability and processing power of the cloud to deliver impressive graphics without the need for expensive gaming hardware.

```
// Example pseudocode for cloud-based rendering using DirectX

void RenderFrame(CloudGraphicsServer server, RenderParameters params) {

CloudGraphicsData renderedFrame = server.RenderFrame(params);

DisplayOnLocalDevice(renderedFrame);

}
```

2. Game Streaming Services

CLOUD GAMING PLATFORMS, such as Microsoft's Project xCloud and Google Stadia, use DirectX to provide users with access to a library of games via streaming. DirectX handles rendering on remote servers, while users interact with the game through their devices. This approach eliminates the need for powerful local hardware and allows gamers to play graphically demanding titles on smartphones, tablets, or low-end PCs.

3. Multiplayer and Synchronization

CLOUD COMPUTING CAN enhance the multiplayer experience in DirectX games. It facilitates the synchronization of game states across multiple players by acting as a centralized server for game data. DirectX's networking capabilities, combined with cloud servers, enable real-time multiplayer gaming with minimal latency.

```
// Example pseudocode for cloud-based multiplayer synchronization

void UpdateGameState(CloudServer cloud, GameState currentState, InputCommands input) {

cloud.SyncGameState(currentState, input);

}
```

4. Content Delivery and Updates

CLOUD-BASED CONTENT delivery systems are essential for modern gaming. DirectX games can benefit from cloud-hosted updates, patches, and downloadable content (DLC). This approach ensures that players have access to the latest game assets and features without the need for manual downloads and installations.

```
// Example pseudocode for cloud-based content delivery

void CheckForUpdates(CloudContentServer server) {

if (server.HasNewContent()) {

DownloadContent(server.GetNewContent());

}
```

```
}
```

5. Cost-Efficient Development

CLOUD RESOURCES CAN aid game development by providing on-demand access to powerful hardware for testing and optimization. Game developers can use cloud-based DirectX environments to fine-tune graphics settings, test performance on various devices, and reduce development costs associated with maintaining local hardware.

The integration of DirectX with cloud computing technologies opens up new possibilities for game developers and players alike. It allows for more accessible gaming experiences, improved graphics quality, and efficient content delivery. As cloud computing continues to evolve, its synergy with DirectX is expected to play a significant role in shaping the future of gaming.

Section 13.2: Leveraging the Cloud for Enhanced Graphics Processing

IN THIS SECTION, WE will delve deeper into how game developers can harness the power of cloud computing to enhance graphics processing using DirectX. Cloud-based graphics processing can significantly improve the visual quality and performance of games, making them accessible to a broader audience.

1. Distributed Rendering

ONE OF THE KEY ADVANTAGES of cloud computing is its ability to distribute rendering tasks across multiple servers or virtual machines. Game developers can leverage this capability to achieve real-time ray tracing, advanced lighting effects, and high-resolution textures that would be challenging to render on a single local device. By offloading rendering to the cloud, games can provide stunning visuals even on low-end hardware.

```
// Pseudocode for distributing rendering tasks to the cloud

void RenderFrame(CloudRenderFarm farm, RenderParameters params) {

CloudRenderedFrame renderedFrame = farm.RenderFrame(params);

DisplayOnLocalDevice(renderedFrame);

}
```

2. AI-Enhanced Graphics

CLOUD COMPUTING ALLOWS developers to integrate artificial intelligence (AI) into the graphics pipeline to enhance visuals further. AI algorithms can upscale lower-resolution textures in real-time, remove noise from rendered images, and even predict object movements to improve anti-aliasing. DirectX can seamlessly integrate with cloud-based AI services to deliver these enhancements.

3. Scalability and Performance

CLOUD INFRASTRUCTURE provides scalability and on-demand resources, ensuring consistent game performance regardless of the player's hardware. During periods of high demand, cloud resources can be dynamically allocated to maintain a smooth gaming experience. DirectX's adaptability to varying hardware configurations makes it a natural fit for cloud-based gaming solutions.

4. Cloud-Based Assets

STORING GAME ASSETS in the cloud allows developers to reduce the size of game installations and accelerate load times. As players explore different game environments, cloud-based assets can be streamed on-the-fly, providing a seamless and immersive experience.

```
// Example pseudocode for streaming cloud-based assets in DirectX

void LoadGameEnvironment(CloudAssetStorage cloudStorage, Environment environment) {

GameAssets assets = cloudStorage.GetAssetsForEnvironment(environment);

LoadAssets(assets);

}
```

5. Dynamic Environments

CLOUD COMPUTING ENABLES dynamic, procedurally generated environments that can adapt to player actions. DirectX can render these dynamic environments in real-time, ensuring that players experience a world that evolves based on their choices and interactions.

6. Cost-Efficiency

WHILE CLOUD-BASED GRAPHICS processing offers many advantages, developers should be mindful of cost considerations. Cloud resources are typically billed based on usage, so efficient resource management and optimization are essential to control expenses. DirectX's flexibility allows developers to fine-tune graphics settings to achieve the desired visual quality while minimizing costs.

In conclusion, leveraging the cloud for enhanced graphics processing with DirectX opens up exciting possibilities for game developers. From distributed rendering to AI-powered enhancements, cloud computing can elevate the visual quality and performance of games, making them accessible to a wider audience and ensuring a more immersive gaming experience. Developers should carefully balance the benefits of cloud-based graphics with cost-efficiency to create compelling and cost-effective gaming experiences.

Section 13.3: DirectX in Cloud-Based Game Streaming Services

IN THIS SECTION, WE will explore the integration of DirectX with cloud-based game streaming services. Game streaming has gained popularity as it allows players to enjoy high-quality gaming experiences on a variety of devices, even those with limited computing power. DirectX plays a crucial role in delivering these experiences to players through the cloud.

1. Cloud Gaming Infrastructure

CLOUD-BASED GAME STREAMING services rely on powerful data centers equipped with high-end GPUs and CPUs. These data centers handle the heavy lifting of rendering and processing game graphics. DirectX is at the core of this infrastructure, as it provides the graphics rendering capabilities required to stream games to players' devices.

2. Low Latency Rendering

ONE OF THE PRIMARY challenges in cloud gaming is minimizing latency, ensuring that player input is reflected in the game's visuals with minimal delay. DirectX's efficiency and optimizations play a vital role in achieving low-latency rendering. Techniques like frame prediction and adaptive frame rates help reduce the perception of latency in cloud-based gaming.

```
// Pseudocode for frame prediction in cloud-based gaming

void RenderFrameWithPrediction(CloudRenderFarm farm, PlayerInput input) {

PredictedFrame predictedFrame = PredictFrame(input);

CloudRenderedFrame renderedFrame = farm.RenderFrame(predictedFrame);

DisplayOnPlayerDevice(renderedFrame);

}
```

3. Device Agnosticism

CLOUD GAMING SERVICES support a wide range of devices, from smartphones to smart TVs. DirectX's versatility allows game developers to create titles that can adapt to different screen sizes, resolutions, and input methods seamlessly. This device agnosticism enhances the accessibility of games, as players can switch between devices without losing their progress.

4. Multiplayer and Social Features

CLOUD GAMING SERVICES often include multiplayer and social features, such as real-time voice chat and cross-platform play.

DirectX facilitates the integration of these features by providing APIs for audio processing and network communication. This ensures that players can connect and interact seamlessly in the cloud gaming environment.

5. Scalability

CLOUD-BASED GAME STREAMING services are designed to scale according to demand. DirectX's compatibility with cloud infrastructure allows game providers to allocate resources dynamically. During peak usage, additional servers can be brought online to maintain performance, and when demand subsides, resources can be scaled down to optimize costs.

```
// Pseudocode for dynamically scaling cloud resources

void ScaleCloudResources(CloudResourceManager manager, int currentPlayers) {

if (currentPlayers > HighDemandThreshold) {

manager.AddCloudServers(AdditionalServers);

} else if (currentPlayers < LowDemandThreshold) {

manager.RemoveCloudServers(UnneededServers);

}

}
```

6. Security and Data Privacy

SECURING CLOUD-BASED game streaming services is of utmost importance. DirectX supports encryption and secure communication protocols, ensuring that player data and interactions remain private and protected from potential threats.

In summary, DirectX plays a pivotal role in cloud-based game streaming services, enabling low-latency rendering, device agnosticism, and scalability. With its support for multiplayer features and security measures, DirectX empowers game developers to create immersive and accessible gaming experiences that can be enjoyed on various devices through the cloud.

Section 13.4: Security Considerations in Cloud-Based DirectX Applications

IN THIS SECTION, WE will delve into the critical topic of security considerations when developing cloud-based applications that use DirectX. Ensuring the security of your application is paramount to protect user data, maintain trust, and prevent vulnerabilities that can be exploited.

1. Data Encryption

WHEN DEALING WITH CLOUD-based applications, especially in the gaming industry, sensitive user data such as login credentials and payment information are transmitted over the internet. To safeguard this data, it's essential to implement strong encryption protocols. DirectX does not directly handle encryption, but it provides APIs that allow developers to work with encryption libraries and ensure secure data transmission.

```
// Pseudocode for encrypting sensitive data using DirectX

void EncryptUserData(DirectXDevice device, UserData userData) {

EncryptionLibrary encryption = CreateEncryptionLibrary();
```

```
EncryptedData encryptedData = encryption.Encrypt(userData);

SendEncryptedDataToCloud(device, encryptedData);

}
```

2. Authentication and Authorization

CLOUD-BASED APPLICATIONS often require robust authentication and authorization mechanisms to prevent unauthorized access. DirectX applications can utilize these mechanisms by integrating with identity providers and access control systems. Multi-factor authentication and role-based access control should be considered to enhance security further.

```
// Pseudocode for authentication using DirectX

bool AuthenticateUser(DirectXDevice device, UserCredentials credentials) {

IdentityProvider identityProvider = GetIdentityProvider();

bool isAuthenticated = identityProvider.ValidateCredentials(credentials);

if (isAuthenticated) {

AuthorizeUser(device, credentials);

}

return isAuthenticated;

}
```

3. Code Obfuscation

TO PROTECT YOUR DIRECTX application from reverse engineering and tampering, consider code obfuscation techniques. Obfuscation makes it harder for attackers to understand the code's logic and modify it. There are third-party tools and libraries that can be integrated into the development pipeline to obfuscate your application's binary code.

4. Regular Security Audits

PERFORM REGULAR SECURITY audits and penetration testing on your cloud-based DirectX application. Identify vulnerabilities and address them promptly. Continuous monitoring and vulnerability scanning can help detect and mitigate security risks before they are exploited.

```
// Pseudocode for automated security scanning

void PerformSecurityScan(DirectXApplication app) {

SecurityScanner scanner = CreateSecurityScanner();

VulnerabilityReport report = scanner.Scan(app);

if (report.HasVulnerabilities()) {

MitigateVulnerabilities(report);

}

}
```

5. Secure Communication

ENSURE THAT COMMUNICATION between your DirectX application and the cloud infrastructure is secure. Use secure protocols like HTTPS for data transmission and implement certificate pinning to prevent man-in-the-middle attacks. DirectX's compatibility with secure communication libraries and protocols facilitates this process.

6. Regular Updates

FREQUENTLY UPDATE YOUR DirectX application to patch security vulnerabilities and incorporate the latest security measures. Encourage users to keep their client applications up to date to maintain a secure environment.

In conclusion, security is a top priority when developing cloud-based applications that use DirectX. Implementing data encryption, authentication, code obfuscation, regular security audits, secure communication, and updates are essential practices to protect user data and maintain the integrity of your application. By following these security considerations, you can offer a safer and more trustworthy experience to your users in the cloud gaming ecosystem.

Section 13.5: Future of Cloud Gaming with DirectX

THE FUTURE OF CLOUD gaming with DirectX is an exciting and rapidly evolving landscape. As technology advances and consumer demands change, cloud gaming is poised to play a more significant role in the gaming industry. In this section, we'll explore the potential developments and trends that will shape the future of cloud gaming powered by DirectX.

1. Improved Latency Reduction

ONE OF THE PRIMARY challenges in cloud gaming has been latency, which can affect the responsiveness of games. Future advancements in network infrastructure, including the deployment of 5G and low-latency edge computing, will contribute to reducing latency further. DirectX, with its efficient rendering capabilities, will continue to play a crucial role in mitigating latency issues.

```
// Pseudocode for latency reduction in cloud gaming

void ReduceLatency(DirectXDevice device, LatencyReductionTechniques techniques) {

if (techniques == LatencyReductionTechniques.EdgeComputing) {

EnableEdgeComputing(device);

}

// Other latency reduction techniques here

}
```

2. Enhanced Graphics Quality

WITH THE INCREASING power of cloud servers and GPUs, cloud gaming platforms will offer even more stunning and realistic graphics. DirectX's ability to harness the capabilities of high-end GPUs will be crucial in delivering visually impressive games to players.

```
// Pseudocode for enabling high-quality graphics in cloud gaming

void EnableHighQualityGraphics(DirectXDevice device) {

DirectXRenderer renderer = CreateHighQualityRenderer();

renderer.Configure(device);

}
```

3. Cross-Platform Gameplay

CLOUD GAMING HAS THE potential to bridge the gap between different gaming platforms. Gamers may be able to seamlessly switch between playing on their PC, console, or mobile device while maintaining their progress and achievements. DirectX's cross-platform compatibility will be essential in achieving this level of interoperability.

```
// Pseudocode for cross-platform gameplay

void EnableCrossPlatformPlay(DirectXDevice device) {

CrossPlatformService platformService = CreateCrossPlatformService();

platformService.Configure(device);

}
```

4. Augmented Reality (AR) and Virtual Reality (VR)

THE INTEGRATION OF AR and VR into cloud gaming is on the horizon. DirectX is well-equipped to handle the demanding rendering requirements of these immersive technologies. Gamers can expect more AR-enhanced and VR-enabled cloud gaming experiences in the future.

```
// Pseudocode for AR/VR support in cloud gaming

void EnableARVRSupport(DirectXDevice device, ARVREnhancements enhancements) {

ARVRManager arvrManager = CreateARVRManager();

arvrManager.Configure(device, enhancements);
```

```
}
```

5. Enhanced AI Integration

THE USE OF AI IN CLOUD gaming will continue to grow, enhancing game experiences. DirectX can facilitate AI-driven features such as intelligent NPCs, adaptive gameplay, and personalized content generation.

```
// Pseudocode for AI integration in cloud gaming

void EnableAIIntegration(DirectXDevice device, AIEnhancements enhancements) {

AIManager aiManager = CreateAIManager();

aiManager.Configure(device, enhancements);

}
```

6. Evolving Cloud Services

CLOUD GAMING SERVICES like Microsoft's Xbox Cloud Gaming and NVIDIA GeForce NOW will continue to expand and offer more games, features, and subscription options. These services leverage DirectX for game rendering and will evolve to meet the demands of a broader audience.

In conclusion, the future of cloud gaming with DirectX holds immense potential for innovation and growth. Reduced latency, improved graphics, cross-platform gameplay, AR/VR integration, AI enhancements, and evolving cloud services are some of the key trends that will shape the cloud gaming landscape. As technology continues to advance, DirectX will remain a vital component in delivering high-quality gaming experiences to players around the world. Gamers can look forward to a future where cloud gaming becomes an even more integral part of the gaming ecosystem, offering convenience and accessibility like never before.

Chapter 14: DirectX and Artificial Intelligence

Section 14.1: AI in Game Development: An Introduction

ARTIFICIAL INTELLIGENCE (AI) plays a pivotal role in modern game development, enhancing the realism, complexity, and engagement of video games. In this section, we'll delve into the fundamental concepts of AI in game development and explore how DirectX can be leveraged to visualize and interact with AI-driven elements in games.

1. The Role of AI in Games

AI IN GAMES IS RESPONSIBLE for creating intelligent behavior and decision-making for non-player characters (NPCs), opponents, and allies. It adds life to the game world by simulating human-like responses and adaptability. Common AI tasks in games include pathfinding, decision trees, behavior trees, and procedural content generation.

```
// Pseudocode for AI decision-making in a game

void MakeDecision(Character character) {

if (character.health < 30) {

character.Flee();

} else {

character.Attack();

}
```

```
}
```

2. AI for Realistic Game Worlds

DIRECTX'S ROLE IN AI development lies in rendering and visualization. It provides the tools and capabilities to create visually appealing representations of AI-controlled characters and their interactions within the game world. DirectX's rendering capabilities bring AI-driven entities to life, making them more immersive and believable.

```
// Pseudocode for rendering AI-driven characters

void RenderAICharacter(DirectXRenderer renderer, Character character) {

renderer.SetCharacterPose(character);

renderer.RenderCharacter(character);

}
```

3. Integrating AI Engines with DirectX

GAME DEVELOPERS OFTEN integrate specialized AI engines or libraries into their games. DirectX serves as the bridge between the AI logic and visual representation. Developers can use DirectX to visualize the decisions and actions of AI agents, making it easier to debug and fine-tune AI behavior.

```
// Pseudocode for integrating an AI engine with DirectX

void IntegrateAIWithDirectX(AIEngine aiEngine, DirectXRenderer renderer) {

aiEngine.Initialize();
```

```
aiEngine.Configure(renderer);

}
```

4. Procedural Content Generation

AI TECHNIQUES, SUCH as procedural content generation, can create vast and dynamic game worlds. DirectX aids in rendering procedurally generated content, whether it's terrain, textures, or objects. This allows for diverse and visually appealing game environments.

```
// Pseudocode for rendering procedurally generated terrain

void RenderProceduralTerrain(DirectXRenderer renderer, Terrain terrain) {

renderer.RenderTerrain(terrain);

}
```

5. Future Directions for AI and DirectX

THE FUTURE OF AI IN game development holds exciting possibilities. As AI algorithms become more sophisticated, games will feature even more realistic and adaptable NPCs. DirectX will continue to evolve to support advanced rendering techniques, enabling developers to create increasingly immersive AI-driven game experiences.

In conclusion, AI is a fundamental component of modern game development, and DirectX serves as a crucial tool for visualizing and interacting with AI-driven elements in games. Whether it's rendering intelligent characters, integrating AI engines, or generating procedural content, DirectX empowers developers to bring AI to life in their games. As AI technology continues to advance, we can expect AI-driven game experiences to become more engaging and realistic, further enhancing the gaming industry.

Section 14.2: Using DirectX for AI Visualization

IN THE REALM OF GAME development, AI plays a crucial role in creating lifelike and engaging experiences. Visualizing AI behavior is essential for debugging, testing, and enhancing the overall quality of games. DirectX, with its powerful graphics capabilities, can be harnessed to visualize AI-driven elements effectively. In this section, we'll explore how DirectX can be used to visualize AI in games.

1. Debugging AI Behavior

DEBUGGING AI BEHAVIOR is a common challenge in game development. DirectX provides developers with the means to visually inspect AI decisions and actions, making it easier to identify and address issues. By rendering AI-controlled entities, developers can observe how they navigate the game world and interact with other objects.

```
// Pseudocode for rendering AI debug information

void RenderAIDebugInfo(DirectXRenderer renderer, AICharacter aiCharacter) {

renderer.DrawDebugPath(aiCharacter.Path);

renderer.DrawBehaviorTree(aiCharacter.BehaviorTree);

}
```

2. Visualizing Decision Trees

DECISION TREES ARE a prevalent AI technique for modeling NPC behavior. DirectX can be used to visualize decision trees by rendering the tree structure and highlighting the path taken by an AI agent during runtime. This visual representation aids in understanding and fine-tuning AI decision-making.

```
// Pseudocode for visualizing a decision tree in DirectX
void VisualizeDecisionTree(DirectXRenderer renderer, DecisionTree decisionTree, AICharacter aiCharacter) {
renderer.RenderTreeStructure(decisionTree);
renderer.HighlightPath(aiCharacter.SelectedPath);
}
```

3. Displaying Sensory Information

AI AGENTS OFTEN RELY on sensory information, such as vision or hearing, to make decisions. DirectX can be employed to display sensory data, such as vision cones or sound radii, allowing developers to verify that AI perception aligns with the game's design.

```
// Pseudocode for displaying AI sensory information
void DisplaySensoryInfo(DirectXRenderer renderer, AISensoryData sensoryData) {
renderer.RenderVisionCone(sensoryData.VisionCone);
renderer.RenderSoundRadius(sensoryData.SoundRadius);
}
```

4. AI Animation and Expression

VISUALIZING AI BEHAVIOR isn't limited to decision-making. DirectX can also be used to render AI character animations and expressions. Whether it's facial expressions, body language, or dynamic animations, DirectX's rendering capabilities bring AI-driven characters to life.

```
// Pseudocode for rendering AI character animations

void RenderAICharacterAnimations(DirectXRenderer renderer, AICharacter aiCharacter) {

renderer.PlayAnimation(aiCharacter.CurrentAnimation);

renderer.RenderFacialExpressions(aiCharacter.FacialExpressions);

}
```

5. Creating AI Debug Tools

DEVELOPERS OFTEN BUILD custom debugging tools to visualize AI behavior. DirectX provides the foundation for creating such tools, allowing developers to design user interfaces and overlays that display AI-related information directly within the game.

```
// Pseudocode for creating a custom AI debugging tool using DirectX

void CreateAIDebugTool(DirectXRenderer renderer, AIDebugger debugger) {

renderer.CreateDebugOverlay(debugger);

renderer.RenderDebugUI(debugger.GetUI());

}
```

6. Enhancing Player Experience

VISUALIZING AI BEHAVIOR isn't just for developers; it can enhance the player experience as well. DirectX can be used to create visual cues that help players understand AI intentions and actions, improving gameplay clarity.

```
// Pseudocode for enhancing player experience with AI visual cues

void EnhancePlayerExperience(DirectXRenderer renderer, Player player, AICharacter aiCharacter) {

renderer.RenderAIIntentions(aiCharacter.Intentions);

renderer.RenderAIActions(aiCharacter.Actions);

renderer.RenderPlayerFeedback(player.Feedback);

}
```

In summary, DirectX's capabilities extend beyond rendering graphics; they are instrumental in visualizing AI behavior and decision-making in games. Debugging, decision tree visualization, sensory data display, animation rendering, and custom debugging tools are all made possible by DirectX. By leveraging these features, developers can create more immersive and polished AI-driven gaming experiences.

Section 14.3: Integrating AI Engines with DirectX

INTEGRATING AI ENGINES with DirectX is a pivotal aspect of modern game development, as it empowers developers to leverage specialized AI tools and libraries while benefiting from DirectX's powerful rendering capabilities. In this section, we will delve into the process of integrating AI engines with DirectX to create smarter and more engaging game characters.

1. Choosing an AI Engine

BEFORE INTEGRATION, you need to select an AI engine or framework that aligns with your game's requirements. Popular choices include Unity ML-Agents, Unreal Engine's AI system, and custom-built AI libraries. Each engine has its strengths, so consider factors like ease of use, community support, and integration options.

```
// Example of selecting an AI engine

AIEngine chosenEngine = UnityMLAgents;
```

2. AI Model Training

MANY AI ENGINES ARE designed to train AI models using various techniques, such as reinforcement learning, neural networks, or decision trees. Train your AI models within the chosen engine, ensuring they learn the desired behaviors and decision-making processes.

```
// Pseudocode for training an AI model in an AI engine

void TrainAIModel(AIEngine engine, AIModule aiModule, TrainingData trainingData) {

engine.LoadAIModule(aiModule);

engine.TrainModel(trainingData);

}
```

3. Exporting AI Models

ONCE AI MODELS ARE trained and optimized, export them in a format compatible with DirectX. Common formats include TensorFlow's .pb format for neural networks or custom formats for decision trees. Ensure that the exported models contain all necessary parameters for inference.

```
// Pseudocode for exporting an AI model to a compatible format

void ExportAIModel(AIEngine engine, AIModule aiModule, string exportPath) {

engine.SaveModel(aiModule, exportPath);

}
```

4. DirectX Integration

TO INTEGRATE AI ENGINES with DirectX, you'll need to create a bridge that facilitates communication between the two systems. This bridge should handle AI model inference and provide results that can be used for character animation, decision-making, and other in-game actions.

```
// Pseudocode for creating a DirectX-AI bridge

class DirectXAIBridge {

public:

void LoadAIModel(string modelPath);

void PerformInference(InputData inputData, OutputData& outputData);

void UpdateCharacterAnimations(OutputData outputData);
```

```
};
```

5. Inference and AI Behavior

DURING GAMEPLAY, DIRECTX can call the AI engine through the bridge to perform inference using the loaded AI models. The AI engine will provide decisions, actions, or character behavior based on the input data it receives from the game environment.

```
// Pseudocode for performing AI inference in DirectX

DirectXAIBridge aiBridge = new DirectXAIBridge();

aiBridge.LoadAIModel("trained_model.pb");

// During gameplay loop

InputData currentInput = CollectInputData();

OutputData aiOutput;

aiBridge.PerformInference(currentInput, aiOutput);

// Apply AI behavior to game characters

aiBridge.UpdateCharacterAnimations(aiOutput);
```

6. Handling AI State Changes

AI ENGINES OFTEN SUPPORT state machines or finite state controllers to manage AI behavior. DirectX can communicate with the AI engine to trigger state changes, such as transitioning from "patrolling" to "attacking" when an enemy is detected.

```
// Pseudocode for handling AI state changes in DirectX

void HandleAIStateChange(DirectXAIBridge aiBridge, AICharacter aiCharacter, AIState newState) {
```

```
aiBridge.SendStateChangeRequest(aiCharacter, newState);

}
```

7. Debugging and Testing

INTEGRATING AI ENGINES with DirectX provides ample opportunities for debugging and testing. You can visualize AI decision-making, inspect AI behavior, and fine-tune AI models using DirectX's rendering capabilities, as discussed in previous sections.

```
// Pseudocode for debugging AI behavior with DirectX

void DebugAIBehavior(DirectXAIBridge aiBridge, AICharacter aiCharacter) {

aiBridge.EnableDebugMode();

aiBridge.RenderAIModelVisualizations(aiCharacter);

aiBridge.VisualizeDecisionTrees(aiCharacter.DecisionTrees);

}
```

Integrating AI engines with DirectX opens up a world of possibilities for creating intelligent and immersive game characters. By selecting the right AI engine, training models, exporting them, and establishing a robust communication bridge, you can infuse your games with advanced AI capabilities that enhance player experiences and make your virtual worlds come to life.

Section 14.4: Procedural Content Generation with DirectX

PROCEDURAL CONTENT generation (PCG) is a technique widely used in modern game development to create diverse and dynamic game worlds and assets. When combined with DirectX, PCG can result in visually stunning and immersive experiences. In this section, we'll explore the integration of procedural content generation techniques with DirectX.

1. Understanding Procedural Content Generation

PROCEDURAL CONTENT generation involves using algorithms to create game content such as terrain, textures, meshes, levels, and more. This approach allows developers to generate content on-the-fly, reducing storage requirements and enabling the creation of vast and unique game worlds.

2. Terrain Generation

ONE COMMON APPLICATION of PCG is terrain generation. DirectX can render procedurally generated terrains with realistic landscapes, including mountains, valleys, and bodies of water. Perlin noise, fractal algorithms, and simplex noise are popular methods for generating terrain heightmaps.

```
// Pseudocode for procedural terrain generation

Heightmap GenerateTerrain(int width, int height) {

Heightmap heightmap(width, height);

for (int x = 0; x < width; x++) {

for (int y = 0; y < height; y++) {

float noiseValue = PerlinNoise(x, y);

heightmap.SetHeight(x, y, noiseValue * maxHeight);

}
```

```
}
return heightmap;
}
```

3. Texture Synthesis

PROCEDURAL TEXTURES can be synthesized in real-time using DirectX. Algorithms like Voronoi diagrams, cellular automata, or noise functions can generate textures for terrain, materials, or visual effects. These textures can be applied to 3D models or used as part of post-processing effects.

```
// Pseudocode for procedural texture synthesis
Texture GenerateProceduralTexture(int width, int height) {
Texture texture(width, height);
for (int x = 0; x < width; x++) {
for (int y = 0; y < height; y++) {
Color pixelColor = CellularAutomataColor(x, y);
texture.SetPixel(x, y, pixelColor);
}
}
return texture;
}
```

4. Dynamic Level Design

PCG CAN ALSO BE APPLIED to level design, creating diverse and challenging game levels. By defining rules and algorithms, you can generate dungeons, mazes, or open-world environments dynamically. DirectX then renders these levels, making each playthrough unique.

```
// Pseudocode for procedural level generation

Level GenerateProceduralLevel() {

Level level;

DungeonGenerator generator;

level = generator.GenerateDungeon();

return level;

}
```

5. Particle Systems and Effects

PROCEDURAL TECHNIQUES can enhance particle systems and special effects in DirectX. For example, procedural noise functions can control particle motion, creating realistic fire, smoke, or fluid simulations. These effects can significantly improve the visual appeal of your game.

```
// Pseudocode for procedural particle motion

void UpdateParticles(ParticleSystem particles) {

for (Particle particle : particles) {

Vector3 noiseOffset = PerlinNoise3D(particle.Position);
```

```
particle.Velocity += noiseOffset * turbulenceFactor;
particle.Position += particle.Velocity * deltaTime;
}
}
```

6. Debugging and Visualization

WHEN INTEGRATING PCG with DirectX, it's essential to have debugging tools to visualize and fine-tune the generated content. DirectX's rendering capabilities can be leveraged to display procedurally generated assets and tweak generation parameters in real-time.

```
// Pseudocode for debugging procedural content
void DebugProceduralContent(ProceduralAsset asset) {
asset.DebugRender();
asset.TweakParametersWithGUI();
}
```

Procedural content generation combined with DirectX can lead to limitless possibilities for game development. By leveraging PCG techniques for terrain, textures, levels, and effects, you can create games with dynamic and visually stunning environments that keep players engaged and coming back for more.

Section 14.5: Future Trends and DirectX in VR

VIRTUAL REALITY (VR) is a rapidly evolving field in the world of game development and interactive experiences. In this section, we'll explore the future trends and the role of DirectX in the world of VR.

1. Evolving VR Technologies

AS TECHNOLOGY CONTINUES to advance, VR hardware is becoming more accessible and capable. Higher-resolution displays, improved tracking systems, and more immersive input devices are making VR experiences increasingly realistic. DirectX plays a crucial role in rendering these high-quality visuals and delivering smooth VR interactions.

2. DirectX and VR Rendering

DIRECTX IS WELL-SUITED for rendering VR content due to its low-level access to hardware. It allows developers to optimize rendering pipelines for VR headsets, ensuring low-latency and high frame rates, which are critical for a comfortable VR experience. Techniques such as foveated rendering, which reduces rendering workload for the peripheral vision, are made possible with DirectX.

```
// Pseudocode for foveated rendering with DirectX

void RenderSceneForVR(Camera vrCamera) {

DirectX.RenderScene(vrCamera);

DirectX.RenderPeripheralBlurred(vrCamera);

DirectX.ComposeFinalImage();
```

```
}
```

3. VR Audio with DirectX

IMMERSIVE AUDIO IS essential in VR experiences. DirectX's capabilities in audio rendering and 3D spatialization can create realistic soundscapes, enhancing the sense of presence in VR environments. Integration with VR audio SDKs further improves audio quality and spatial accuracy.

```
// Pseudocode for VR audio rendering with DirectX

void RenderVRAudio(SpatialAudioEngine audioEngine) {

DirectX.RenderAudioListener(vrCamera);

audioEngine.Render3DSounds();

audioEngine.ApplyHead-Related Transfer Functions(vrHeadset);

audioEngine.PlaySpatialAudio();

}
```

4. Mixed Reality and AR Integration

MIXED REALITY (MR) and Augmented Reality (AR) are expanding the possibilities of interactive experiences. DirectX provides the graphics capabilities required for mixed reality headsets that blend digital content with the real world. This technology has applications in gaming, education, training, and more.

5. DirectX Ray Tracing in VR

THE INTEGRATION OF real-time ray tracing with DirectX introduces new opportunities for VR visuals. Ray tracing enables more realistic lighting, reflections, and shadows, resulting in highly immersive VR environments. This technology is expected to play a significant role in the future of VR game development.

```
// Pseudocode for ray-traced reflections in VR

void RenderRayTracedReflections(Camera vrCamera) {

DirectX.EnableRayTracing();

DirectX.RenderSceneWithReflections(vrCamera);

DirectX.DisableRayTracing();

}
```

6. Social and Multiplayer VR with DirectX

COLLABORATIVE AND MULTIPLAYER VR experiences are on the rise. DirectX's networking capabilities (as discussed in Chapter 6) can be leveraged to create shared VR environments, where users from around the world can interact in real-time. This opens up possibilities for social VR, virtual conferences, and collaborative workspaces.

As the VR landscape continues to evolve, DirectX remains a crucial tool for developers looking to create immersive and visually stunning virtual reality experiences. Its low-level access to hardware, rendering capabilities, and support for emerging technologies position it at the forefront of VR development. By staying updated with the latest VR trends and integrating DirectX effectively, developers can deliver compelling VR content that captivates users and pushes the boundaries of what's possible in virtual reality.

Chapter 15: Advanced Texturing Techniques

Section 15.1: Detailed Look at Texture Mapping

TEXTURE MAPPING IS a fundamental concept in computer graphics and game development. It involves applying 2D images, called textures, to 3D models to add visual detail and realism. In this section, we'll take a closer look at texture mapping and explore various techniques and considerations for advanced texturing.

1. The Basics of Texture Mapping

TEXTURE MAPPING IS the process of wrapping a 2D image around a 3D object's surface. Each point (vertex) on the object's surface is associated with a corresponding point (texel) on the texture map. When rendering the object, the texels' colors are applied to the surface, creating the illusion of detail, color, and texture.

2. Types of Textures

TEXTURES COME IN VARIOUS types, each serving a specific purpose:

- **Diffuse Textures:** These represent the color and surface detail of an object. They are used to simulate materials like wood, metal, or fabric.
- **Normal Maps:** Normal maps encode surface normals in an RGB color format. They are used to simulate fine surface details and improve the lighting of 3D objects.

- **Specular Maps:** Specular maps control the shininess and reflectivity of an object's surface. They determine where highlights appear.

- **Height Maps:** Height maps encode height or displacement information for terrain or surfaces. They are used in tessellation and parallax mapping.

3. UV Mapping

UV MAPPING IS THE PROCESS of assigning 2D texture coordinates (U and V) to the 3D vertices of a model. These coordinates determine how the texture is wrapped around the object. UV mapping can be done manually or generated automatically by 3D modeling software.

```
// Pseudocode for applying UV coordinates in DirectX

vertex.position = Vector3(x, y, z);

vertex.texCoord = Vector2(u, v);
```

4. Tiling and Texture Coordinates

TILING IS A TECHNIQUE where textures are repeated across an object's surface. Texture coordinates outside the range [0, 1] can be used to achieve tiling effects. This is common for surfaces like floors and walls.

```
// Pseudocode for applying tiling in DirectX

vertex.texCoord = Vector2(u * tilingFactor, v * tilingFactor);
```

5. Texture Filtering

TEXTURE FILTERING METHODS control how texels are sampled and interpolated when rendering. Common filtering techniques include:

- **Point Sampling:** Uses the nearest texel's color value. It can result in a pixelated look when textures are scaled up.

- **Bilinear Filtering:** Computes the weighted average of four nearest texels. It smooths texture transitions but can still appear blurry.

- **Trilinear Filtering:** Combines bilinear filtering with mipmapping to improve texture quality at different distances from the camera.

6. Anisotropic Filtering

ANISOTROPIC FILTERING is a more advanced technique that enhances texture quality, especially at oblique angles. It reduces blurriness and maintains sharpness in textures, making them look better in various viewing conditions.

7. Texture Compression

TEXTURE COMPRESSION techniques reduce memory usage and improve rendering performance. DirectX supports various texture compression formats, such as DXT1, DXT5, and BC7. Choosing the right format depends on the texture's characteristics and the desired quality.

8. Shader Effects and Texture Blending

SHADERS CAN BE USED to apply advanced effects to textures, such as blending multiple textures together based on certain conditions (e.g., terrain textures based on slope or height). This allows for complex and dynamic surface appearances.

Texture mapping is a versatile tool in game development, and mastering advanced texturing techniques can significantly enhance the visual quality of your 3D environments. Understanding the different types of textures, UV mapping, filtering, and shader effects empowers developers to create immersive and visually stunning virtual worlds. As hardware and software capabilities continue to advance, texture mapping remains a crucial aspect of game graphics, contributing to the realism and appeal of modern games.

Section 15.2: Bump Mapping and Normal Mapping

BUMP MAPPING AND NORMAL mapping are advanced texturing techniques used in computer graphics to simulate surface details and improve the lighting of 3D objects without significantly increasing the polygon count. These techniques are widely used in video games and real-time applications to create the illusion of complex surface geometry.

1. Bump Mapping

BUMP MAPPING IS A TECHNIQUE that simulates surface irregularities and fine details by perturbing the normal vectors of a 3D object's vertices. Instead of modifying the actual geometry, bump mapping adjusts the surface normals used in lighting calculations. This gives the appearance of a bumpy or rough surface.

In bump mapping, a grayscale texture called a "bump map" is used. The brightness values in the bump map represent the height variations at each texel. Light calculations are performed based on the perturbed normals, creating the illusion of depth and detail.

Here's a simplified example of bump mapping in HLSL shader code:

```
// Input structure

struct VSInput {

float4 position : POSITION;

float2 texCoord : TEXCOORD0;

};

// Output structure

struct PSOutput {

float4 position : SV_POSITION;

float2 texCoord : TEXCOORD0;

float3 normal : NORMAL;

};

// Bump map texture

Texture2D<float> bumpMap : register(t0);

SamplerState sampler : register(s0);

// Vertex shader

PSOutput VSMain(VSInput input) {
```

```
PSOutput output;

// Sample the bump map

float height = bumpMap.Sample(sampler, input.texCoord).r;

// Perturb the normal based on the bump map

float3 normal = normalize(input.normal + float3(0, 0, height));

// Pass data to the pixel shader

output.position = float4(input.position.xyz, 1.0f);

output.texCoord = input.texCoord;

output.normal = normal;

return output;

}
```

2. Normal Mapping

NORMAL MAPPING IS ANOTHER technique used to simulate surface details and enhance lighting. Instead of modifying the vertex normals, normal mapping directly encodes perturbed surface normals in a texture known as the "normal map." Each RGB color in the normal map represents the direction of the surface normal at that texel.

In the pixel shader, normal vectors are sampled from the normal map and used for lighting calculations. This allows for intricate surface details, such as scratches, bumps, and crevices, without adding geometric complexity.

Here's a simplified example of normal mapping in HLSL shader code:

```
// Input structure

struct VSInput {

float4 position : POSITION;

float2 texCoord : TEXCOORD0;

};

// Output structure

struct PSOutput {

float4 position : SV_POSITION;

float2 texCoord : TEXCOORD0;

float3 normal : NORMAL;

};

// Normal map texture

Texture2D<float3> normalMap : register(t0);

SamplerState sampler : register(s0);

// Vertex shader (assuming the normal map is in tangent space)

PSOutput VSMain(VSInput input) {

PSOutput output;

// Sample the normal map
```

```
float3 normalMapValue = normalMap.Sample(sampler, input.texCoord);

// Transform the normal map value to world space

float3 normal = normalize(normalMapValue * 2.0f - 1.0f);

// Pass data to the pixel shader

output.position = float4(input.position.xyz, 1.0f);

output.texCoord = input.texCoord;

output.normal = normal;

return output;

}
```

Both bump mapping and normal mapping techniques are powerful tools for enhancing the realism of 3D objects in real-time applications. These methods allow developers to create intricate surface details and improve the lighting of objects without the computational cost of increasing polygon counts. When used effectively, bump mapping and normal mapping can make a significant difference in the visual quality of games and simulations.

Section 15.3: Environment and Reflection Mapping

ENVIRONMENT MAPPING and reflection mapping are advanced rendering techniques that enhance the visual realism of 3D objects by simulating their interaction with the surrounding environment. These techniques are widely used in computer graphics to create reflective surfaces and capture the ambiance of a scene.

1. Environment Mapping

ENVIRONMENT MAPPING, also known as reflection mapping, is a technique used to simulate the reflection of the environment on the surface of 3D objects. This creates the illusion of reflective surfaces, such as mirrors or glass, without the need for complex geometry.

In environment mapping, a cube map or spherical map of the environment is used as a texture. Each face or section of the map corresponds to a direction in 3D space (e.g., up, down, front, back). When rendering an object, the environment map is sampled based on the object's surface normal, and the reflected color is used in the shading calculation.

Here's a simplified example of environment mapping in HLSL shader code:

```
// Input structure

struct VSInput {

float4 position : POSITION;

float3 normal : NORMAL;

};

// Output structure

struct PSOutput {

float4 position : SV_POSITION;

float3 normal : NORMAL;

float3 reflection : TEXCOORD0;
```

```
};

// Environment map texture (cube map)

TextureCube<float3> environmentMap : register(t0);

SamplerState sampler : register(s0);

// Vertex shader

PSOutput VSMain(VSInput input) {

PSOutput output;

// Pass position and normal to the pixel shader

output.position = mul(input.position, mul(World, ViewProjection));

output.normal = input.normal;

return output;

}

// Pixel shader

float4 PSMain(PSOutput input) : SV_TARGET {

float3 reflectedColor = environmentMap.Sample(sampler, reflect(input.normal, float3(0, 1, 0)));

return float4(reflectedColor, 1.0f);

}
```

In this example, the environment map is sampled based on the reflected direction, creating the appearance of reflective surfaces.

Environment mapping is commonly used for rendering objects with metallic or glass-like materials.

2. Reflection Mapping

REFLECTION MAPPING is a subset of environment mapping that focuses on simulating reflective surfaces more efficiently. Instead of using a full cube map, reflection mapping often employs a simpler 2D texture, known as a reflection map or reflection probe.

Reflection maps store precomputed reflections for specific points or objects in the scene. When rendering an object, the reflection map is sampled based on the object's position or surroundings, providing quick and visually convincing reflections.

Here's a simplified example of reflection mapping in HLSL shader code:

```
// Input structure (similar to environment mapping example)

struct VSInput {

float4 position : POSITION;

float3 normal : NORMAL;

};

// Output structure (similar to environment mapping example)

struct PSOutput {

float4 position : SV_POSITION;

float3 normal : NORMAL;

float3 reflection : TEXCOORD0;
```

```
};

// Reflection map texture (2D)

Texture2D<float3> reflectionMap : register(t0);

SamplerState sampler : register(s0);

// Vertex shader (similar to environment mapping example)

PSOutput VSMain(VSInput input) {

PSOutput output;

// ...

return output;

}

// Pixel shader

float4 PSMain(PSOutput input) : SV_TARGET {

float3 reflectedColor = reflectionMap.Sample(sampler, input.position.xy).rgb;

return float4(reflectedColor, 1.0f);

}
```

Reflection mapping is a valuable technique for creating realistic reflections on surfaces like water, polished floors, or metal objects. It provides a balance between visual quality and computational efficiency.

Both environment mapping and reflection mapping are essential tools for achieving realistic lighting and reflections in 3D graphics.

These techniques contribute significantly to the visual fidelity of modern games and simulations by simulating how objects interact with their surroundings.

Section 15.4: Dynamic Texturing Strategies

DYNAMIC TEXTURING IS a powerful technique in computer graphics that allows for real-time updates and modifications of textures applied to 3D objects. It is commonly used to create interactive and visually engaging experiences in games and simulations. In this section, we'll explore various strategies and considerations when implementing dynamic texturing.

1. Procedural Texturing

PROCEDURAL TEXTURING involves generating textures algorithmically rather than using pre-designed image textures. This approach is highly flexible and can be used for various purposes, such as simulating natural phenomena (e.g., clouds, terrain) or creating abstract patterns.

One common method for procedural texturing is to use shaders, such as HLSL in DirectX. Shaders can generate textures on the fly based on mathematical formulas or noise functions. Here's a simplified example of procedural texture generation in HLSL:

```
// Input structure (similar to previous examples)

struct VSInput {

float4 position : POSITION;

float2 texCoord : TEXCOORD0;

};
```

```
// Output structure (similar to previous examples)

struct PSOutput {

float4 position : SV_POSITION;

float4 color : COLOR0;

};

// Procedural texture generation in the pixel shader

float4 PSMain(VSInput input) : SV_TARGET {

// Calculate texture color procedurally based on input parameters

float4 textureColor = CalculateProceduralTexture(input.texCoord);

return textureColor;

}

// Procedural texture function (e.g., Perlin noise)

float4 CalculateProceduralTexture(float2 texCoord) {

// ... Procedural texture generation logic ...

return /* Generated texture color */;

}
```

Procedural texturing is ideal for situations where textures need to change dynamically based on in-game events or environmental factors.

2. Video Textures

VIDEO TEXTURES INVOLVE using video files as textures on 3D objects. This technique is often used for displaying dynamic content, such as videos, animations, or live camera feeds, on surfaces within a game or application.

To implement video textures in DirectX, you can use video playback libraries or frameworks that provide DirectX integration. These libraries enable you to load video files and update the texture with each frame of the video. This approach is particularly useful for creating interactive screens or displays within virtual environments.

3. Render-to-Texture (RTT)

RENDER-TO-TEXTURE (RTT) is a technique where you render a scene or specific objects to a texture instead of directly to the screen. This rendered texture can then be used as a dynamic texture on other objects or as a source for further image processing.

In DirectX, RTT is achieved by rendering to a render target texture (RTT). You set up a render target, render the scene or objects to it, and then use the resulting texture elsewhere. RTT is useful for implementing effects like mirrors, security cameras, or real-time reflections, where you need to capture and display a portion of the scene from a different perspective.

4. Texture Streaming

TEXTURE STREAMING IS a strategy to efficiently manage large textures, particularly in open-world games or applications with extensive environments. It involves loading only the necessary portions of textures into memory as they are needed, rather than loading entire textures at once.

Texture streaming helps reduce memory usage and loading times. When a player or camera approaches a specific area, the required textures are loaded or streamed in progressively to maintain a smooth gaming experience. DirectX provides functionality to manage texture streaming efficiently.

In conclusion, dynamic texturing techniques like procedural texturing, video textures, render-to-texture, and texture streaming offer versatile ways to enhance the visual appeal and interactivity of DirectX applications and games. These strategies allow developers to create immersive and engaging experiences with changing and responsive textures, contributing to the realism and engagement of 3D environments.

Section 15.5: Texture Compression and Management

TEXTURE COMPRESSION and management play crucial roles in optimizing the performance and memory usage of DirectX applications, especially when dealing with large textures and a wide range of assets. In this section, we'll delve into the importance of texture compression, various compression formats, and best practices for texture management.

1. Importance of Texture Compression

TEXTURE COMPRESSION is the process of reducing the memory footprint of textures while maintaining acceptable visual quality. It's essential for real-time applications like games, where large textures can consume a significant amount of memory and impact performance. Texture compression helps in the following ways:

- **Reduced Memory Usage:** Compressed textures require less GPU memory, allowing more textures to be loaded simultaneously.

- **Faster Loading Times:** Smaller texture sizes lead to quicker loading times, improving the overall user experience.

- **Enhanced Performance:** Smaller textures can be transferred and rendered more efficiently, resulting in better frame rates.

2. Texture Compression Formats

DIRECTX SUPPORTS SEVERAL texture compression formats, each with its strengths and trade-offs. Some common formats include:

- **BC (Block Compression) Formats:** These formats, such as BC1, BC3, BC5, etc., are widely used for color textures. They offer good compression ratios with minimal loss in quality. BC7 is a more recent format known for its high quality and flexibility.

- **ASTC (Adaptive Scalable Texture Compression):** ASTC is a versatile format that supports a wide range of compression ratios and quality levels. It's suitable for both color and normal maps.

- **ETC (Ericsson Texture Compression):** Primarily used in mobile platforms, ETC formats provide decent compression and quality for mobile games and applications.

- **PVRTC (PowerVR Texture Compression):** Another mobile-oriented format, PVRTC offers good compression and is compatible with PowerVR GPUs.

- **DXT Formats:** These legacy formats, such as DXT1, DXT5, etc., are less commonly used nowadays due to their lower quality compared to BC formats. However, they are still supported for compatibility reasons.

The choice of compression format depends on factors like target platform, memory budget, and visual quality requirements. It's often a trade-off between compression ratio and visual fidelity.

3. Texture Streaming and Level of Detail (LOD)

TO MANAGE MEMORY EFFICIENTLY, consider implementing texture streaming and LOD techniques. Texture streaming loads textures dynamically as they come into view, reducing the initial memory load. LOD involves using lower-resolution textures for distant objects, switching to higher-resolution versions as objects get closer. This maintains visual quality while conserving memory.

4. Mipmapping

MIPMAPPING INVOLVES creating a set of pre-filtered, lower-resolution versions of a texture, known as mipmaps. Mipmaps help improve rendering quality, reduce aliasing, and enhance performance by allowing the GPU to select the appropriate mipmap level based on the screen space size of the texture.

Here's how you can enable mipmapping when creating a texture in DirectX:

```
// Assuming you have a texture resource 'pTextureResource'
```

```
// Create a texture with mipmaps

D3D11_TEXTURE2D_DESC texDesc;

texDesc.Width = width;

texDesc.Height = height;

texDesc.MipLevels = 0; // Automatically generate full chain of mipmaps

texDesc.ArraySize = 1;

texDesc.Format = DXGI_FORMAT_R8G8B8A8_UNORM;

texDesc.SampleDesc.Count = 1;

texDesc.SampleDesc.Quality = 0;

texDesc.Usage = D3D11_USAGE_DEFAULT;

texDesc.BindFlags = D3D11_BIND_SHADER_RESOURCE;

texDesc.CPUAccessFlags = 0;

texDesc.MiscFlags = D3D11_RESOURCE_MISC_GENERATE_MIPS; // Enable mipmap generation

pDevice->CreateTexture2D(&texDesc, nullptr, &pTextureResource);
```

Ensure that you regenerate mipmaps whenever the base texture is updated or changed.

5. Texture Atlases

TEXTURE ATLASES ARE collections of smaller textures packed into a single larger texture. They are often used to reduce the number of texture switches during rendering, which can improve performance. When using texture atlases, you need to manage texture coordinates carefully to access the correct sub-texture within the atlas.

In summary, texture compression and management are critical aspects of DirectX development, impacting both performance and memory usage. By choosing the right compression formats, implementing texture streaming, LOD techniques, mipmapping, and considering texture atlases, developers can create DirectX applications that deliver optimal performance and visual quality while efficiently utilizing hardware resources.

Chapter 16: Real-Time Rendering Techniques

Section 16.1: Understanding Real-Time Rendering

REAL-TIME RENDERING plays a crucial role in modern computer graphics, particularly in the realm of video games and interactive simulations. Unlike offline rendering, which can take hours or even days to produce a single frame of high-quality imagery, real-time rendering aims to generate images at a rapid pace, typically 30 frames per second or higher, to provide a seamless and responsive user experience. In this section, we will delve into the fundamental concepts of real-time rendering.

Rendering in Real Time

AT ITS CORE, REAL-TIME rendering involves the process of converting a three-dimensional scene into a two-dimensional image that can be displayed on a screen. This process must occur quickly enough to maintain the illusion of continuous motion and responsiveness, which is critical for interactive applications such as games. Achieving real-time rendering is a challenging task due to the complex computations required for tasks like lighting, shading, and visibility determination.

The Graphics Pipeline

REAL-TIME RENDERING follows a well-defined pipeline, often referred to as the graphics pipeline, which consists of a series of stages where various computations and transformations are performed. The graphics pipeline takes a three-dimensional representation of a scene and transforms it into a two-dimensional image suitable for display. The pipeline stages include vertex processing, primitive assembly, rasterization, pixel processing, and frame buffer output.

Vertex Processing

THE FIRST STAGE OF the graphics pipeline, vertex processing, involves transforming the 3D coordinates of vertices in the scene into a common coordinate system known as clip space. During this stage, transformations like modeling transformations, viewing transformations, and projection transformations are applied to the vertices. Additionally, vertex shaders, programmed using languages like HLSL (High-Level Shader Language), can be used to perform custom operations on vertices.

Primitive Assembly and Rasterization

AFTER VERTEX PROCESSING, the next stages are primitive assembly and rasterization. Primitive assembly groups vertices into geometric primitives such as triangles, lines, or points. Rasterization then converts these primitives into fragments or pixels that will be shaded and eventually displayed on the screen. This stage also handles tasks like depth testing and back-face culling.

Pixel Processing

PIXEL PROCESSING IS where the actual rendering of each pixel takes place. During this stage, pixel shaders are employed to calculate the color, opacity, and other attributes of each pixel. These shaders can perform complex operations like texture mapping, lighting calculations, and special effects. Pixel processing is a computationally intensive stage and is often a focus of optimization efforts.

Frame Buffer Output

FINALLY, THE RENDERED pixels are combined and written to the frame buffer, which represents the image that will be displayed on the screen. The contents of the frame buffer are typically refreshed at a high rate to create the illusion of motion.

Real-Time Rendering Challenges

REAL-TIME RENDERING faces several challenges, including the need for efficient algorithms, optimization techniques, and hardware acceleration. Balancing visual quality with performance constraints is an ongoing concern. As hardware capabilities continue to evolve, real-time rendering techniques also advance to take advantage of new features and capabilities.

In the sections that follow, we will explore various aspects of real-time rendering, including techniques for implementing real-time shadows, lighting effects, particle systems, environmental effects, and strategies for optimizing rendering performance. Understanding these concepts is essential for anyone involved in the field of computer graphics and game development.

Stay tuned as we delve deeper into the exciting world of real-time rendering in the chapters ahead.

Section 16.2: Implementing Real-Time Shadows and Lighting

REAL-TIME SHADOWS AND lighting are crucial elements in creating immersive and visually appealing 3D environments. In this section, we will explore the concepts and techniques behind implementing real-time shadows and lighting effects in computer graphics.

Shadows in Real-Time Rendering

SHADOWS PLAY A SIGNIFICANT role in conveying depth, realism, and immersion in 3D scenes. Real-time shadows aim to replicate the way objects cast shadows onto one another and their environments in real life. Achieving convincing shadows in real-time rendering is a complex task that involves several techniques:

Shadow Mapping

SHADOW MAPPING IS ONE of the most commonly used techniques for real-time shadow rendering. It involves rendering the scene from the perspective of a light source and storing depth information in a texture, known as the shadow map. During the rendering of the main scene, each fragment's depth is compared to the corresponding depth in the shadow map. If the fragment is in shadow, it is darkened, creating the appearance of a shadow.

```
// Pseudocode for shadow mapping in shaders

float depthFromLight = texture(shadowMap, shadowCoord).r;

if (shadowCoord.z > depthFromLight + bias) {

// Fragment is in shadow

fragmentColor = vec3(0.0);

} else {

// Fragment is lit

// Apply lighting calculations here

}
```

Soft Shadows

REAL-WORLD SHADOWS often have soft edges, especially when the light source is not a point light. Soft shadows can be achieved by introducing techniques like Percentage Closer Filtering (PCF) or Variance Shadow Mapping (VSM). These methods involve sampling multiple points within a shadow map and interpolating shadow values, creating a smoother transition between shadowed and lit areas.

Shadow Techniques for Different Light Sources

THE TYPE OF LIGHT SOURCE can affect shadow rendering. Point lights, directional lights, and spotlights each require different shadow mapping techniques to produce realistic results. For example, point lights require cube shadow maps, while directional lights can use a cascaded shadow map approach to handle large outdoor environments efficiently.

Lighting Effects

REAL-TIME LIGHTING effects enhance the visual quality of a 3D scene. Key lighting techniques include:

Phong Shading

PHONG SHADING IS A straightforward method for simulating specular highlights on surfaces. It uses the Phong reflection model to calculate the reflection direction and determine the intensity and color of specular highlights.

```
// Pseudocode for Phong shading in shaders

vec3 viewDir = normalize(cameraPosition - fragmentPosition);

vec3 lightDir = normalize(lightPosition - fragmentPosition);

vec3 reflectionDir = reflect(-lightDir, normal);

float specular = pow(max(dot(viewDir, reflectionDir), 0.0), shininess);
```

Normal Mapping

NORMAL MAPPING IS USED to add surface detail by perturbing the normals of a model's vertices. This creates the illusion of finer details without increasing the model's polygon count.

```
// Pseudocode for normal mapping in shaders

vec3 tangentSpaceNormal = texture(normalMap, texCoord).rgb * 2.0 - 1.0;

vec3 worldSpaceNormal = normalize(tangentSpaceNormal * TBN);
```

Deferred Rendering

DEFERRED RENDERING is a technique that separates the rendering process into multiple passes, allowing for more complex lighting effects. It involves rendering and storing various attributes (e.g., position, normal, color) into intermediate textures and then performing lighting calculations in a separate pass.

```
// Pseudocode for deferred rendering

// Pass 1: Geometry pass

// Render scene into G-buffer (position, normal, color)

// Pass 2: Lighting pass

// For each light, calculate lighting contributions based on G-buffer data
```

Performance Considerations

IMPLEMENTING REAL-TIME shadows and lighting effects can be computationally expensive. Developers often need to strike a balance between visual fidelity and performance. Techniques like Level of Detail (LOD), occlusion culling, and efficient rendering algorithms play crucial roles in achieving real-time rendering at a consistent frame rate.

In the upcoming sections, we will explore advanced rendering techniques, particle systems, environmental effects, and performance optimization strategies to help you create stunning real-time graphics in your applications and games.

Section 16.3: Particle Systems and Effects

PARTICLE SYSTEMS ARE essential tools for creating a wide range of visual effects in real-time rendering, including fire, smoke, rain, explosions, and more. They simulate the behavior of individual particles within a 3D environment to achieve convincing and dynamic effects. In this section, we will explore the principles and techniques behind particle systems in computer graphics.

Understanding Particle Systems

A PARTICLE SYSTEM CONSISTS of a collection of small, independent entities known as particles. Each particle has properties such as position, velocity, size, color, and lifetime. By continuously updating and rendering these particles, various effects can be generated. Here are some key concepts related to particle systems:

Emission

EMISSION DEFINES HOW particles are initially spawned or emitted into the scene. Particles can be emitted from a point, a surface, or a volume within the 3D space. Emission rates, directions, and patterns determine the initial behavior of particles.

Simulation

PARTICLE SIMULATION involves updating the properties of particles over time. Common updates include changing positions based on velocities, adjusting sizes or colors, and decreasing lifetimes. Physics-based simulations may include forces like gravity, wind, or collisions with other objects.

Rendering

PARTICLES ARE RENDERED as textured billboards or 3D models. Billboards are often used for simple effects, while 3D models can be employed for more complex and detailed particles. Proper rendering techniques ensure that particles blend seamlessly into the scene.

Particle Effects

PARTICLE SYSTEMS ARE versatile and can be used to create a wide range of effects:

Fire and Smoke

CREATING REALISTIC fire and smoke effects involves using particle systems to simulate the motion, appearance, and dissipation of individual fire and smoke particles. Particle lifetimes, colors, and sizes can be manipulated to achieve convincing results.

Explosions

EXPLOSIONS ARE DYNAMIC and chaotic events. Particle systems can simulate debris, sparks, and shockwaves resulting from an explosion. By carefully controlling the emission and behavior of particles, impressive explosion effects can be achieved.

Weather Effects

RAIN, SNOW, AND OTHER weather effects can be simulated using particle systems. Particle density, size, and motion patterns can mimic the appearance of precipitation, enhancing the environmental realism in a scene.

Magical Spells and Special Abilities

IN VIDEO GAMES AND animations, magical spells and special abilities often involve visual effects like glowing particles, sparkles, or auras. Particle systems are ideal for creating these magical and otherworldly visuals.

Optimization and Realism

EFFICIENCY IS CRUCIAL when implementing particle systems to maintain real-time performance. Techniques such as level of detail (LOD), culling, and batching can help manage large numbers of particles. Additionally, optimizing rendering and updating code is essential for smooth performance.

Balancing realism and performance is a constant challenge. While high-quality particle systems can be visually stunning, they can also be computationally expensive. Developers must decide on the appropriate level of detail and complexity based on the target hardware and desired visual fidelity.

In summary, particle systems are invaluable tools for adding dynamic and visually engaging effects to real-time graphics. Understanding how to create, simulate, and render particles allows developers to bring life and excitement to their games, simulations, and interactive applications.

Section 16.4: Real-Time Environmental Effects

REAL-TIME ENVIRONMENTAL effects play a crucial role in enhancing the realism and immersion of computer graphics and gaming experiences. These effects simulate interactions between light, materials, and the environment to create stunning visuals. In this section, we will explore various real-time environmental effects commonly used in computer graphics.

Reflections

REALISTIC REFLECTIONS are essential for simulating the interaction between surfaces and their surroundings. There are two primary types of reflections: screen-space reflections (SSR) and cube map reflections.

Screen-Space Reflections (SSR): SSR is a technique that calculates reflections based on the information available on the screen. It works by ray tracing from the camera's viewpoint to determine what is reflected on the screen. SSR is computationally efficient but may not capture all reflection details accurately.

Cube Map Reflections: Cube map reflections involve pre-rendering six views of the environment (up, down, left, right, front, and back) into a cube map texture. This cube map is then used to calculate accurate reflections based on the 3D environment. Cube map reflections are more precise but can be computationally expensive.

Refractions

REFRACTIONS SIMULATE the bending of light as it passes through transparent materials like water or glass. This effect is often used to create realistic underwater scenes, glass objects, and heat distortion.

To achieve refractions, developers can use techniques like screen-space refraction or ray marching. Screen-space refraction is a simpler approach but may not provide highly accurate results, while ray marching is more computationally intensive but offers greater realism.

Depth of Field

DEPTH OF FIELD (DOF) is a visual effect that simulates the blurring of objects that are not in focus. This effect is commonly used in photography and cinematography to draw the viewer's attention to a specific subject.

In computer graphics, DOF is calculated based on the distance from the camera to objects in the scene. It can be achieved using techniques like Gaussian blur or bokeh rendering. DOF enhances the realism of scenes and adds an artistic touch to graphics.

Ambient Occlusion

AMBIENT OCCLUSION (AO) is a shading technique that simulates how ambient light is blocked or occluded by nearby surfaces, creating soft shadows in crevices and corners. It helps improve the perception of depth and adds realism to scenes.

There are two primary types of ambient occlusion: screen-space ambient occlusion (SSAO) and baked ambient occlusion. SSAO is a real-time technique that calculates occlusion based on the information available on the screen. Baked ambient occlusion involves precomputing occlusion data and baking it into textures for use in the rendering process.

Global Illumination

GLOBAL ILLUMINATION (GI) refers to the simulation of indirect lighting in a scene. It takes into account how light bounces off surfaces and affects the overall illumination. GI techniques include radiosity, ray tracing, and photon mapping.

Real-time global illumination can be challenging to implement due to its computational complexity. However, it greatly contributes to the realism of scenes by accurately modeling how light interacts with the environment.

Dynamic Weather and Time of Day

DYNAMIC WEATHER AND time-of-day systems change the lighting, sky, and environmental conditions in real-time. These systems can create dynamic day-night cycles, varying weather conditions, and atmospheric effects.

Implementing dynamic weather and time of day involves altering the lighting, skybox, and other environmental parameters over time. This can greatly enhance the immersive qualities of games and simulations.

In summary, real-time environmental effects are essential for creating visually captivating and realistic computer graphics. Understanding and implementing these effects can elevate the quality of graphics in games, simulations, and interactive applications, providing users with more engaging and immersive experiences.

Section 16.5: Optimizing Real-Time Rendering Performance

OPTIMIZING REAL-TIME rendering performance is a critical aspect of computer graphics development, especially in video games and interactive applications where smooth and responsive visuals are crucial for a positive user experience. In this section, we will explore various strategies and techniques for optimizing real-time rendering performance.

1. Level of Detail (LOD)

LEVEL OF DETAIL IS a technique that involves using simplified versions of 3D models or textures for objects that are distant from the camera. LOD reduces the computational load by rendering less detailed geometry or textures for objects that are less visible to the player. Implementing LOD systems can significantly improve rendering performance, especially in open-world games.

2. Occlusion Culling

OCCLUSION CULLING IS a method for determining which objects are not visible to the camera and, therefore, should not be rendered. This technique prevents unnecessary rendering of objects hidden behind others, leading to performance improvements. Techniques like frustum culling and portal culling are commonly used in occlusion culling.

3. Batch Rendering

BATCH RENDERING INVOLVES grouping together objects with similar shaders and rendering them in a single draw call. Reducing the number of draw calls can significantly improve rendering performance. Properly organizing and batching objects can reduce CPU overhead and improve GPU efficiency.

4. GPU Instancing

GPU INSTANCING ALLOWS you to render multiple instances of the same object with a single draw call. This technique is particularly useful for rendering large numbers of identical objects, such as trees, grass, or particles. GPU instancing minimizes CPU-GPU communication and can significantly boost performance.

5. Deferred Rendering

DEFERRED RENDERING is a rendering technique that splits the rendering process into multiple passes, allowing for efficient lighting calculations and post-processing effects. Deferred rendering can optimize performance by reducing redundant calculations and enabling more complex lighting and shading effects.

6. Texture Compression

USING COMPRESSED TEXTURES can reduce memory bandwidth and GPU memory usage. Modern graphics APIs and hardware support various texture compression formats, such as DXT, BCn, and ASTC. Choosing the appropriate texture compression format can help optimize rendering performance without sacrificing visual quality.

7. Multithreading

LEVERAGING MULTI-CORE CPUs for rendering tasks can significantly improve performance. Implementing multithreaded rendering allows parallel execution of rendering tasks, such as scene traversal, physics simulations, and AI updates. However, proper synchronization and load balancing are essential to avoid race conditions and ensure smooth performance.

8. GPU Profiling

PROFILING GPU PERFORMANCE is crucial for identifying bottlenecks and optimizing rendering code. Tools like GPU profilers provide insights into GPU utilization, shader performance, and draw call statistics. By identifying performance bottlenecks, developers can make informed optimizations.

9. Dynamic Resolution Scaling

DYNAMIC RESOLUTION scaling adjusts the rendering resolution based on the GPU load or frame rate. When the GPU is under heavy load, the resolution is lowered temporarily to maintain smooth frame rates. This adaptive technique ensures a consistent user experience, even during performance-intensive scenes.

10. Resource Management

EFFICIENT RESOURCE management, including texture streaming, mesh LOD management, and efficient memory allocation, is essential for maintaining a balanced GPU workload. Properly managing resources can reduce memory overhead and prevent resource thrashing.

In conclusion, optimizing real-time rendering performance is a multifaceted process that involves a combination of techniques and strategies. By implementing these optimizations, developers can achieve smoother frame rates, reduce input latency, and provide a better overall user experience in graphics-intensive applications and games. Balancing visual quality with performance is a continuous endeavor, and modern graphics APIs and hardware offer a wide range of tools and techniques to help achieve these goals.

Chapter 17: Physics in DirectX

Section 17.1: Basics of Game Physics

GAME PHYSICS PLAYS a fundamental role in creating realistic and interactive virtual worlds. It governs how objects move, collide, and interact within a game environment. Understanding the basics of game physics is crucial for game developers working with DirectX to create immersive and believable experiences. In this section, we will explore the fundamentals of game physics and how DirectX can be utilized to implement physics simulations.

1. Newtonian Physics

AT THE CORE OF GAME physics lies Newtonian physics, which describes the behavior of objects in terms of forces, mass, and acceleration. Newton's laws of motion, particularly the second law (F = ma), are fundamental to understanding how objects move and interact in the game world. Game developers use these principles to simulate the motion of characters, vehicles, projectiles, and more.

2. Rigid Body Dynamics

RIGID BODY DYNAMICS is a common approach to simulating the movement and collisions of solid objects in games. In this approach, objects are treated as if they are rigid and do not deform. Key components of rigid body dynamics include mass, inertia, and angular velocity. DirectX provides libraries and APIs for implementing rigid body physics simulations.

3. Collision Detection

COLLISION DETECTION is a critical aspect of game physics. It involves identifying when two or more objects in the game world intersect or collide. Efficient collision detection algorithms are essential for maintaining good performance in real-time games. DirectX offers features and libraries for collision detection, including bounding volume hierarchies, ray tracing, and more.

4. Collision Response

ONCE A COLLISION IS detected, the game must determine how the objects involved respond to the collision. This includes calculating forces, velocities, and directions of movement after the collision occurs. Physics engines integrated with DirectX can handle complex collision response calculations, allowing developers to create realistic interactions between objects.

5. Constraints and Joints

IN MANY GAMES, OBJECTS are interconnected with constraints and joints, such as hinges, springs, and ropes. These components add complexity to the physics simulation and are used to create mechanical systems like vehicles, articulated characters, and dynamic structures. DirectX offers tools for implementing constraint-based physics systems.

6. Fluid Dynamics and Soft Bodies

ADVANCED PHYSICS SIMULATIONS can include fluid dynamics for liquids and gases, as well as soft body physics for deformable objects like cloth and flesh. While DirectX itself doesn't provide extensive support for these simulations, it can be integrated with third-party physics libraries and plugins to achieve these effects.

7. Performance Considerations

REAL-TIME PHYSICS SIMULATIONS can be computationally intensive. Game developers must consider performance optimization techniques, such as multithreading, spatial partitioning, and level of detail (LOD), to ensure that physics simulations run smoothly even in complex scenes. DirectX's parallel processing capabilities can be leveraged for efficient physics calculations.

8. Integration with DirectX

DIRECTX PROVIDES APIS and tools for integrating physics engines into game development. Many game engines and middleware solutions offer DirectX support and simplify the process of implementing physics simulations. Developers can choose from various physics engines like NVIDIA PhysX, Havok, or custom-built solutions based on DirectX.

In summary, game physics is a fundamental aspect of creating realistic and interactive virtual environments. Understanding the principles of Newtonian physics, collision detection, and collision response is essential for game developers working with DirectX. DirectX offers the necessary tools and libraries for integrating physics simulations into games, allowing developers to create immersive and dynamic experiences for players.

Section 17.2: Implementing Physics with DirectX

IMPLEMENTING PHYSICS in a DirectX-based game involves utilizing libraries, tools, and principles to create realistic and engaging simulations. In this section, we will explore how DirectX can be leveraged to integrate physics into your game development process.

1. Physics Libraries and Engines

TO IMPLEMENT PHYSICS in a DirectX game, developers often rely on dedicated physics libraries and engines. These libraries provide pre-built solutions for simulating the behavior of objects in the game world, handling collisions, and calculating forces and motion. Some popular physics libraries compatible with DirectX include NVIDIA PhysX, Havok, and Bullet Physics.

2. Integration with DirectX

PHYSICS LIBRARIES ARE typically designed to work seamlessly with DirectX. They provide APIs and SDKs that allow developers to integrate physics simulations into their DirectX-based games. This integration enables realistic interactions between game objects, including collision detection and response, ragdoll physics for characters, and the simulation of complex physical systems.

3. Collision Detection

ONE OF THE KEY ASPECTS of physics in games is collision detection. DirectX provides features for efficiently detecting collisions between objects, such as bounding volume hierarchies (e.g., bounding boxes, spheres) and ray casting. Physics engines often include optimized collision detection algorithms that can handle complex shapes and environments.

4. Physics Materials and Properties

OBJECTS IN A GAME WORLD often have physical properties like mass, friction, restitution (bounciness), and density. These properties define how objects react when they collide or interact with forces. DirectX and physics libraries allow developers to assign these properties to game objects, ensuring that they behave realistically.

5. Ragdoll Physics

RAGDOLL PHYSICS IS commonly used for character animations and death sequences in games. It simulates the movement and behavior of a character's limbs and body when they are affected by external forces or collisions. DirectX and physics engines offer tools for creating and controlling ragdoll simulations, adding realism to character animations.

6. Joint and Constraint Systems

MANY GAMES REQUIRE objects to be interconnected, forming complex systems. DirectX-based physics engines support the creation of joints and constraints, such as hinges, springs, and ropes, allowing developers to build mechanical systems, vehicles, and dynamic structures.

7. Performance Optimization

REAL-TIME PHYSICS SIMULATIONS can be computationally intensive, especially in complex game environments. Developers must consider performance optimization techniques, including multithreading, spatial partitioning, and culling, to ensure that physics calculations run smoothly. DirectX's support for parallel processing can be advantageous in optimizing physics simulations.

8. Debugging and Visualization

DEBUGGING PHYSICS SIMULATIONS is crucial to identify and resolve issues. DirectX-based tools and debugging frameworks offer features for visualizing physics interactions, collision shapes, and forces. This aids developers in fine-tuning physics parameters and troubleshooting physics-related bugs.

9. Integrating Physics with Gameplay

ULTIMATELY, THE GOAL of integrating physics into a DirectX game is to enhance gameplay and immersion. Developers should carefully design game mechanics that leverage physics, such as destructible environments, realistic vehicle handling, and dynamic interactions with the game world. Physics can be a powerful tool for creating memorable gaming experiences.

In conclusion, implementing physics in a DirectX-based game involves selecting a physics library or engine, integrating it with DirectX, defining physical properties, handling collision detection, and optimizing performance. By effectively incorporating physics into gameplay, developers can create more engaging and immersive experiences for players. DirectX's compatibility with physics engines simplifies the process of adding realistic physics simulations to games, allowing developers to focus on creating compelling content and interactions.

Section 17.3: Collision Detection and Response

COLLISION DETECTION and response are fundamental aspects of physics in DirectX-based games. This section explores the techniques and methodologies used to handle collisions between objects within the game world and how to respond to these collisions realistically.

1. Collision Detection Algorithms

COLLISION DETECTION is the process of identifying when two or more objects intersect in the game world. DirectX provides several methods and algorithms for efficient collision detection, including:

- **Bounding Volume Hierarchies**: These hierarchical structures, such as bounding boxes, spheres, or octrees, help speed up collision checks by narrowing down potential collision candidates.

- **Ray Casting**: Used for detecting collisions between a ray (a straight line with an origin and direction) and objects in the scene. It's commonly used for shooting mechanics and picking objects in the game world.

- **Mesh Intersection**: DirectX allows for detailed mesh-based collision detection, enabling precise detection of collisions on complex 3D models. This is particularly useful for character-environment interactions.

2. Handling Collisions

ONCE COLLISIONS ARE detected, it's essential to handle them appropriately. Here are some collision response techniques:

- **Physics-Based Response**: For realistic physics simulations, objects may react according to physical principles like conservation of momentum, friction, and restitution (how bouncy an object is). These principles govern how objects should move after a collision.

- **Simple Displacement**: In some cases, objects may simply need to be moved away from each other to prevent overlap. This is common in 2D games or simplified 3D scenarios.

- **Impulse Resolution**: This technique calculates and applies impulses (changes in momentum) to objects involved in a collision to achieve realistic reactions. Impulse-based methods are prevalent in physics engines.

- **Constraints and Joints**: When dealing with interconnected objects, constraints and joints are used to simulate mechanical systems like hinges, springs, or ropes. These elements control how objects interact and move together.

3. Continuous Collision Detection

IN FAST-MOVING GAMES or simulations, objects can move so quickly that they pass through each other between frames, causing missed collisions. Continuous collision detection (CCD) addresses this issue by predicting potential collisions along an object's path. CCD methods ensure that fast-moving objects correctly interact with their environment.

4. Optimization Techniques

EFFICIENT COLLISION detection is crucial for maintaining a game's performance. Developers often employ optimization techniques such as:

- **Bounding Volume Culling**: By using bounding volumes like spheres or boxes, objects that are far from each other can be quickly excluded from collision checks.

- **Spatial Partitioning**: Dividing the game world into spatial partitions (e.g., grids, octrees) helps reduce the number of collision checks by only considering objects in nearby partitions.

- **Parallel Processing**: Utilizing multi-threading or GPU acceleration can significantly speed up collision detection in complex scenes.

5. Collision Response in Game Mechanics

COLLISIONS ARE NOT limited to preventing objects from passing through each other; they also play a crucial role in game mechanics. For example:

- **Damage and Health**: Collisions can cause damage to characters or objects, affecting their health or durability.

- **Triggering Events**: Certain collisions can trigger in-game events, such as opening doors, activating traps, or advancing the storyline.

- **Score and Rewards**: Colliding with collectibles or achieving specific collision-related objectives can earn players scores or rewards.

- **Environmental Interactions**: Collisions can alter the game environment, like breaking obstacles or causing explosions.

In conclusion, collision detection and response are vital components of physics in DirectX-based games. Properly implementing these mechanisms ensures that objects in the game world interact realistically, enhancing player immersion and gameplay. DirectX offers various collision detection methods and tools, allowing developers to create engaging and dynamic game experiences with complex physical interactions. Whether it's simulating realistic physics or triggering in-game events, mastering collision handling is essential for game development with DirectX.

Section 17.4: Simulating Realistic Environments

CREATING REALISTIC environments is a key aspect of modern game development, and DirectX provides various tools and techniques to achieve this goal. Simulating real-world physics, such as gravity, friction, and materials, is essential to immerse players in a convincing game world. In this section, we'll explore how DirectX enables developers to simulate realistic environments.

1. Physics Simulation

PHYSICS SIMULATION in DirectX allows you to apply physical laws and principles to objects in your game world. This includes:

- **Gravity**: You can simulate gravity's effect on objects by applying a downward force that accelerates them toward the ground. This is crucial for realistic jumping, falling, and object dynamics.

- **Friction**: Controlling friction between objects and surfaces is essential for accurate movement. DirectX provides ways to adjust friction coefficients to simulate various materials like ice, sand, or concrete.

- **Material Properties**: You can define material properties, such as elasticity and hardness, to determine how objects react to collisions and forces. Soft materials may deform, while hard materials remain rigid.

- **Rigid Body Dynamics**: DirectX allows you to simulate rigid body physics, enabling objects to move, rotate, and collide realistically. Rigid body dynamics consider mass, inertia, and external forces.

2. Particle Systems

PARTICLE SYSTEMS ARE used to simulate various natural phenomena, such as fire, smoke, rain, or sparks. DirectX provides tools to create and control particle systems, allowing developers to design visually compelling effects that enhance the realism of the game environment.

3. Realistic Lighting

LIGHTING PLAYS A CRUCIAL role in creating realistic environments. DirectX supports various lighting techniques, including:

- **Global Illumination**: Advanced lighting models like radiosity and global illumination simulate the indirect lighting and reflections that occur in the real world.

- **Dynamic Lighting**: Real-time dynamic lighting allows for moving light sources, changing shadows, and realistic day-night cycles, enhancing immersion and visual quality.

- **HDR Rendering**: High Dynamic Range (HDR) rendering provides a broader range of color and luminance values, resulting in more realistic and visually stunning environments.

4. Weather Effects

SIMULATING WEATHER effects like rain, snow, fog, and wind can significantly impact a game's atmosphere. DirectX offers the tools to create these effects by manipulating shaders, textures, and particle systems. Weather effects can also affect gameplay by altering visibility, movement, or physics.

5. Terrain Generation

CREATING REALISTIC terrains is essential for open-world games and outdoor environments. DirectX supports terrain generation techniques like heightmaps, tessellation, and procedural generation. These methods allow developers to create vast and diverse landscapes with detailed textures and natural features.

6. Sound and Environment

REALISTIC ENVIRONMENTS are not limited to visuals alone; sound plays a crucial role in immersion. DirectX provides audio libraries for spatial audio, allowing developers to position sound sources in 3D space. This enables players to perceive sounds as if they originate from objects or directions within the game world.

7. Optimization and Performance

WHILE CREATING REALISTIC environments is essential, performance optimization is equally important. DirectX offers tools and techniques for optimizing graphics and physics calculations, ensuring that realistic simulations don't come at the cost of smooth gameplay.

In conclusion, DirectX empowers game developers to simulate realistic environments by incorporating physics, lighting, particle systems, weather effects, terrain generation, and spatial audio. These tools and techniques enable the creation of immersive game worlds that captivate players and enhance gameplay experiences. Balancing realism with performance optimization is a key challenge, but mastering these aspects is crucial for modern game development with DirectX.

Section 17.5: Integrating Physics Engines with DirectX

INTEGRATING PHYSICS engines with DirectX is a common practice in game development to achieve realistic and interactive simulations. Physics engines handle the complex calculations required for simulating real-world physics, including collision detection, rigid body dynamics, and more. In this section, we'll explore how to integrate physics engines with DirectX for enhanced realism in your games.

1. Choosing a Physics Engine

BEFORE INTEGRATING a physics engine with DirectX, you need to choose the right physics engine for your project. Popular physics engines in the game development industry include NVIDIA PhysX, Havok, Bullet Physics, and more. Consider factors like licensing, platform support, performance, and the specific features required for your game when making your selection.

2. Setting Up the Integration

INTEGRATING A PHYSICS engine with DirectX typically involves the following steps:

- **Initialization**: Initialize both DirectX and the physics engine in your game. Ensure that they use compatible units and scales to avoid issues with physics simulations.

- **Creating Physics Objects**: Define objects in the physics engine that correspond to your game objects. These objects should have properties like mass, shape, and initial position.

- **Collision Detection**: Physics engines excel at collision detection. They can accurately detect collisions between objects, helping you handle complex interactions, such as character-to-environment collisions or object-to-object collisions.

- **Rigid Body Dynamics**: Physics engines handle rigid body dynamics, including applying forces, calculating accelerations, and updating positions and rotations. This is essential for realistic object movement.

3. Synchronization

TO ENSURE THAT THE physics simulations are synchronized with your DirectX graphics, you must establish a frame-by-frame synchronization mechanism. This usually involves updating the physics simulation before rendering each frame. Consider using fixed or variable time steps to maintain synchronization, depending on the requirements of your game.

4. Callbacks and Events

PHYSICS ENGINES OFTEN provide callbacks and events to notify your game code of significant events like collisions, triggers, and joint constraints. Utilize these callbacks to trigger specific actions in response to physics events, such as playing sound effects, triggering animations, or altering gameplay.

5. Debugging and Visualizing

DEBUGGING PHYSICS INTERACTIONS is crucial during development. Most physics engines offer tools to visualize physics objects, collision shapes, and forces. Integrate these debugging features into your game to identify and resolve physics-related issues efficiently.

6. Performance Considerations

WHILE PHYSICS ENGINES are powerful, they can be computationally expensive. To maintain smooth gameplay, optimize physics calculations by implementing techniques like broad-phase collision culling, object pooling, and multithreading.

7. Advanced Features

SOME PHYSICS ENGINES offer advanced features like soft body dynamics, cloth simulation, fluid dynamics, and more. Depending on your game's requirements, you can explore these features to add additional layers of realism.

8. Examples

HERE'S A SIMPLE CODE snippet in C++ that demonstrates initializing the NVIDIA PhysX physics engine and performing a basic physics simulation step:

```
// Initialize PhysX

physx::PxFoundation* foundation = PxCreateFoundation(PX_PHYSICS_VERSION, allocatorCallback, errorCallback);

physx::PxPhysics* physics = PxCreatePhysics(PX_PHYSICS_VERSION, *foundation, physx::PxTolerancesScale());

// Create a dynamic actor (rigid body)

physx::PxTransform transform(physx::PxVec3(0.0f, 10.0f, 0.0f));

physx::PxRigidDynamic* dynamicActor = physics->createRigidDynamic(transform);

// Add the actor to the scene

physicsScene->addActor(*dynamicActor);

// Simulate physics

physicsScene->simulate(deltaTime);

physicsScene->fetchResults(true);
```

In this example, we initialize PhysX, create a dynamic actor, add it to the physics scene, and simulate physics for a specified deltaTime.

Integrating a physics engine with DirectX can greatly enhance the realism and interactivity of your games. It enables you to create dynamic, physics-driven environments that respond realistically to player actions. Careful consideration of synchronization, performance, and debugging is essential for a successful integration.

Chapter 18: DirectX and Cross-Platform Development

Section 18.1: Challenges of Cross-Platform DirectX Development

CROSS-PLATFORM GAME development has gained significant importance in the gaming industry due to the diverse range of platforms available to gamers today. DirectX, traditionally associated with Windows, presents both opportunities and challenges when it comes to developing games that run on multiple platforms, including Windows, Xbox, and more. In this section, we'll explore the challenges of cross-platform DirectX development and strategies to overcome them.

1. Platform Dependencies

ONE OF THE PRIMARY challenges in cross-platform DirectX development is dealing with platform-specific dependencies. DirectX is tightly integrated with the Windows operating system, making it challenging to port DirectX-based games to other platforms seamlessly. Platform-specific APIs, windowing systems, and input handling need to be addressed.

2. Graphics API Variations

DIFFERENT PLATFORMS may use varying graphics APIs, such as Vulkan, OpenGL, or Metal, instead of DirectX. Adapting your rendering code to these APIs while maintaining performance and visual quality can be complex and time-consuming.

3. Hardware Differences

PLATFORMS OFTEN HAVE different hardware capabilities and performance characteristics. Optimizing your game to run smoothly on a range of hardware configurations without compromising visual quality is a significant challenge.

4. Input and User Interface

CROSS-PLATFORM GAMES must account for diverse input methods and user interfaces across devices. Supporting keyboard and mouse, game controllers, touch screens, and more requires careful design and implementation.

5. Testing and Debugging

TESTING AND DEBUGGING across multiple platforms can be resource-intensive. Ensuring consistent gameplay and performance on each platform while identifying and fixing platform-specific issues is a substantial effort.

6. Codebase Maintenance

MAINTAINING A SINGLE codebase that targets multiple platforms can lead to code complexity. Managing platform-specific code branches and ensuring feature parity across platforms can be demanding.

7. Performance Optimization

EACH PLATFORM MAY HAVE unique performance bottlenecks and optimization techniques. Profiling and optimizing your game for each target platform is essential for delivering a smooth gaming experience.

8. Deployment and Distribution

DEPLOYING AND DISTRIBUTING a cross-platform game involves dealing with different app stores, certification processes, and distribution channels. Each platform has its requirements and restrictions that need to be addressed.

9. Third-Party Library Compatibility

COMPATIBILITY WITH third-party libraries and middleware can vary across platforms. Ensuring that all external dependencies work consistently on different platforms is crucial.

10. Version and Update Management

MANAGING GAME VERSIONS and updates across multiple platforms can be complex. Coordinating simultaneous releases and updates while adhering to platform-specific requirements is a logistical challenge.

Strategies for Cross-Platform DirectX Development

TO ADDRESS THESE CHALLENGES, game developers often employ the following strategies:

- **Abstraction Layers**: Using abstraction layers or middleware can help isolate platform-specific code and provide a unified API for game development. Tools like SDL (Simple DirectMedia Layer) or game engines that support cross-platform development can simplify this process.

- **Conditional Compilation**: Employing conditional compilation and preprocessor directives to include platform-specific code sections in your codebase allows you to maintain a single codebase while addressing platform differences.

- **Feature Flags**: Using feature flags or configuration settings can enable or disable platform-specific features at runtime, providing flexibility without modifying the codebase.

- **Cross-Platform Libraries**: Leveraging cross-platform libraries and frameworks for rendering, input, and other core functionalities can reduce the complexity of supporting multiple platforms.

- **Continuous Testing**: Implementing continuous integration and automated testing across multiple platforms helps catch and fix issues early in the development process.

- **Multiplatform Development Tools**: Using integrated development environments (IDEs) and tools that support multiplatform development can streamline the process by providing platform-specific project configurations and deployment options.

- **Community and Documentation**: Engaging with developer communities and utilizing platform-specific documentation and resources can help overcome platform-specific challenges.

Cross-platform DirectX development requires careful planning, a deep understanding of platform differences, and the use of appropriate tools and strategies. While it presents challenges, it also offers the opportunity to reach a broader audience and maximize the impact of your game across various platforms.

Section 18.2: Strategies for Writing Portable DirectX Code

WRITING PORTABLE DIRECTX code that can run seamlessly across different platforms is a complex but rewarding endeavor. To achieve cross-platform compatibility while using DirectX, game developers can employ various strategies and best practices:

1. Abstraction Layers and Frameworks:

- Consider using cross-platform abstraction layers like SDL (Simple DirectMedia Layer) or game development frameworks like Unity or Unreal Engine, which offer support for multiple platforms, including DirectX.

- These tools provide a unified interface for game development, helping developers focus on gameplay and reducing the need for platform-specific code.

2. Conditional Compilation:

- Utilize conditional compilation and preprocessor directives to isolate platform-specific code segments. By encapsulating platform-specific code in conditional blocks, you can maintain a single codebase while accommodating different platforms.

- For example, you can use #ifdef and #endif directives to include or exclude Windows-specific code sections when compiling for other platforms.

```
#IFDEF _WIN32
```

```
// Windows-specific code

#include <Windows.h>

#endif

// Cross-platform code
```

3. Feature Flags:

- Implement feature flags or configuration settings that allow you to enable or disable platform-specific features at runtime. This approach provides flexibility without the need for code changes.

- For instance, you can create a configuration file that specifies which platform-specific features to enable, and your game can read this file and adjust its behavior accordingly.

4. Cross-Platform Libraries:

- Leverage cross-platform libraries and middleware for various aspects of game development, such as rendering, input, and audio. These libraries abstract platform-specific details and provide a consistent API.

- Libraries like GLFW for window and input management or OpenAL for audio can simplify cross-platform development.

5. Separate Platform Modules:

- Organize your codebase into separate modules or libraries for each target platform. Each module can encapsulate platform-specific functionality and can be compiled and linked based on the target platform.

- This modular approach keeps platform-specific code isolated and makes it easier to manage.

6. Testing and Continuous Integration:

- Implement automated testing across different platforms as part of your development pipeline. Continuous integration (CI) tools can help automate the building and testing of your game on various platforms.

- Detecting and addressing platform-specific issues early in development reduces debugging time later.

7. Cross-Platform Development Tools:

- Use integrated development environments (IDEs) and tools that support cross-platform development. These tools often provide project configurations and deployment options tailored to different platforms.

- Visual Studio, for example, offers support for multiplatform development, allowing you to manage platform-specific settings within a single project.

8. Documentation and Community Resources:

- Engage with developer communities and forums focused on cross-platform game development. Share experiences and seek advice from developers who have successfully tackled cross-platform challenges.

- Leverage platform-specific documentation and resources to understand the nuances of each platform and the best practices for achieving compatibility.

9. Version Control and Collaboration:

- Utilize version control systems such as Git to manage your codebase efficiently. Version control allows for collaboration among team members working on different platforms.

- Proper branching and merging strategies help maintain a coherent codebase while accommodating platform-specific changes.

WRITING PORTABLE DIRECTX code is a multifaceted process that requires a combination of technical expertise, careful planning, and the right tools. By adopting these strategies and best practices, game developers can navigate the complexities of cross-platform development and deliver engaging gaming experiences to a broad audience.

Section 18.3: Leveraging DirectX in Cross-Platform Game Engines

CROSS-PLATFORM GAME engines have become invaluable tools for game developers seeking to create games that can run on various operating systems and devices. These engines often provide the infrastructure and tools necessary to streamline cross-platform development, and they also offer support for DirectX, making it easier for developers to work with this graphics API while targeting multiple platforms. In this section, we will explore how DirectX is leveraged within cross-platform game engines and the benefits it brings.

Integration of DirectX:

CROSS-PLATFORM GAME engines, such as Unity and Unreal Engine, are known for their ability to abstract the underlying graphics APIs. However, they also include DirectX support for targeting Windows-based platforms. The integration of DirectX within these engines allows developers to take advantage of DirectX's advanced features and optimizations while maintaining cross-platform compatibility.

Benefits of DirectX Integration:

1. **Performance Optimization:** DirectX offers fine-grained control over GPU resources and rendering pipelines. By using DirectX within a cross-platform engine, developers can optimize graphics rendering for Windows platforms, ensuring that games run smoothly on Windows-based devices.
2. **Advanced Graphics Features:** DirectX provides access to advanced graphics features, such as tessellation, shader models, and DirectX Raytracing (DXR). These features can be used to enhance the visual quality of games when running on Windows.
3. **Tooling and Debugging:** DirectX integration includes access to debugging tools like PIX (Performance Investigator for Xbox) and GPU debugging tools in Visual Studio. These tools aid in diagnosing and optimizing graphics performance issues on Windows platforms.
4. **Compatibility with Windows Features:** DirectX also allows game engines to take advantage of Windows-

specific features like DirectInput for input handling, DirectSound for audio, and Windows-specific UI libraries. This integration ensures that games feel native on Windows platforms.

Cross-Platform Abstraction:

WHILE DIRECTX INTEGRATION is valuable for Windows development, cross-platform engines maintain a layer of abstraction to ensure compatibility with other platforms. This abstraction ensures that game logic and content are portable, and developers can write code that works across Windows, macOS, Linux, and consoles like PlayStation and Xbox.

Engine-Specific DirectX Support:

DIFFERENT ENGINES MAY provide varying degrees of DirectX support and optimization. Developers should review the engine's documentation and DirectX-related features to make informed decisions on how to leverage DirectX capabilities effectively.

Testing and Quality Assurance:

WHEN USING DIRECTX within a cross-platform engine, it's crucial to thoroughly test the game on all target platforms. This ensures that DirectX-specific optimizations do not negatively impact performance or compatibility on non-Windows platforms.

Conclusion:

DIRECTX INTEGRATION within cross-platform game engines empowers developers to harness the power of DirectX while maintaining the ability to target a wide range of platforms. By leveraging this integration, game developers can create visually stunning and performant games that run smoothly on Windows-based devices, offering players a seamless gaming experience. However, it's essential to strike a balance between DirectX optimizations and cross-platform compatibility to ensure that the game reaches a broader audience.

Section 18.4: Case Studies: Successful Cross-Platform DirectX Projects

IN THIS SECTION, WE'LL delve into some case studies of successful projects that have utilized DirectX within cross-platform game development. These examples illustrate how game developers have effectively leveraged DirectX to achieve their goals while ensuring compatibility across different platforms.

1. Hollow Knight:

- *Platform(s):* Windows, macOS, Linux, Nintendo Switch, PlayStation 4, Xbox One
- *Engine:* Unity
- *DirectX Integration:* Hollow Knight, a critically acclaimed indie game, utilized Unity as its game engine. While Unity abstracts graphics APIs, the developers incorporated DirectX for Windows platforms to optimize rendering and achieve a higher level of visual fidelity. This strategic use of DirectX contributed to the game's success on Windows while maintaining compatibility with other platforms.

2. Ori and the Blind Forest:

- *Platform(s):* Windows, Xbox One, Nintendo Switch

- *Engine:* Unity

- *DirectX Integration:* Ori and the Blind Forest, another Unity-powered game, targeted both Windows and Xbox One platforms. The developers leveraged DirectX for Windows to ensure the game's performance and visual quality were exceptional on Windows devices. Simultaneously, Unity's cross-platform capabilities allowed them to bring the game to Xbox One, providing a seamless gaming experience across different systems.

3. Stardew Valley:

- *Platform(s):* Windows, macOS, Linux, Nintendo Switch, PlayStation 4, Xbox One, iOS, Android

- *Engine:* Custom Engine (MonoGame)

- *DirectX Integration:* Stardew Valley is a standout example of a game that started as a Windows-exclusive project but eventually expanded to various platforms. Initially developed for Windows using the MonoGame framework, the game relied on DirectX for graphics rendering. The successful integration of DirectX ensured optimal performance on Windows systems. Subsequently, the game was ported to other platforms while maintaining a consistent gaming experience.

4. Risk of Rain 2:

- *Platform(s):* Windows, macOS, Linux, Nintendo Switch, PlayStation 4, Xbox One

- *Engine:* Unity

- *DirectX Integration:* Risk of Rain 2, a Unity-based game, employed DirectX for Windows to deliver high-quality visuals and performance. The game's compatibility with Windows was a key factor in its success, and its transition to other platforms was facilitated by Unity's cross-platform capabilities.

5. Dead Cells:

- *Platform(s):* Windows, macOS, Linux, Nintendo Switch, PlayStation 4, Xbox One, iOS, Android

- *Engine:* Custom Engine (HaxeFlixel)

- *DirectX Integration:* Dead Cells, developed using the HaxeFlixel framework, initially targeted Windows as its primary platform, making extensive use of DirectX for rendering. The game's success on Windows paved the way for its expansion to various platforms, with the developers optimizing the graphics pipeline for each target system while maintaining consistent gameplay mechanics.

THESE CASE STUDIES highlight how DirectX can be effectively utilized within cross-platform game development to achieve superior graphics performance on Windows while ensuring compatibility across a wide range of devices and operating systems. Successful game developers strategically implement DirectX to enhance the gaming experience for Windows users without sacrificing the ability to reach a broader audience.

Section 18.5: Future of Cross-Platform Gaming with DirectX

AS TECHNOLOGY CONTINUES to advance, the landscape of cross-platform gaming is poised for significant changes, and DirectX will play a crucial role in shaping its future. In this section, we'll explore the emerging trends and developments that are expected to influence the cross-platform gaming industry and the role DirectX will play in this evolving landscape.

1. DirectX 12 Ultimate:

WITH THE RELEASE OF DirectX 12 Ultimate, Microsoft introduced a unified standard for PC and Xbox Series X/S gaming. This technology brings feature parity between the two platforms, making it easier for developers to create cross-platform games that take full advantage of the latest hardware capabilities. DirectX 12 Ultimate includes support for ray tracing, variable rate shading, mesh shaders, and other advanced rendering techniques, providing a consistent and high-quality gaming experience across Windows and Xbox platforms.

2. Cloud Gaming:

THE ADVENT OF CLOUD gaming services, such as Xbox Cloud Gaming (formerly known as Project xCloud) and NVIDIA GeForce NOW, is reshaping the way games are played and delivered. These services enable players to stream games across a variety of devices, including smartphones, tablets, and low-end PCs. DirectX will continue to be essential in delivering rich graphics and low-latency experiences through the cloud, ensuring that players can enjoy high-quality gaming regardless of their hardware.

3. Cross-Platform Play:

CROSS-PLATFORM PLAY has become a popular feature, allowing gamers on different platforms to play together in multiplayer games. DirectX will continue to facilitate this trend by providing a consistent graphics and performance foundation across platforms. Developers can leverage DirectX to ensure that players on Windows, Xbox, and other platforms have a seamless gaming experience when playing together.

4. VR and AR Integration:

VIRTUAL REALITY (VR) and Augmented Reality (AR) are becoming more prominent in gaming. DirectX will play a pivotal role in VR and AR gaming experiences by providing the necessary rendering capabilities to create immersive virtual worlds. As cross-platform VR and AR gaming expand, DirectX will be integral in ensuring compatibility and performance across a wide range of devices.

5. Machine Learning and AI:

MACHINE LEARNING (ML) and Artificial Intelligence (AI) are increasingly being used in game development for tasks like NPC behavior, procedural content generation, and player analytics. DirectX's support for compute shaders and AI-focused features will enable developers to harness the power of AI for cross-platform gaming, enhancing gameplay and creating more dynamic and engaging experiences.

6. Evolving Hardware Standards:

DIRECTX WILL CONTINUE to adapt to evolving hardware standards, ensuring that game developers can take full advantage of the latest technologies. As new hardware innovations emerge, DirectX will provide the necessary tools and APIs to leverage these advancements for cross-platform gaming, delivering higher-quality graphics and improved performance.

In conclusion, DirectX remains a vital component in the future of cross-platform gaming. As technology evolves and the gaming industry continues to grow, DirectX will adapt to meet the changing demands of game developers and players alike. It will play a pivotal role in enabling cross-platform gaming experiences that are immersive, high-quality, and accessible to players across a wide range of devices and platforms.

Chapter 19: The Community and Ecosystem around DirectX

Section 19.1: The DirectX Developer Community

THE DIRECTX DEVELOPER community is a vibrant and active group of professionals and enthusiasts dedicated to graphics and game development using Microsoft's DirectX technology. This section explores the various aspects of this community, its importance, and the resources it provides to developers.

1. Community Forums and Websites:

THE DIRECTX COMMUNITY is known for its numerous forums and websites where developers can seek help, share knowledge, and discuss the latest developments in graphics programming. Websites like Stack Overflow and GameDev.net host dedicated DirectX sections where developers can ask questions and find solutions to common issues.

2. Open-Source Projects:

MANY DIRECTX DEVELOPERS actively contribute to open-source projects related to graphics programming. These projects often provide valuable resources, libraries, and tools that can streamline the development process. GitHub hosts numerous DirectX-related repositories, making it easy for developers to collaborate and leverage open-source solutions.

3. Tutorials and Educational Content:

THE COMMUNITY CREATES and shares tutorials, articles, and educational content to help both beginners and experienced developers improve their DirectX skills. These resources cover a wide range of topics, from getting started with DirectX to advanced rendering techniques. Websites like LearnOpenGL[1] and DirectXTutorial[2] offer comprehensive learning materials.

4. Meetups and Conferences:

DIRECTX DEVELOPERS often participate in industry events, conferences, and local meetups to network, share knowledge, and stay updated on the latest DirectX advancements. Events like the Game Developers Conference (GDC) and SIGGRAPH provide valuable opportunities for DirectX enthusiasts to connect with peers and experts in the field.

5. Development Communities:

GAME DEVELOPMENT COMMUNITIES, such as Unity[3] and Unreal Engine[4], also have sections dedicated to DirectX. These communities offer a platform for developers using game engines that incorporate DirectX to share their experiences, tips, and techniques for creating games with stunning graphics.

6. Online Courses and Certifications:

SEVERAL ONLINE COURSES and certifications focused on DirectX programming are available. These courses are offered by

---

1. https://learnopengl.com/
2. https://www.directxtutorial.com/
3. https://unity.com/
4. https://www.unrealengine.com/

educational platforms like edX[5], Coursera[6], and Udemy[7], allowing developers to formalize their knowledge and skills in DirectX development.

7. Developer Tools and Utilities:

THE DIRECTX COMMUNITY has developed and shared various tools and utilities that simplify game development processes. These tools range from debugging aids to performance optimization utilities, helping developers create more efficient and polished DirectX applications.

8. Beta Testing and Feedback:

DEVELOPERS WITHIN THE community often engage in beta testing for DirectX-related products and services. Providing feedback and participating in beta programs allows developers to influence the direction of DirectX and ensure it meets the needs of the community.

In summary, the DirectX developer community is a diverse and supportive ecosystem that fosters collaboration, learning, and innovation in the field of graphics and game development. Whether you are a novice seeking guidance or an experienced developer looking to share your expertise, the DirectX community offers a wealth of resources and opportunities to enhance your skills and contribute to the advancement of DirectX technology.

---

5. https://www.edx.org/

6. https://www.coursera.org/

7. https://www.udemy.com/

Section 19.2: Resources and Learning Materials for DirectX

IN THE DIRECTX DEVELOPER community, access to valuable learning resources and materials is essential for both beginners and seasoned developers. This section explores the diverse range of educational content and references available to help developers master DirectX.

1. Official Documentation:

MICROSOFT OFFERS COMPREHENSIVE and up-to-date documentation for DirectX on its official website. This documentation covers DirectX 12 and includes guides, reference materials, and code samples. It serves as an authoritative source for understanding DirectX's core concepts and functionality.

2. Books and eBooks:

NUMEROUS BOOKS AND eBooks dedicated to DirectX programming are available, catering to different skill levels and DirectX versions. These resources provide in-depth explanations, tutorials, and practical examples. Some popular titles include "Introduction to 3D Game Programming with DirectX" by Frank D. Luna and "Practical Rendering and Computation with Direct3D 11" by Jason Zink.

3. Video Tutorials:

VIDEO TUTORIALS ON platforms like YouTube[8] and Pluralsight[9] offer visual, step-by-step guidance for various DirectX topics. These tutorials often walk you through the development

8. https://www.youtube.com/

9. https://www.pluralsight.com/

process, helping you understand DirectX by watching code in action.

4. Online Forums and Communities:

AS MENTIONED IN THE previous section, online forums and communities like Stack Overflow, GameDev.net, and Reddit's r/GraphicsProgramming serve as valuable resources. Developers can seek answers to specific questions, share knowledge, and engage in discussions related to DirectX.

5. GitHub Repositories:

GITHUB HOSTS A PLETHORA of DirectX-related repositories that contain source code, samples, and projects. These repositories are valuable for exploring real-world implementations and learning best practices. You can search for DirectX projects and repositories using GitHub's search functionality.

6. Online Courses and MOOCs:

ONLINE LEARNING PLATFORMS such as edX[10], Coursera[11], and Udemy[12] offer DirectX courses and Massive Open Online Courses (MOOCs). These courses often provide structured learning paths, assignments, and assessments to enhance your DirectX skills.

7. API and SDK Samples:

DIRECTX SDKS INCLUDE a wealth of sample applications and code snippets. These samples showcase DirectX features and techniques, making them valuable resources for hands-on learning.

10. https://www.edx.org/

11. https://www.coursera.org/

12. https://www.udemy.com/

Developers can explore these samples to gain practical insights into DirectX programming.

8. Blogs and Articles:

MANY DIRECTX EXPERTS maintain blogs or write articles sharing their experiences, tips, and advanced techniques. These resources offer practical insights and often delve into specific DirectX challenges and solutions. Regularly following DirectX-focused blogs can keep you updated on the latest developments.

9. Online Courses and Certifications:

DIRECTX-FOCUSED ONLINE courses and certifications are offered by educational platforms, universities, and training institutes. These courses provide structured learning paths and may include assessments and certificates upon completion.

10. Documentation in Game Engines:

IF YOU ARE DEVELOPING games using engines like Unity or Unreal Engine, these engines often have documentation and resources related to DirectX integration. Refer to the respective engine's documentation to learn how DirectX is used within the engine's framework.

In conclusion, the availability of diverse learning resources and materials empowers DirectX developers to continually expand their knowledge and skills. Whether you prefer official documentation, books, videos, or interactive online courses, there are ample opportunities to master DirectX and stay updated with the latest developments in graphics programming.

Section 19.3: Contributing to the DirectX Ecosystem

ACTIVE PARTICIPATION and contribution within the DirectX ecosystem can be a rewarding experience for developers. This section explores ways in which you can contribute to the DirectX community, share your knowledge, and collaborate on projects.

1. Open-Source Projects:

MANY OPEN-SOURCE DIRECTX projects are hosted on platforms like GitHub. Contributing to these projects is a great way to give back to the community and gain experience. You can help with bug fixes, feature enhancements, or even start your own open-source DirectX project.

2. Code Contributions:

IF YOU'VE DEVELOPED useful libraries, utilities, or tools related to DirectX, consider sharing your code with the community. Open-source repositories and forums are excellent platforms to publish your work. This can benefit other developers and receive feedback for improvements.

3. Answering Questions:

ACTIVELY PARTICIPATING in forums like Stack Overflow, GameDev.net, and Reddit can help answer questions from fellow DirectX developers. Sharing your expertise by providing solutions and guidance can be invaluable to those seeking assistance.

4. Tutorials and Documentation:

WRITING TUTORIALS OR improving existing documentation can help newcomers grasp DirectX concepts more easily. Sharing your insights and knowledge through tutorials, articles, or contributions to official documentation can be highly beneficial.

5. Sample Projects:

CREATE AND SHARE SAMPLE DirectX projects that demonstrate specific techniques or solutions. These projects can serve as learning resources and examples for others. Platforms like GitHub allow you to easily share your projects with the community.

6. Contribute to Frameworks:

MANY DIRECTX FRAMEWORKS and libraries are open source and maintained by the community. Contributing to these projects can help improve the overall DirectX ecosystem. It can involve adding features, fixing issues, or optimizing code.

7. Technical Blogs and Presentations:

CONSIDER STARTING A technical blog or giving presentations at conferences or meetups to share your DirectX experiences and insights. This can help educate others and promote discussions within the community.

8. Mentoring and Collaboration:

MENTOR NEWER DEVELOPERS interested in DirectX programming. Collaborate on projects or work with others on solving challenging DirectX-related problems. Mentorship can be a rewarding way to contribute to the growth of the community.

9. Feedback to Microsoft:

IF YOU ENCOUNTER ISSUES or have suggestions for improving DirectX, provide feedback to Microsoft through official channels. Microsoft values input from developers and uses it to enhance DirectX in future releases.

10. Participate in DirectX Communities:

JOIN DirectX-related communities, forums, **and** social media **groups**. Engaging **in** discussions, sharing your expertise, **and** helping others can foster a sense **of** belonging within **the** DirectX ecosystem.

By actively contributing to the DirectX ecosystem, you not only help improve the toolkit for everyone but also enhance your own skills and reputation as a DirectX developer. Sharing knowledge and collaborating with the community can lead to a deeper understanding of DirectX and its applications in graphics programming.

Section 19.4: DirectX in Academia and Research

DIRECTX HAS A SIGNIFICANT presence in academia and research, contributing to various fields beyond game development. This section explores how DirectX is utilized in educational institutions and research projects.

1. Teaching Graphics Programming:

MANY UNIVERSITIES AND colleges incorporate DirectX into their computer science and game development curricula. Students learn graphics programming, shader development, and real-time rendering techniques using DirectX. Professors often create coursework and assignments centered around DirectX to provide hands-on experience.

2. Research Projects:

DIRECTX IS A VALUABLE tool for research in computer graphics, simulations, and scientific visualization. Researchers use DirectX to develop applications for scientific simulations, medical imaging, architectural modeling, and more. It enables real-time visualization of complex data.

3. Academic Projects:

STUDENTS AND RESEARCHERS frequently undertake academic projects involving DirectX. These projects may include developing interactive educational software, virtual reality simulations, or graphics-based tools for data analysis.

4. Thesis and Dissertations:

GRADUATE STUDENTS PURSUING degrees in computer science, computer graphics, or related fields often choose DirectX as a focal point for their theses and dissertations. These works contribute to the existing knowledge and understanding of DirectX capabilities.

5. Collaboration with Industry:

ACADEMIC INSTITUTIONS often collaborate with the game industry and other sectors that leverage DirectX technology. Such partnerships can lead to research projects, internships, and career opportunities for students.

6. DirectX Research Publications:

RESEARCH FINDINGS AND breakthroughs related to DirectX are published in academic journals and presented at conferences.

Topics may include advanced rendering techniques, performance optimization, or novel uses of DirectX in scientific domains.

7. Hackathons and Competitions:

SOME EDUCATIONAL INSTITUTIONS host DirectX-focused hackathons and competitions. These events challenge students to apply DirectX knowledge to create innovative projects within a limited timeframe.

8. Guest Lectures and Workshops:

DIRECTX EXPERTS FROM the industry are often invited to give guest lectures and workshops at academic institutions. This provides students with insights into real-world DirectX applications and industry practices.

9. Collaborative Projects:

COLLABORATIONS BETWEEN academia and the game industry may result in joint projects. Students and researchers work alongside industry professionals on DirectX-powered games or applications.

10. Industry-Academia Partnerships:

DIRECTX DEVELOPERS in the game industry collaborate with academic institutions to offer internships, sponsor research projects, or provide access to cutting-edge DirectX technology. These partnerships bridge the gap between academia and industry.

DirectX's versatility and real-time rendering capabilities make it an essential tool in both education and research. It continues to play a vital role in advancing computer graphics, simulations, and interactive applications across various domains. Students and researchers alike benefit from the rich features and extensive documentation provided by DirectX, enabling them to explore and innovate in the world of graphics programming and beyond.

Section 19.5: The Business Aspect of DirectX Development

DIRECTX DEVELOPMENT not only impacts the technical aspects of game and software development but also has significant implications on the business side of the industry. In this section, we delve into the business aspects of DirectX development.

1. Cost Considerations:

DEVELOPING WITH DIRECTX can have cost implications. Companies must invest in skilled developers, hardware, and software licenses. Balancing the cost of development with potential returns is crucial for project success.

2. Revenue Generation:

DIRECTX-POWERED APPLICATIONS, especially games, can generate substantial revenue. Revenue streams include game sales, in-app purchases, subscription models, and microtransactions. Effective monetization strategies are essential for profitability.

3. Intellectual Property (IP) Protection:

PROTECTING INTELLECTUAL property is vital in the DirectX development business. This involves safeguarding game assets, proprietary technology, and adhering to copyright and licensing agreements.

4. Market Competitiveness:

THE GAME INDUSTRY IS highly competitive. DirectX developers must analyze market trends, competitor offerings, and consumer preferences to create products that stand out and appeal to a broad audience.

5. Marketing and Promotion:

EFFECTIVE MARKETING and promotion are key to a product's success. DirectX developers need to invest in marketing strategies, including advertisements, social media campaigns, and participation in gaming events.

6. User Engagement:

USER ENGAGEMENT AND retention are essential for DirectX applications. Developers must continually update and enhance their products based on user feedback to keep players engaged over time.

7. Monetization Models:

CHOOSING THE RIGHT monetization model is critical. Options include free-to-play with in-app purchases, premium pricing, subscription models, and ad-supported models. Each has its own advantages and challenges.

8. Distribution Platforms:

SELECTING DISTRIBUTION platforms is a strategic decision. Popular platforms like Steam, Epic Games Store, Xbox Live, and others offer access to a broad user base. However, complying with platform-specific requirements is necessary.

9. Community Building:

BUILDING A COMMUNITY around DirectX-powered products can enhance brand loyalty and user engagement. This includes forums, social media groups, and engaging with fans and players.

10. Legal and Regulatory Compliance:

DIRECTX DEVELOPERS must adhere to legal and regulatory requirements, including age ratings, privacy policies, and international laws when distributing their products globally.

11. Long-Term Support:

PROVIDING LONG-TERM support **for** DirectX applications **is** essential to maintain user satisfaction. Regular updates, bug fixes, and compatibility with **new** DirectX versions are part of **this** commitment.

12. Revenue Sharing:

IN SOME CASES, DEVELOPERS may enter revenue-sharing agreements with platform providers. Understanding the terms and implications of revenue-sharing **is** crucial **for** financial planning.

13. Indie Development:

INDIE DEVELOPERS OFTEN rely on DirectX **for** creating innovative games. Balancing creative freedom with business success can be challenging but rewarding **for** indie studios.

14. Global Reach:

DIRECTX DEVELOPMENT allows products to reach a global audience. Understanding cultural differences and localization is important for international success.

15. Evolving Business Models:

THE GAME INDUSTRY'S business models are constantly evolving. Staying updated on industry trends and adapting business strategies accordingly is crucial for DirectX developers.

DirectX development is not just about coding and graphics; it's a multifaceted endeavor that involves careful consideration of business aspects. Success in DirectX development requires a combination of technical expertise, effective business strategies, and a deep understanding of the gaming industry's dynamics. Balancing creativity, technology, and business acumen can lead to the creation of successful and impactful DirectX-powered products.

Chapter 20: The Future of DirectX

In this final chapter, we explore the future of DirectX and its role in the ever-evolving landscape of graphics and game development. DirectX has a rich history, and as technology advances, it continues to adapt and innovate.

Section 20.1: Emerging Trends in Graphics Technology

GRAPHICS TECHNOLOGY is in a constant state of evolution, and DirectX plays a crucial role in shaping its future. Here, we take a look at some emerging trends and technologies that are likely to impact DirectX development in the coming years.

1. Ray Tracing Advancements:

RAY TRACING, A TECHNOLOGY that simulates the behavior of light, has gained significant attention. DirectX is at the forefront of integrating ray tracing into real-time rendering, offering stunning visual realism.

2. Real-Time AI Integration:

ARTIFICIAL INTELLIGENCE is becoming increasingly important in graphics and game development. DirectX is expected to further integrate AI for tasks like character behavior, procedural content generation, and dynamic world creation.

3. VR and AR Evolution:

VIRTUAL REALITY (VR) and Augmented Reality (AR) are poised for growth. DirectX will continue to support these technologies, enabling more immersive and interactive experiences.

4. Cross-Platform Development:

CROSS-PLATFORM DEVELOPMENT is on the rise. DirectX will likely expand its capabilities to facilitate development for various platforms, including consoles, PC, mobile, and emerging platforms.

5. Cloud Gaming Integration:

CLOUD GAMING SERVICES are gaining traction. DirectX may play a vital role in cloud gaming platforms, delivering high-quality graphics and low-latency experiences to players.

6. Advanced Multi-GPU Support:

DIRECTX IS EXPECTED to continue improving multi-GPU support, making it easier for developers to harness the power of multiple graphics cards for enhanced performance.

7. Real-Time Collaboration Tools:

COLLABORATION TOOLS within DirectX development environments are likely to improve, enabling developers to work together seamlessly, even across different geographic locations.

8. Advanced Rendering Techniques:

DIRECTX WILL KEEP PUSHING the boundaries of real-time rendering techniques, allowing for more detailed environments, advanced lighting, and realistic physics simulations.

9. Enhanced Developer Tools:

DIRECTX DEVELOPMENT tools will evolve to provide better debugging, profiling, and optimization capabilities, streamlining the development process.

10. API Efficiency:

OPTIMIZATIONS **in** the DirectX API will focus on reducing overhead and improving performance, ensuring that developers can make the most of modern hardware.

11. Machine Learning Integration:

MACHINE LEARNING AND deep learning models will find more applications in graphics and physics simulations, further enhancing realism in DirectX-powered experiences.

12. Dynamic World Generation:

DIRECTX MAY ENABLE dynamic world generation, where game environments evolve in response to player actions and in-game events, creating more immersive narratives.

13. Global Illumination:

REALISTIC GLOBAL ILLUMINATION techniques will become more accessible through DirectX, enhancing the visual quality of games and simulations.

14. Haptic Feedback Integration:

DIRECTX MAY INCORPORATE more advanced haptic feedback support, allowing developers to create more immersive and tactile experiences.

15. Environmental Sustainability:

WITH GROWING CONCERN **for** environmental impact, DirectX development may include tools and practices **for** optimizing energy consumption and carbon footprint.

The future of DirectX is marked by innovation and adaptation to emerging technologies. As graphics hardware becomes more powerful and diversified, DirectX will continue to be a driving force in enabling developers to create visually stunning and immersive experiences across a wide range of platforms. Developers and enthusiasts alike can look forward to exciting advancements in the world of DirectX development.

Section 20.2: DirectX and Next-Generation Hardware

DIRECTX HAS ALWAYS been closely tied to the latest advancements in graphics hardware. As we look toward the future, it's essential to consider how DirectX will continue to leverage and adapt to next-generation hardware.

One of the most significant drivers of innovation in graphics technology is the hardware it runs on. The following are some key aspects of DirectX's relationship with next-gen hardware:

1. Ray Tracing Acceleration:

NEXT-GEN GPUS ARE LIKELY to feature dedicated hardware for ray tracing acceleration. DirectX will continue to take advantage of these capabilities, making real-time ray tracing even more accessible and performant.

2. Advanced Tensor Cores:

MODERN GPUS ARE EQUIPPED with Tensor Cores designed for deep learning workloads. DirectX will explore new ways to integrate AI-driven features, like advanced upscaling, denoising, and animation, into games and applications.

3. High Refresh Rates and Resolution:

NEXT-GEN DISPLAYS SUPPORT higher refresh rates and resolutions, such as 8K. DirectX will provide the tools necessary to harness the full potential of these displays while maintaining performance.

4. Variable Rate Shading (VRS):

VRS IS A TECHNOLOGY that allows different parts of the screen to be rendered at varying levels of detail, reducing rendering workload. DirectX will continue to expand VRS support for better performance on next-gen hardware.

5. Hardware-Accelerated Machine Learning:

AS MACHINE LEARNING becomes more integrated into graphics workflows, DirectX will facilitate hardware-accelerated machine learning, enabling real-time AI-driven effects and optimizations.

6. Advanced Memory Management:

NEXT-GEN GPUS WILL feature improved memory management capabilities, allowing for more efficient texture streaming and dynamic loading. DirectX will provide APIs to take full advantage of these features.

7. Hardware Ray Tracing in Consoles:

CONSOLES, SUCH AS THE Xbox Series X, have embraced hardware ray tracing. DirectX will ensure seamless cross-platform development, allowing developers to target both consoles and PCs with ray tracing effects.

8. Realistic Physics Simulations:

DIRECTX WILL CONTINUE to support hardware-accelerated physics simulations, enabling more realistic and immersive gameplay experiences.

9. Mesh Shaders:

NEXT-GEN HARDWARE INTRODUCES mesh shaders, which provide more flexibility and efficiency in geometry processing. DirectX will incorporate mesh shaders into its feature set for enhanced performance.

10. Advanced Audio Processing:

WITH DEDICATED AUDIO hardware becoming more prevalent, DirectX will provide APIs for efficient audio processing, including realistic spatial audio and immersive soundscapes.

DirectX's ability to leverage next-generation hardware is crucial for staying relevant in the ever-advancing field of graphics and game development. By embracing these hardware advancements, DirectX will continue to empower developers to create cutting-edge visuals, realistic simulations, and immersive experiences that push the boundaries of what's possible. As hardware technology evolves, so too will the capabilities of DirectX, ensuring its continued role as a cornerstone of the gaming and graphics industry.

Section 20.3: Evolving Standards in Game Development

GAME DEVELOPMENT IS an ever-evolving field, and DirectX, as a critical component of this industry, must adapt to changing standards and trends. In this section, we'll explore the evolving standards that DirectX will need to address in the coming years.

1. Cross-Platform Development:

CROSS-PLATFORM GAME development has gained immense popularity. DirectX will need to continue supporting cross-platform development, ensuring that developers can target various platforms, including consoles, PC, mobile devices, and the cloud.

2. API Abstraction Layers:

ABSTRACTION LAYERS like Vulkan and Metal have gained traction, especially on non-Windows platforms. DirectX may need to evolve to provide better interoperability with these APIs, enabling more flexibility for developers.

3. Open Standards and Open Source:

THE GAME DEVELOPMENT community has shown a growing interest in open standards and open-source tools. DirectX could explore open initiatives to foster collaboration and innovation within the community.

4. Web Integration:

WEB TECHNOLOGIES ARE increasingly being used for game development, thanks to WebGL and WebAssembly. DirectX may consider better integration with web-based gaming to reach a broader audience.

5. VR and AR Standards:

WITH THE CONTINUED growth of virtual reality (VR) and augmented reality (AR), DirectX should stay aligned with evolving industry standards to ensure seamless integration with VR and AR hardware and software.

6. Accessibility and Inclusivity:

THE GAMING INDUSTRY is becoming more inclusive, with a focus on accessibility features. DirectX should encourage the implementation of accessibility standards to make gaming experiences accessible to a broader audience.

7. Real-Time Ray Tracing Standards:

AS REAL-TIME RAY TRACING becomes more common, DirectX must work on standardized approaches to ray tracing techniques, ensuring compatibility across different hardware and platforms.

8. Globalization and Localization:

TO CATER TO A GLOBAL audience, DirectX should support localization standards, making it easier for developers to create games in multiple languages and adapt content for various regions.

9. Security and Privacy Standards:

WITH INCREASING CONCERNS about security and user privacy, DirectX should provide tools and guidelines for developers to adhere to the latest security and privacy standards, protecting both players and their data.

10. Ethical Game Development:

ETHICAL CONSIDERATIONS in game development, such as addressing diversity, inclusion, and responsible monetization, are becoming more significant. DirectX can encourage ethical game development practices through guidelines and resources.

Adapting to these evolving standards will be crucial for DirectX's continued relevance and effectiveness in the game development industry. By staying flexible and responsive to industry trends, DirectX can empower developers to create innovative, cross-platform, and inclusive gaming experiences that cater to the diverse and evolving expectations of players worldwide.

Section 20.4: The Role of DirectX in Future Gaming Experiences

THE FUTURE OF GAMING is an exciting landscape filled with innovation, new technologies, and immersive experiences. DirectX will play a significant role in shaping this future by providing the tools and frameworks necessary for game developers to push the boundaries of what is possible. In this section, we will explore the role of DirectX in crafting the gaming experiences of tomorrow.

1. Realistic Graphics and Ray Tracing:

DIRECTX WILL CONTINUE to evolve to deliver even more realistic graphics. Real-time ray tracing, which has already made significant strides, will become a standard feature, enhancing lighting, reflections, and shadows in games.

2. Virtual Reality (VR) and Augmented Reality (AR):

DIRECTX WILL BE AT the forefront of VR and AR development. As these technologies mature, DirectX will offer improved support, making it easier for developers to create immersive virtual worlds and enhance real-world experiences with AR.

3. Cloud Gaming:

CLOUD GAMING IS GAINING momentum, and DirectX will be instrumental in delivering high-quality, low-latency gaming experiences streamed from the cloud. This shift will expand gaming accessibility to devices with limited hardware capabilities.

4. Artificial Intelligence (AI):

AI-DRIVEN NPCS, DYNAMIC storytelling, and procedural content generation will become more prevalent. DirectX will provide interfaces for developers to integrate AI seamlessly into their games, creating more lifelike and engaging experiences.

5. Cross-Platform Play:

THE DEMAND FOR CROSS-platform multiplayer gaming will continue to grow. DirectX will facilitate cross-platform play, allowing gamers on various devices to connect and compete in the same virtual worlds.

6. Accessibility Features:

DIRECTX WILL PRIORITIZE accessibility features, ensuring that games are playable by individuals with disabilities. This includes improved support for voice commands, haptic feedback, and customizable controls.

7. Blockchain and NFT Integration:

THE INTEGRATION OF blockchain technology and non-fungible tokens (NFTs) into gaming will offer new ways for players to own, trade, and interact with in-game assets. DirectX will provide the infrastructure for secure and efficient blockchain integration.

8. Sustainability and Energy Efficiency:

WITH INCREASING CONCERNS about the environmental impact of technology, DirectX will focus on energy-efficient rendering techniques, reducing the carbon footprint of gaming while maintaining quality.

9. Ethical Game Development Practices:

DIRECTX WILL ENCOURAGE ethical game development practices, promoting diversity and inclusion, responsible monetization, and fair treatment of players.

10. User-Generated Content and Modding:

USER-GENERATED CONTENT and modding communities will continue to thrive. DirectX will support these communities with tools that make it easier to create and share content, expanding the lifespan of games.

DirectX's adaptability and commitment to innovation will make it an essential platform for game developers in the ever-evolving gaming industry. As technology advances, DirectX will empower developers to create richer, more immersive, and socially connected gaming experiences that captivate players across the globe. The future of gaming is bright, and DirectX will be there every step of the way, enabling developers to turn their creative visions into reality.

Section 20.5: Preparing for the Next Wave of DirectX Innovations

AS WE LOOK AHEAD TO the future of DirectX, it's essential for developers and the gaming industry as a whole to prepare for the next wave of innovations. While we've discussed several aspects of

DirectX's future in previous sections, this final section will focus on how developers can stay ahead of the curve and leverage emerging trends in graphics technology effectively.

1. Continuous Learning and Skill Development:

EMBRACING NEW DIRECTX features and techniques requires ongoing learning. Developers should invest in staying up-to-date with the latest DirectX releases, attending conferences, and participating in online communities to share knowledge.

2. Hardware Upgrades:

KEEPING HARDWARE UP-to-date is crucial for taking advantage of DirectX's latest capabilities. As DirectX evolves, it may require more powerful GPUs and CPUs to deliver cutting-edge graphics and performance.

3. Adaptability and Flexibility:

DIRECTX'S VERSATILITY means that developers must adapt to changing requirements. Being flexible in your development approach and willing to experiment with new techniques will be essential.

4. Collaboration and Networking:

COLLABORATION WITHIN the game development community can lead to innovative solutions. Building a network of developers, artists, and designers can help exchange ideas and foster creativity.

5. Ethical Considerations:

AS DIRECTX AND GAMING technology advance, ethical considerations become more critical. Developers should prioritize ethical practices, including diversity, responsible monetization, and player well-being.

6. Environmental Responsibility:

THE GAMING INDUSTRY, including DirectX, will face increased scrutiny regarding its environmental impact. Developers should explore eco-friendly development practices and consider the sustainability of their projects.

7. Market Research and Player Feedback:

STAYING CONNECTED WITH player preferences and market trends is vital. Conducting market research and actively seeking player feedback can guide development decisions and ensure games remain relevant.

8. Security and Data Privacy:

WITH THE RISE OF ONLINE and cloud-based gaming, security and data privacy will become paramount. Developers should prioritize secure coding practices and user data protection.

9. Accessibility and Inclusivity:

THE IMPORTANCE OF ACCESSIBLE gaming experiences will continue to grow. Developers should strive to make their games inclusive and accessible to players of all abilities.

10. Innovation and Risk-Taking:

INNOVATIONS IN GAMING often come from taking risks. Developers should not be afraid to experiment with new ideas and gameplay concepts, pushing the boundaries of what's possible.

As DirectX evolves, it will provide new tools and opportunities for game developers to create exciting and immersive experiences. However, these opportunities come with the responsibility to embrace new technologies responsibly, prioritize ethical development practices, and consider the broader impact of gaming on society and the environment.

In conclusion, the future of DirectX promises incredible innovations and experiences in the world of gaming. Developers who stay curious, adaptable, and committed to responsible development practices will be well-positioned to ride the waves of innovation and continue delivering memorable gaming experiences to players worldwide. The journey ahead is filled with exciting possibilities, and DirectX will remain at the forefront of this ever-evolving landscape.

www.ingramcontent.com/pod-product-compliance
Lightning Source LLC
LaVergne TN
LVHW090303210926
848480LV00001B/117

* 9 7 9 8 2 2 4 5 6 2 5 8 9 *